D1882291

THE TRUT
ABOUT WOMAN

Owing to the antiquity and rarity of this book, certain pages are regrettably absent, and readability is compromised due to the blurring of the original text. If you possess any insights regarding the availability of these missing sections, kindly inform us. Your assistance is crucial in ensuring the completion of this significant work for the benefit of future generations.

THE TRUTH ABOUT WOMAN

CATHERINE GASQUOINE HARTLEY

GYAN

Published by

Gyan Publishing House
5, Ansari Road
Daryaganj, New Delhi-110002
Phone: 011-47034999, 9811692060
E-mail: books@gyanbooks.com

Distribution Network
gyanbooks.com
India, USA, Canada, UK, Australia

© Publisher
All rights reserved. No part of this work may be reproduced, stored, adapted, or transmitted in any form or by any means, electronic, mechanical, photocopying, micro-filming, recording or otherwise, or translated in any language, without the prior written permission of the copyright owner and the publisher.

ISBN: 978-93-7447-295-8 (PB)

First Published, 1913

2nd Impression 2026

Printed at: Gyan Press, Delhi.

The book is sold subject to the condition that it shall not, by way of trade or otherwise, be lent, resold, hired out, or otherwise circulated without the prior publisher's written consent.

THE TRUTH ABOUT WOMAN
Author: CATHERINE GASQUOINE HARTLEY

THE TRUTH ABOUT WOMAN

THE TRUTH ABOUT WOMAN

BY

C. GASQUOINE HARTLEY

(MRS. WALTER M. GALLICHAN)

1914

DEDICATION

TO

LESLIE, MY LITTLE ADOPTED SON

In writing at last this book on Woman, which for so many years has had a place in my thoughts, one truth has forced itself upon me: the predominant position of Woman in her natural relation to the race. The mother is the main stream of the racial life. All the hope of the future rests upon this faith in motherhood.

To whom, then, but to you, my little son, can I dedicate my book? You came to me when I was still seeking out a way in the futility of Individual ends; you reconciled my warring motives and desires; you brought me a new guiding principle. You taught me that the Individual Life is but as a bubble or cluster of foam on the great tide of humanity. I knew that the redemption of Woman rests in the growing knowledge and consciousness of her responsibility to the race.

PREFACE

It is very difficult to write a preface to a work which is expressly intended as a revelation of the faith of the writer. The successive stages of thought and emotion that have been passed through are still too near, and one feels too deeply. I have made several futile attempts to concentrate into a short note the Truths about Woman that I have tried to convey in my book. I find it impossible to do this. The explanation of one's own book would really require the writing of another book, as Mr. Bernard Shaw has proved to us in his delightful prefaces. But to do this one must be freed altogether from the limits of length and time. The fragments of what I wish to say would be of no service to any one.

I then tried to place myself, as it were, outside the book, and to look at it as a stranger might. But the difficulties here were even greater. I grew so interested in criticising my own opinions that my notes soon outran the possibilities of a preface. In this spirit of genuine discrimination, I became aware how easy it would be for any one who does not share my faith to find apparent contradictions of statement and errors in thought—much that is feeble here, extravagant there; to notice some salient fault and to take it as decisive of the writer's incompetence. I am tempted to point these out myself to guide and protect the reader.

Now that my book is done I feel that I have touched only the veriest fringe of a vast subject. But one thing I may say, I have tried to express the truth as I have come to see it. The conception I have of Woman is not new; it is very old. And for that reason it will be rejected by many women to-day. At present the inspiration towards freedom in the Woman's Movement has involved a tendency to follow individual paths, without waiting to consider to what end they lead. There has arisen a sort of glamour about freedom. No one of us can be free, for no one of us stands alone; we are all members one of another. And woman's destiny is rooted in the race. This, rightly considered, is the most vital of all vital facts. I appeal to women to realise more clearly their true place and gifts, as representing that original racial motherhood, out of which the masculine and feminine characters have arisen.

My book is a statement of my faith in Woman as the predominant and responsible partner in the relations of the sexes. To such a belief my opinion was driven, as it were, not deliberately set from the beginning. The time when the resolve to write a book upon Woman first took a place in my thoughts goes back for many years. The child of a Puritan father, who died for the faith in which he believed, the desire to teach was born in my blood. Our character is forged in the past, we cannot escape our inheritance. I began my work as the head-mistress of a school for girls. I was young in experience and very ignorant of life. In my enthusiasm I was quite unconscious of my own limitations. I believed that I was able to train up a new type of free woman. Of course I failed. Looking back now I wonder if I ever taught my pupils one-hundredth part of what they taught me. Perhaps if any of them, separated from me by time and circumstances, chance to read my book, they may be glad to know that it was largely due to them and what I learnt from them that it has come to be written. Certainly it was in those days, when saddened by my own failures, that the purpose came to me, dimly but insistently, to seek out the Truth about Woman and the relations of the sexes. I began to read and to collect material at first for my own guidance and instruction, and as a necessary preparation for my work. I needed it: I must have been slow to learn. For a long time I wandered in the wrong path. My desire was to find proofs that would enable me to ignore all those facts of woman's organic constitution which makes her unlike man. I stumbled blindly into the fatal error of following masculine ideals. I desired freedom for women to enable them to live the same lives that men live and to do the same work that men do. I did not understand that this was a wastage of the force of womanhood; that no freedom can be of service to woman unless it is a freedom to follow her own nature. I am very glad that the book that is now finished was not written in that period of my belief. I have waited and I have lived.

Five years ago I took up definitely the task of writing the book. At that time the plan of the work was made and the first Introductory chapter written. Circumstances into which I need not enter caused the work again to be put aside. I am glad: I have learnt much in these last years.

There is little more that I need to say.

The book is divided into three parts—the first biological, the second historical. These two parts are preliminary to the third part, which deals with the present-day aspects of the Woman Problem, the differences between woman and man, and the relations of the sexes.

This arrangement of my inquiry into three parts was necessary. It may seem to some that I should have done better to confine my investigations to the present. But the claim of woman for freedom is rooted deep in the past. This fact had to be established. I have tried to give the earlier sections such lighter qualities and interest as would commend them to my readers. It is hardly necessary for me to say I can make no claim to personal scientific knowledge. Probably I have made many mistakes.

It is perhaps foolish to make apologies for work that one has done. But the inclusion of so wide a field has had a disadvantage. My investigations may be objected to as in certain points not being supported by sufficient proof. I know this. My stacks of unused notes remind me of how much I have had to leave out. This is especially the case in the final part. The subject of every chapter treated here could easily form a volume in itself. I hope that at least I have opened up suggestions of many questions on which I could not dwell at length.

Some remarks may be necessary as to the nature of my material. It has been drawn from a variety of sources. I have tried to acknowledge in footnotes the great amount of help I have received. But my notes have been taken during many years, and if any acknowledgment has been forgotten, it is my memory that is at fault, and not my gratitude. The Bibliography (which has been drawn up chiefly from the works I have consulted, and is merely representative) will show how many fields there are from which the student may glean. In particular I am indebted to the works of Havelock Ellis, of Iwan Bloch and Ellen Key. To these writers I would express my warmest thanks for the help and guidance I have gained from their work.

The opinions expressed are in all cases my own. I say this without any apology of modesty. I hold that the one justification of writing a book at all is to state those truths one has learnt from one's own experience of life. For we can give to others only what we have received ourselves; the vision rising in our own eyes, the passion born in our own hearts.

C. Gasquoine Hartley.

7, Carlton Terrace,
Child's Hill, N.W.
March, 1913.

CONTENTS

N.B.—A complete synopsis of contents will be found at the beginning of each chapter

PART III—MODERN SECTION: PRESENT-DAY ASPECTS OF THE WOMAN PROBLEM

CONTENTS OF CHAPTER I

INTRODUCTION—THE STARTING-POINT OF THE INQUIRY

The twentieth century the age of hurrying progress—The change in the position of women—Reasons for the revolution—First efforts towards emancipation—Outlook of the Woman Movement—Its fundamental error—Possibilities of future development—Motherhood and the Woman Movement—Schopenhauer's view of woman—He asserts an absurdity—The predominance of man over woman not to be regarded as a natural and inviolable law—An examination of the mastery of the male—Can we look forward to a remedy ?—Our own time a turning-point in the history of women—Assumed inferiority of the female sex—Necessity for biological knowledge in forming an estimate of the present sex-relationship—Two kinds of influences to be considered—Nature and Nurture—The different play of the environmental forces, or Nurture, upon women and upon men—The importance of Nature—Galton's *Law of Inheritance*—Woman's responsibility as race-bearer—Sexual differences between the female and the male—Primitive woman and her position in early civilisations—Remarks and conclusion—The immense importance of motherhood.

CHAPTER I

INTRODUCTION—THE STARTING-POINT OF THE INQUIRY

"The method of investigating truth commonly pursued at this time, therefore, is to be held erroneous and almost foolish, in which so many inquire what others have said, and omit to ask whether the things themselves be actually so or not."—WILLIAM HARVEY.

THE twentieth century will, we may well believe, be stamped in the records of the future as "the age of hurrying change." In certain directions this change has resulted in a profounder transformation of thought than has been effected by all the preceding centuries. Never, probably, in the history of the world were the meanings and ambitions of progress so prevalent as they are to-day. An energy of inquiry and an endless curiosity is sweeping away the complacent Victorian attitude, which in its secure faith and tranquil self-confidence accepted the conditions of living without question and without emotion. Stripped of its masks, this phase of individual egoism was perhaps the most villainous page of recorded human history; yet, with strange confidence, it regarded itself as the very summit of civilisation. It may be that such a phase was necessary before the awakening of a social conscience could arise. Old conceptions have become foolish in a New Age. A great motive, an enlarging dream, a quickening understanding of social responsibility, these are what we have gained.

Above all, this common Faith of Progress has brought

a new birth to women. Many are feeling this force. There are two, says Professor Karl Pearson,[1] and it might almost be said only two great problems of modern social life—they are the problem of woman and the problem of labour. Regarded with fear by many, they are for the younger generation the sole motors in life, and the only party cries which in the present can arouse enthusiasm, self-sacrifice, and a genuine freemasonry of class and sex.

There is something almost staggering in the range and greatness of the changes in belief and feeling, in intellectual conclusions and social habits, which are now disturbing the female part of humankind. How complete is the divorce between the attitude of the woman of this generation towards society and herself, and that of the generation that has passed—yes, passed as completely as if hundreds and not units represent the years that separate it from the present.

It is instructive to note in passing what was written about woman at the time immediately preceding the present revolt of the sex. The virtue upon which most stress was laid was that of "delicacy," a word which occurs with nauseous frequency in the books written both by women and men in the two last centuries.[2] "Propriety," wrote Mrs. Hannah More, "is to a woman what the great Roman citizen said action is to an orator: it is the first, the second, and the third requisite."[3]

[1] "Woman and Labour," *The Chances of Death*, Vol. I. p. 226.

[2] Quoted from *The Emancipation of English Women*, by W. Lyon Blease, a book which gives an unbiased, and in many respects excellent, account of the struggle of English women to gain freedom from the seventeenth century to the present day.

[3] *Strictures*, I. 6, Gregory.

"This delicacy or propriety," it has been well said,[1] "implied not only modesty, but ignorance; and not only decency of conduct, but false decency of mind. Nothing was to be thoroughly known, nothing to be frankly expressed. The vicious concealment was not confined to physical facts, but pervaded all forms of knowledge. Not only must the girl be kept ignorant of the principles of physiology, but she must also abstain from penetrating thoroughly into the mysteries of history, of politics, of science, and of philosophy. Even her special province of religion must be lightly surveyed. She was not required to think for herself, therefore she was deprived of all training which would enable her to think at all. The girl must appear to be dependent upon the mental strength of a man, as well as upon his physical strength."

It is necessary to remember this attitude if we are to understand the direction that woman's emancipation has largely—and, as some of us think, mistakenly—taken in this country. It explains the demand for equality of opportunity with men, which has become the watch-cry of so many women, thinking that here was the way to solve the problem. A cry good and right in itself, but one which is a starting-point only for woman's freedom, and can never be its end.

Little more than fifty years have passed since Miss Jex-Blake undertook her memorable fight to obtain medical training for herself and her colleagues at the University of Edinburgh.[2] At about the same time arose women's demand for the right of higher education, and colleges for women were opened at Oxford and Cambridge. These were the practical results which followed the revolt of Mary Wollstonecraft, and later, the great

[1] *The Emancipation of English Women.*

[2] For an account of this struggle see *Sketch of the Foundation and Development of the London School of Medicine for Women*, by Isabel Thorne; also *The Emancipation of English Women.*

revival due to the publication of John Stuart Mill's epoch-marking book, the *Subjection of Women.*

During the first period of the woman's movement the centre of restlessness was amongst unmarried women, who rebelled at the old restrictions, eager for self-development and a more intellectually active life. These women undertook their own cause, insisting that their humanity came before their sex. They were picked women, much above the average woman, and to a certain extent abnormal in so far as they denied the important factor of sex. To them the average male was not a subject of overwhelming interest, and marriage and motherhood were not of prominent importance in their thought. For them "equality of opportunity for women with men" seemed to solve the problem of woman's emancipation. The constructive result of their campaign was the winning of the higher education of woman, the right to work, and the rush of women into the professions. Much, indeed, was gained, though it may be said with equal truth that much was lost. With this solution—the increased power of self-realisation in a narrow class of picked women, chiefly unmarried women of the middle-class—the woman's movement might well begin, but in this alone it can never end. The movement was incomplete as far as woman's emancipation went, because it was won by ignoring sex. In spite of the great advance in freedom and in scope of activity of life, the stigma attached to woman was not removed. To-day we have arrived at a point where instead of ignoring sex we must affirm it, and claim emancipation on the ground of our sex alone. Our mothers taught acceptance, and asked for privileges; the pioneers of revolt raised the cry "acceptance is a sin and all privilege evil"; we, the blood in our veins beating more strongly and understanding at last the true inwardness of our power, found our claim for complete emancipation upon that special work in the world and for the State which our differentiation from men imposes upon us. This differentiation is our potentiality for motherhood, and is the endowment of every woman, whether realised or not. We claim as our glory what our mothers accepted as their burden of shame.

No sudden causeless changes ever happen, or ever have happened. And the question, Why? arises. What is this dynamic force which has been, and is still sweeping in a great wave of emancipation across the civilised world, joining women in one common purpose? On the outside the revolutionary character of women's modern thought and modern practice means nothing more than that they claim the rights of adult human beings—political enfranchisement, the right of education and freedom to work. But the facts are far too complex to enable us thus to rush hastily to an answer. There is a pitiful monotony in much that is written and spoken about women's emancipation. The real causes are deep to seek, and not infrequently they have been missed even by those who have been most instrumental in bringing a new hope to women. The most advanced women champions, the martyrs of revolt, show no greater sense of the meanings and issues of the struggle in which they are engaged than the complaisant supporters of the worn-out customs they combat. They exhibit only the energies of an admirable impulse, without the control of a guiding law. Speculation, which should be carried to a comprehension of general facts, is concentrated upon the immediate gain of the hour. The tendency is to trifle with truth, and to disguise its reach and consequences. We have read, and spoken, and thought so much about the special character of woman that we have become almost wearied of the subject. Like Narcissus, we stand in some danger of falling in love with our own image. Perhaps the truth is we speculate too much instead of trying to find out the facts. The woman question is as old as sex itself and as young as mankind.

The future position of woman in society is a question that carries with it biological and psychological, as well as social and practical, issues of the widest significance, and further, it is bound up intimately with the profoundest riddles of existence. The problems remain to a great extent unsolved. But the conviction forces itself that the emancipation of woman will ultimately involve a revolution in many of our social institutions. It is this that brings fear to many. Yet we must remember that woman's emancipation is no new movement, but has always been with us, although with varying prominence at different times in history. In the past, civilisations have fallen, in part at least, because they failed to develop in equal freedom their women with their men. It is also certain that no civilisation in the future can remain the highest if another civilisation adds to the intelligence of its male population the intelligence of its women. This in itself is enough to condemn all ideas of sex inequality.

The struggle for the Suffrage has intensified many problems which it will take all the intellectual and emotional energy of both men and women to solve. Up till now there has been little more than a fight for mere rights against male monopolies. In the near future this struggle must lead to a realisation of the duties of woman, founded on a level-headed facing of the physiological realities of her nature. It is a complete disregard of sexualogical difficulties which renders so superficial and unconvincing much of the talk which proceeds from the "Woman's Rights" platform. All efforts made to understand the sex problem, which is the woman question, must be based on the full knowledge of the physical capacity of woman and the effect that her emancipation will have on her function of race production. All effort ought to be directed towards the future welfare and happiness of the children who are to follow us. This is the goal of woman's struggle for progress, it is the sole end worthy of it.

To assume as Schopenhauer and so many others have done, down to Sir Almroth Wright's recent hysterical wail in *The Times*, that woman, on account of her womanhood is incapable of intellectual or social development, paying her sole debt of Nature in bearing and caring for children, is really to state a belief in decay for humankind. Any stigma attached to women is really a stigma attached to their potentiality as mothers, and we can only remove it by beginning with the emancipation of the actual mother. No sharp cleavage can be made between qualities that are good and masculine on the one side, and all that is feminine on the other. The view is entirely erroneous. How, for instance, can ignorance and weakness constitute at once the perfection of womankind, and the imperfection of mankind? The matter is not so simple. Man must fall with woman, and rise with her.

My first purpose is to make this clear.

To-day we are faced with the question whether the predominance of man over woman is to be regarded as a natural, and therefore inviolable, law of the male and female. Some will deny this mastery of the male. It may be said that woman sways man more than he rules her. This is true. The influence of woman is important—fearfully important. Yet the fitting answer to such glossing—if it be necessary really to point out that sexual privilege is not personal power—is that such government is exercised in one direction alone, and arises not from woman's strength, but out of her subjection. Women have rendered back to men the ill that this long sex domination has wrought upon them. None the less have we to reckon with the despotism of the male side of life. "The softening influence of woman!" . . . It is a pretty phrase; but all the same women and men have been doing their best to degrade each other to a pitiful mediocrity. It is not the purifying influence of women—the theory of chivalrous moralists—but an unguided and therefore deteriorating sexual tyranny that regulates society. Let us have done with this absurd catch-phrase of "Woman's Influence." No influence worth naming as such can be exercised but by an independent mind. Women need better fields for the exercise of their love of power. The sexual sphere, which has shaped an impalpable prison around them, has barred them from that part of life which is social and broadly human; the falsely feminine has been developed to the loss of the womanhood in them. It is only in obedience to man that woman has gained her power of life. She has borne children at his will and for his pleasure. She has received her very consciousness from man: this has been her womanhood, to feel herself under another's will. There is no possible hiding of the truth; if women influence men, men command life.

But is it possible, looking forward to new conditions of society, now approaching like a long-delayed spring, to foresee a remedy? Can the woman of the future belong to herself? What are her natural disabilities, and to what extent are they modifiable by new arrangements of social and domestic life? Must she be content for the future with that dependence on the individual man which has been her fate in the past; or, on the other hand, can she take up her economic and social position in society and work therein for her own maintenance as free from considerations of her sex as a man can? These are the questions which must be faced when united womanhood begins to formulate their wants and to realise their power. It is almost idle in the present transition to speculate as to what women should or should not be, or the work they should or should not do. Women do not yet know what they want. All that can be done is to note the changes that are taking place, for we cannot, even do we wish, now change the revolutionary forces. We must seek to understand their causes, so that we may be able to direct them in the future in such ways as will tend to the greater solidarity and happiness of women and men.

In the everlasting controversy as to woman's place in Nature the majority of arguments have been based on an assumed inferiority of the female sex. Appeal has been made to anatomy to establish the difference between the natural endowment of men and women in the hope of fixing by means of anatomical measurements and tests those characters of males and females that are unalterable, because inborn, and those that are acquired, and therefore modifiable. But the obstacles in the way of anatomical investigations are very great, if only on account of the complexity of the material. Often and often it has happened that old conclusions have been overthrown by new knowledge. Indeed, it may be said that such appeal has resulted in uncertainty, and in many instances in confusion. The chief source of error has been the careless acceptance of female inferiority, which has maimed most investigations and seriously retarded the attainment of useful results. And though it is very far from my purpose to wish to deny the fundamentally different nature of the masculine and feminine character, it is still true that a blank separation of human qualities into male qualities and female qualities is no longer possible. In no instance have the anatomists succeeded in determining with absolute distinction between the characters that belong separately to the sexes. Moreover, it has been shown that there is no such thing as a *fixed woman character*, but that women differ according to the circumstances under which they live, just as men differ. This brings us directly against the old problem, inferiority cannot be accepted as the sole reason of woman's present restricted position in society. Other causes must be sought for.

Many features of the social and psychic as well as the physical phenomena of human life have what we may call an organismal mainspring, and become more intelligible when traced back to these. No one, for instance, can appreciate the social significance of sex, or account for the existing sexual relationships in human societies, who does not know something of their biological antecedents. Take again the sex differences, which attain to such complexity and importance in the human civilised races, these can be explained only if their origin is recognisable. To comprehend the higher forms of life we must gain an acquaintance with the lower and more formative types. In this way we shall begin to see something of that continual upward change under the action of love's-selection that has developed the female and the male. Many problems that have brought sorrow and perplexity to us to-day will become recognisable as we ascertain their causes, and then we can do much to remove them. Thus the problem of woman must first be considered from a biological point of view. Explorations must be made into the remote and obscure beginnings of sex. We must carry our investigations back beyond the cycle of man, and trace the growth and uses of the differentiation of the sexes from the lowest forms of life.

Biology, a science hardly more than a century old, is still in the descriptive and comparative stage; it is the scientific study of the present and past history of animal life for the purpose of understanding its future history. It is of vital importance to human welfare in the future that we should learn by this comparative study of origins and of the potent past what are the lines along which progress is to be expected.

This, then, will be the first path of our discovery. We shall have to traverse many past ages of life and to consider certain humble organisms, before we shall be able really to understand woman in her true position in the sexual relationship as we find it to-day.

But the possibility of applying biological results to sociology with any hope of enlightenment depends on an understanding of the questions, How? and Why? It is important to know what the phenomena are, but it is yet more important to know how? and for what reason? they have come about. Thus we are led forward always from facts to their efficient causes. Women are found to differ from men in this or that respect. But this in itself decides nothing. As soon as we are informed as to any one difference, we must seek out its cause; and this we must do over and over again. Hundreds of women must be interrogated, observed and reported upon —and then what? Shall we know the answer to our problem? Certainly not. In each case we must ask: Is this difference we have found between the sexes a natural inborn quality of woman, whether it be physical or psychical, that must be regarded as a right and unalterable part of her woman character, or is it an acquired, and therefore changeable, modification that has been superimposed upon her through the artificial sexual, social and economic circumstances of her environment?

The mere asking of this question will give many new discoveries.

Life is a relation between two forces: on the one hand the organism and on the other the external conditions that form the environment These two processes are known as Nature and Nurture, they are complementary and inseparable, and they act together. Thus the organism modifies its surroundings, and is in turn modified by them. But every life possesses in great degree the power of self-adaptation, and, broadly speaking, it is true that no matter under what conditions it may be compelled to live, it will mould its own life into harmony with those conditions and thus continue its existence, and this whether it is compelled to adopt a more perfect or a less perfect character. It becomes evident that an appropriate environment is necessary if the Nature is to be expressed, or expressed fully; otherwise life cannot realise development. The environment is constantly checking and modifying the inheritance. Nurture supplies the liberating stimulus to the inheritance, and growth is limited, in exact measurement by the Nurture stimuli available. Human advancement is, of course, widely different from the slow progress in the lower forms of life, but it is fundamentally the same. Experience is continually spreading over new fields and bringing about a more wide and exact relation between the individual and the external world. It follows that any change in the environment will cause a change in the individual. To live differently from what one had been living is to be different from what one has been. These are simple biological facts.

Now, how does woman stand in this respect? No one can deny the difference of environment that in the past has acted on women and on men. Speaking from a biological standpoint, it would seem that any present inferiority of woman is mainly social, due to her adaptation to an arbitrary environment. It has been truly said [1] that "man, in supporting woman, has become her economic environment." By her position of economic dependence in the sex relation, sex distinction has become with her "not only a means of attracting a mate, as with all creatures, but a means of gaining her livelihood, as is the case with no other creature under heaven." Can we wonder that the differences between the sexes assume such great and, in certain directions, such unnatural importance? Woman to a far greater extent than man is in process of evolution; her powers dormant for want of liberating Nurture stimuli. We know that Alpine plants brought from their natural soil change their character and become hardly recognisable, and these marked modifications will reappear in many generations of plants, but as soon as the plants are taken back to grow in their natural environment they are transformed to their original Alpine forms. May we not then entertain as a possibility that woman's modern character, with all its acknowledged faults—all its separation from the human qualities of man—is a veneer imposed by an unnatural environment on succeeding generations of women? If the larger social virtues are wanting in her, may it not be because they have not been called for

[1] *Woman and Economics*, Mrs. Stetson, p. 38.

in a parasitic life? How splendid a hope for women rests here! There is a biological truth, not usually suspected by those who quote it, in the popular saying: "Man is the creature of circumstance." And this is even more true of women, who are less emancipated from their surroundings than are men—more saturated with the influences and prejudices of their narrowed environment.

It would seem, then, that Nurture is more important than Nature in seeking to explain the character of woman to-day. Yet, let me not be mistaken, nor let it be thought for one moment that I do not realise the importance of Nature. The first right of every human being is the right of being well-born. This is the goal of all our struggles for progress—it is the sole end worthy of them.

Let me try to make this clearer.

Reproduction carries life beyond the individual. Haeckel has said that the process is nothing more than the growth of the organism beyond its individual mass. But this process in the higher forms of life has become exceedingly complex. All living beings are individual in one respect and composite in another, for the inheritance of each individual is a mosaic of ancestral contributions. Galton's *Law of Inheritance* makes this abundantly clear. Briefly stated, the law is as follows: The two parents of each living being contribute *on the average* one-half of each inherited quality, each of them contributing one-quarter of it. The four grand-parents furnish between them one-quarter, or each of them one-sixteenth; and so on backwards through past generations of ancestors. Now, though, of course, these numbers are purely arbitrary, applying only to averages, and rarely true exactly of individual cases, where the prepotency of any one ancestor may, and often does, upset the balance of the contributions made by the other ancestors, it may certainly be accepted as the most probable theory that biology has given us to explain the grand-parents, great-grand-parents, great-great-grand-difficult problem of Nature--that is the inheritance we receive from our ancestors.

We see that the heredity relation is an extremely complex affair. It is not merely dual from the parents; but it is multiple, through them reaching back to the parents, and so on backwards indefinitely. It is, indeed, a mosaic of many, yes, of uncountable, contributions. The Life Force gathering within itself these multiple sets of heredity contributions is like capital ever growing at compound interest. The importance of this is abundantly clear. For as we come to understand the continuity of our inheritance from generation to generation we realise more vividly how the past has a living hand on and in the present, and how that present will be carried on to the future. We are all links in the one mighty Chain of Life, and on us, and upon women especially, rests a high responsibility. We must hand on our past inheritance unimpaired, so that the new link forged by us may strengthen and not weaken the chain. It is the duty of every woman as a potential mother of men to choose a fitting father for her children, having first educated herself for a freer and more capable maternity. In the past she has done this blindly, following the Life Force without understanding, or hindered from her purpose by the artificial conditions of society. In the future such blindness and such failure of her powers will alike be regarded as sin. With full knowledge, woman will fulfil her great central purpose of breeding the race—ay, breeding it to heights now deemed impossible, not dreamt of even by those of us who look forward through the darkness to the clear sunlight of that time when the sex relation shall be freed from economic pressure and from all coercion of a false morality, and the universal creative energy, no longer finding gratification alone in personal ends, shall at last reach its goal and give birth to a race of new women and new men.

But to come back from this dream of the future.

Certain facts now become evident. In the inheritance of each individual are many latent qualities that do not find expression. It is as if in every life the separate heredity qualities, or groups of qualities, wait in competition, and those that succeed and find an expression in each life owe their success to an incalculable number of small and mostly unknown circumstances. One is tempted to speculate as to a possible direction in the future of women that may arise from the liberating of these unknown forces; but as yet we have not a sufficient basis of facts. But one truth must not be lost sight of; the unsuccessful qualities that do not find their expression in an individual life may remain to be handed on for new competition to a new generation. No one of the forces of our inheritance, be it for good or for evil, is dead; rather it sleeps till that time when the liberating powers of Nurture call it into active expression. There is real biological truth in the saying, "Every man is a potential criminal"; but it is equally true that every one is a possible saint. And there is one point further; we know that those qualities which do succeed in the competition of the inheritance, and which form at birth the character of the individual, are very different from their actual expression in the development of life, where perforce such qualities are modified to the environment. What we are is no certain criterion of what we are capable of becoming. For every item of our inheritance requires an appropriate growth-soil if it is actively to live. Each life is an adjustment of internal character to external conditions. A garden that has been choked with weeds may remain flowerless for many succeeding years, but dig that garden, and sleeping flowers, not known to live within the memory of man, may spring to life. May it not be that in the garden of woman's inheritance there are buried seeds, lying dormant, which at the liberating touch of opportunity may reawaken and assert themselves as forgotten flowers? Yes, to-day this seems a practical fact that already is being accomplished, and not a futile speculation. The re-birth of woman is no dream. At last she is realising the arrest in her development that has followed the acceptance of a position which forces her to be a parasite and a prostitute.

Every one admits the differences of function that separate the female from the male half of humankind. But to assume that the physical, mental, and moral disabilities of women, of which we hear so much, are a necessary part of their inheritance—the debt they pay for being the mothers of the race—is an absurdity it would be difficult to explain except for that strange sex bias, which seems always to colour all opinions as to women, their character and their place in society. Havelock Ellis, who in his admirable work *Man and Woman* has made an exhaustive examination of all the known facts with regard to the real and supposed secondary sexual differences between women and men, comes to this conclusion in his final summary—

> "We have not succeeded," he says, "in determining the radical and essential character of men and women uninfluenced by external modifying conditions. We have to recognise that our present knowledge cannot tell us what they might be, but what they actually are, under the conditions of civilisation. . . . The facts are so numerous that even when we have ascertained the precise significance of some one fact, we cannot be sure that it is not contradicted by other facts. And so many of the facts are modifiable under a changing environment that in the absence of experience we cannot pronounce definitely regarding the behaviour of either the male or female organism under different conditions."

Only a knowledge of the multifarious and complex environmental forces, which in the past have moulded women into what to-day they are, will lead us to our goal. We may examine woman's present character, both physical and mental, with every precision of detail, but the knowledge gained will not settle her inborn Nature. We shall discover what she is, not what she might be. No, rather to do this we must go back through many generations to primitive woman. We must study, in particular, that period known as the Mother-Age, when we find an early civilisation largely built up by woman's activity and developed by her skill. We must find out every fact that we can of woman's physical and mental life in this first period of social growth; we must examine the causes which led to the change from this Mother-rule to that of the Father-rule, or the patriarchate, which succeeded it. Insight into the civilisations of the past is of special value to us in trying to solve our problems of woman's true place in the social life. For one thing, we shall learn that morality and sexual customs and institutions are not fixed, but are peculiar to each age, and are good only in so far as they fulfil the needs of any special period of a people's growth. We must note, in particular, the contributions made by woman to early civilisation, and then seek the reasons why she has lost her former position of power. The savage woman is nearer to Nature than we ourselves are, and in learning of her life we shall come to an understanding of many of the problems of our lives.

This, then, must be the second path of our discovery, and, following it, we shall gain further knowledge of what is artificial and what is real in the character of woman and in the present relations of the sexes.

We find that the external surroundings that influence life are referable to one of two classes: those which tend to increase destructive processes, and find their active expression in expenditure of energy, and those which tend to increase constructive processes, and are passive instead of active, storing energy, not expending it. These two classes of external forces, disruptive and constructive, are called katabolic and anabolic. Looking back on the early natural lives of men and women, we find there has been a very sharp separation in the play of these opposite sets of influences. A hasty survey of the facts suffices to prove that the work of the world was divided into two great parts, the men had the share of killing life, whether that of man or of animals, their attention was given to fighting and hunting; while the women's share was the continuing and nourishing life, their attention being given to the domestic arts—to agriculture and the attendant stationary industries. Woman's position during the matriarchate was largely the result of the need in primitive society of woman's constructive energy, and her power arose from an unfettered use of her special functions. But this divergence of the paths of women from the paths of men continued, and during the patriarchal period became arbitrary with the withdrawal of women from initiative labour, an unnatural arrangement which arose out of later social conditions. The militant side of social activities has belonged to men, the passive to women; and men have been goaded into growth by the conditions and struggles of their lives. They have gathered around themselves a special man-formed environment of institutions and laws, of activities and inventions, of art and literature, of male sentiments, and male systems of opinions, to which they are connected in subtle and numerous relations, and this complex heritage of influences has been reimposed on men generation by generation. In this social working-life women have not had an equal part—and a drag in their development has arisen as the result of this passivity. At a certain period in civilisation women became an inferior class because men with their greater range of opportunities, which brought them within a wider and more variable circle of influences, developed a superior fitness on the motor side. Another contrast is very evident, men's work being performed under more striking circumstances and with more apparent effort and danger, drew to itself prestige, which women's work did not receive; their work, on the contrary, was held in contempt.[1]

Yet, in this connection, it is necessary to say emphatically that, in its origin, there was nothing arbitrary in this division between the sexes. It was, in itself, a natural outcome of natural causes, arising out of the needs of primitive societies. There is nothing derogatory to woman in accepting the passive or, more truly, the constructive power of her nature; rather it is her chief claim for the regaining of her true position in society. I wish at once to say how far it is from my desire to judge woman from a male standpoint. The power and nature that are woman's are not secondary to man's; they are equal, but different, being co-existent and complementary—in fact, just the completion of his.

There is another point that must be made clear.

The separation in the social activities of women and men was not brought about, as is stated so frequently, by men's injustice to women. There is an unfortunate tendency to regard the subjection of woman as wholly due to male selfishness and tyranny. Many leaders of woman's freedom hold to this view as their broad exposition of principle. Such belief is illogical and untrue. It cannot be too often repeated that sex-hatred means retrogression and not progress. I do not mean to say that women have not suffered at men's hands. They

[1] See Thomas, *Sex and Society*, chapter on "Sex and Primitive Industry," pp. 123–146; and Ellis, *Man and Woman*, pp. 1–17.

have, but not more than men have suffered at their hands. No woman who faces facts can deny this truth. Neither sex can afford to bring railing accusations against the other. The old doctrine of blame is insufficient. Women's disabilities are not, in their origin at least, due to any form of male tyranny. I believe, moreover, that any solution of the woman problem, and of woman's rights, is of ridiculous impotence that attempts to see in man woman's perpetual oppressor. The enemy, if enemy there is, of woman's emancipation, is woman herself.

But, on the other side, it is certain that the long-held opinion—what we may call "the male view of women"—which believes that the position woman occupies in society and the duties she performs are, in the main, what they should be, she being what she is, is equally false. Such theorists throw upon Nature the responsibility of the evils consequent on the deviations from equality of opportunity in the past lives of women. Truly we credit Nature with an absurd blunder do we accept this inferiority of the female half of life. *Woman is what she is because she has lived as she has.* And no estimate of her character, no effort to fix the limit of her activities, can carry weight that ignores the totally different relations towards society that have artificially grown up, dividing so sharply the life of woman from that of man.

I am brought back to the object of this book.

What are the conditions that have brought woman to her position of dependence upon man? How far is her state of physical and mental inferiority the result of this position? To what extent is she justified in her present revolt? What result will her freedom have on the sexual relationships? Will the change be likely to work for the benefit of the future? In a word, how far are the new claims woman is making consistent with race permanence? It is not one, but a whole group of questions that have to be answered when once the ideal of the right of the present position of the sexes is shaken. The subject is so entangled that a straightforward step-by-step inquiry will not always be possible. Dogmatic conclusions, and the bringing forward of too hasty remedies must alike be avoided. The past must lead us to the present, and thence we must look to the future. The first need is to find out every fact that we can that will help us in our search for the truth. Most writers on the subject, in their desire to fix on a cause of the evil, have selected one factor, or group of factors, and largely neglected all others. Otto Weininger, for instance, the brilliant modern denouncer of woman, refers the whole great difference between women and men to one cause—the bondage of sexuality. Mrs. Stetson, in *Woman and Economics*, finds a different answer to the same question, and assumes that the whole evil is of economic origin. Both explanations are in part true, but neither is the truth.

To institute reform successfully needs a wider spirit. We must face sex problems with biological and historical knowledge. Before we can understand women's present position in society, or even suggest a future, we must examine the place she has filled in the civilisations of the past; we must fix, too, the part the female half of life has played in the evolution of the sexes. Yet an inquiry into facts is only the first stage, and not the final. When we can go on from these facts to their results, and learn the reasons of what we have discovered, we shall become to some extent, at least, prepared. Then, and then only, can we venture to look forward and intelligently suggest whither the present revolution is leading us.

It is to reach this goal that this book is written. It is an attempt to place the woman question in a wider and more decisive light. It is not an investigation of facts alone, but of causes. The gospel it would preach is a gospel of liberation. And that from which woman must be freed is herself—the unsocial self that has been created by a restricted environment. We have seen that woman's social inferiority in the past has been to a great extent a legitimate thing. To all appearances history would have been impossible without it, just as it would have been impossible without an epoch of slavery and war. Physical strength has ruled in the past, and woman was the weaker. The truth is that woman's time had not come, but now her unconscious evolution must give place to a conscious development. Happiness for women! That must imply wholly independent activities, and complete freedom for the exercise of her work of race production. Woman's duty to society is paramount, she is the guardian of the Race-body and Race-soul. But woman must be responsible to herself; no longer must she follow men. The natural growth force needs to be liberated. Woman must be freed *as woman;* she must die to arise from death a full human being. There is no other solution to the woman question, and there can be no other.

PART I

BIOLOGICAL SECTION

CONTENTS OF CHAPTER II

THE ORIGIN OF THE SEXES

Biology the starting-point of sociology—The irresistible force of Love—The true place of woman and man in the animal kingdom—Analogy between animal love-matings and our own—The Life-force—Reproduction a process of nutrition—Different modes of Reproduction—Cell-division—Successive stages of growth—Theory of sex—Its nature and origin—Incipient sex among the early forms of life—The true office of sex—The principle of fertilisation—Its use to the species in progressive development—Nutrition as a factor determining sex—Illustration of the *volvox*—The dependence of the male-cell upon the female-cell—The well-nourished female—The hungry male—Relation between food supply and the sexes—Illustrations—Lessons to be learnt—All species are invented and tolerated by Nature for parenthood and its service—The part played by the female—The demand laid upon her heavier than that laid upon the male—The female is mainly responsible for the race—The female led and the male followed in the evolution of life.

CHAPTER II

THE ORIGIN OF THE SEXES

"Before studying the sexual relations, and their more or less regulated form in human societies, it will not be out of place to say a few words on reproduction in general, to sketch briefly its physiology in so far as this is fundamental, and, to show how tyrannical are the instincts whose formation has been determined by physiological causes."—LETOURNEAU.

LET us now, as the first path of our inquiry, turn our attention to that biological point of view which is indispensable and fundamental if we are to understand those primary emotions, impulses and differences of the sexes, of deep organic origin, which were rooted long ago in the lowest forms of life, and hence were passed on to man from his pre-human ancestors. No apology is needed for this inquiry; for in these uncounted ancestral forces, dating back to the remote beginnings of life, we shall find hints, at least, of many things which lead up to and explain those problems which must be solved, before we can determine the true position of woman in the complex sexual relations of our social life. We cannot deny our lineage. The force which drove life onwards from the start drives it still to-day. The reproductive impulse is the chief motor of humanity; our seed is eternal. And the point of view that I wish to make clear is that the sex-impulses, which are, as few will deny, the base of the present unrest among women, have an inconceivably long history, and thus spring up within us with a tremendous organic momentum. To deny this force is futile, to suppress it impossible; all that can be done is to so regulate its expression that it may serve life instead of waste it. Implanted in every normal life is an instinctive desire to function in two ways: to grow and to reproduce, from the simple cell to the highest type of life, including man and woman, these two desires are essential and imperative. The irresistible Force of Life has been inherited by us from millions of ancestral lovers. Only when furnished with a re-interpretative clue to the origin of sex and its functioning can we come to realise its strength and its beauty, far stronger, far subtler, than we suspected before. It is the shirking of these life-facts that has resulted so often in error.

And let no one resent or think useless such an analogy between animal love-matings and our own. In tracing the evolution of our love-passions from the sexual relations of other mammals, and back to those of their ancestors, and to the humbler, though scarcely less beautiful, ancestors of these, we shall discover what must be considered as essential and should be lasting, and what is false in the conditions and character of the sexes to-day; and thereby we shall gain at once warning in what directions to pause, and new hope to send us forward. We shall learn that there are factors in our sex-impulses that require to be lived down as out-of-date and no longer beneficial to the social needs of life. But encouragement will come as, looking backwards, we learn how the mighty dynamic of sex-love has evolved in fineness, without losing its intensity, how it is tending to become more mutual, more beautiful, more lasting. And this gives us new hope to press forward on that path which woman even now is travelling, wherein she will be free from the risk of clinging to conditions of the past, which for so long have dragged her evolution in the mire.

The same force that pushed life into existence tends to increase and perpetuate it. For when the great Force of Life has once started, the same movements which constitute that life continue, and give rise to nutrition, the first of the great faculties, or powers, of life. Then, after this growth has been carried to a certain point, the organism from the superabundance of nutrition is furnished with a surplus growing energy, by means of which it reproduces itself, whence arises the second of the great life faculties. We thus have the two essential forces of life—the preservative force and the reproductive force, arising alike from nutrition. Food to assure life and growth for the individual; reproduction, an extension of the same process, to ensure the continuance of the species. We thus see the truth of Haeckel's definition that "reproduction is a nutrition and growth of the organism beyond its individual mass," or in biological formula, "a discontinuous growth."[1]

It is well to grasp at once this first conception of reproduction as simply an extension of nutrition, if we are to free our minds from misconception. It is a common belief that the original purpose of sex is to ensure reproduction, whereas fundamentally it is not necessary to propagation at all. It is perfectly true, of course, that

[1] Haeckel, *Generelle Morphologie der Organismen*, Vol. II. p. 16.

in the majority of animals, and also in many plants, an individual life begins in the union of two minute elements, the mother egg-cell and the sperm father-cell. But this is not the earliest stage, and below these higher forms we find a great world of life reproducing without this sex-process by simple separation and growth. In these unicellular organisms reproduction is known as asexual, because there are no special germ-cells, nor is there anything corresponding to fertilisation. The most common forms are (1) by division into two; (2) by budding, a modified form of division; (3) by sporulation, a division into many units.[1]

It is worth while to wait to learn something of this first stage in the development of life, for in this way we shall gain a clue as to the origin of sex and the real purpose it fulfils in the service of reproduction. In the very simplest forms of unicellular organisms propagation is effected at what is known as "the limit of growth"; when the cell has attained as much volume as its surface can adequately supply with food, a simple division of the cell takes place into two halves or daughter cells, each exactly like the other, which then become independent and themselves repeat the same rupture process. But in some slightly more complex cases differences occur between the two cells into which the organism divides, as in the *slipper animacule*, where one-half goes off with the mouth, while the other has none. In a short time, however, the mouthless half forms a mouth, and each half grows into a replica of the original. We have here one of the earliest examples of differentiation. That

[1] Thomson, J. Arthur, *Heredity*, p. 29.

injured multicellular organisms should be able by re-growth to repair their loss is an analogous phenomenon; thus an earth-worm cut by a spade does not necessarily suffer loss, but the head part grows a tail and the decapitated portion produces a head; sponges, which do not normally propagate by division, may be cut in pieces and bedded out successfully; the arms of a star-fish, torn asunder by a fisherman, will almost always result in several perfect star-fish. Similarly among plants a cut-off portion may readily give rise to new plants—a potato-tuber is one of hundreds of instances. This ability to effect complete repair is one of the powers that life has lost; it persists as high in the scale as reptiles, and a lizard is able to regrow an amputated leg.

It is certainly not the least interest in studying these early forms that one is able to trace the analogy they bear with the higher forms. No rigid line can be drawn between the successive stages of growth. And it should be borne in mind that, simple as is the life-process in these single-celled organisms, many of them are highly differentiated and show great complexity of structure within the narrow limits of their size. Thus among the *protozoa*, the basis of all animal life, we find very definite and interesting modes of behaviour, such as seeking light and avoiding it, swimming in a spiral, approaching certain substances and retreating from others; the organisms often, indeed, trying one behaviour after another.[1] If we realise this it becomes easier to understand how the higher types of life have developed from these primitive types. Indeed, all the bodies of the most complex

[1] Thomson, J. Arthur, *Heredity*, p. 33.

animals—including ourselves—originate as simple cells, and in the individual history of each of us divide and multiply just as do the cells which exist independently; only in multicellular organisms each cell must be regarded as an individual, modified to serve a special purpose, one cell differentiated to start a lineage of nerve cells, another a lineage of digestive cells, yet another for the reproduction of the species, and so on, each group of cells taking on its special use, but the power of division remaining with the modified cell. Thus a new life is built up—a child becomes an adult, by multiplication of these differentiated cells, repeating the original single-cell development.

Budding. the second, and perhaps the most usual mode of asexual propagation, may be said to mark a further step in the development of the reproductive process. Here the mother-cell, instead of dividing into two equal parts and at once rupturing, protrudes a small portion of its substance, which is separated by a constriction that grows deeper and deeper until the bulk becomes wholly detached. This small bud then grows until it attains the size of the parent, when it, in turn, repeats the same process. This mode of reproduction is common to the great majority of plants. In animal life it is not confined to single-celled organism, but takes place in certain multicellulars, such as worms, bryozoans, and ascidians; one very interesting example being the sea-worm (*myrianida*) which buds off a whole chain of individuals.

Nearly allied with budding is the third stage, in which the division is multiple and rapid within the limited space of the mother-cell. This is known as spore formation.

The cells become detached, and do not further develop until they have escaped from the parent. They then increase by division and growth to form independent individuals. This spore reproduction is found among certain types of vegetation; it also occurs in the *protozoa.*

It is probable that these three stages of asexual reproduction are not all the steps actually taken by Nature in the development of the early life-process. There must have been intermediate steps, perhaps many such, but the forms in which they occur either have not persisted, or have not yet been studied.[1] The feature common to all ordinary forms of asexual multiplication is that the reproductive process is independent of sex; what starts the new life is the half, or a liberated portion of the single parent cell. It will be readily seen that by this process the offspring are identical with the parent. Life continues, but it continues unchanged. Thus the power of growth is restricted within extremely narrow limits. Any further development required a new process. With the life-force pushing in all directions every possible process would be tried. We are often met with striking phenomena of adjustments to new conditions, which in some cases, when found to be advantageous to the organism, persist. There is, in fact, abundant evidence that Nature in these early days of life was making experiments. In pursuance of this policy it naturally came about that any process by which the organism gained increased power of growth had the greater likelihood of survival. The number of devices in the way of modification of form and habit to secure advantage

[1] Ward, *Pure Sociology*, p. 307.

is practically infinite; but there was one principle that was eagerly seized upon at a very early stage, and, persisting by this law of advantage, was utilised by all progressive types as an accessory of success. This was the principle of fertilisation, which arose in this way from what would almost seem the chance union of two cells, at first alike, but afterwards more and more highly differentiated, and from whose primordial mating have proceeded by a natural series of ascending steps all the developed forms of sex.

The ways in which this was brought about we have now to see. But even at this point it becomes evident that the true office of sex was not the first need of securing reproduction—that had been done already—rather it was the improving and perfecting of the single-cell process by introducing variation through the commingling of the ancestral hereditary elements of two parents, and, by means of such variations, the production of new and higher forms of life—in fact, progress by the mighty dynamic of sex.[1]

As we should expect, the passing from the sexless mode of reproduction to the definite male and female types is not sharply defined or abrupt. Even among many unicellular organisms the process becomes more elaborate with distinct specialisation of reproductive elements. In some cases conjugation is observed, when two individuals coalesce, and each cell and each nucelus divides into two, and each half unites with the half of the other to form a new cell. This is asexual, since

[1] See Ward, *op. cit.*, pp. 304-314, from whose chapter on this subject I have taken these facts.

the uniting cells are exactly similar, but the effect would seem to be the strengthening of the cells by, as it were, introducing new blood. In somewhat more complex cases these cells do not part company when they divide, but remain attached to one another, and form a kind of commonwealth. Here one can see at once that some cells in a little group will be less advantageously placed for the absorption of nourishment than others. By degrees this differentiation of function brings about differentiation of form, and cells become modified, in some cases, to a surprising extent, to serve special purposes. The next advance is when the uniting cells become somewhat different in themselves. In the early stages this difference appears as one of size; a small weakly cell, though sometimes propagating by union with a similar cell, in other cases seeks out a larger and more developed cell, and by uniting with it in mutual nourishment becomes strong. This may be seen among the *protozoa* where we can trace the distinct beginnings of the male and female elements. A very instructive example is furnished by the case of *volvox*, a multicellular vegative organism of very curious habits. The cells at first are all alike; they are united by protoplasmic bridges and form a colony. In favourable environmental conditions of abundant nutrition this state of affairs continues, and the colony increases only by multiplication and without fertilisation. But when the supply of food is exhausted, or by any cause is checked, sexual reproduction is resorted to, and this in a way that illustrates most instructively the differentiation of the female and male cells. Some of the cells are seen accumulating nourishment at the expense of the others and grow larger, and if this continues, cells which must be regarded as ova, or female cells, result; while other cells, less advantageously placed with more competitors struggling to obtain food, grow smaller and gradually change their character, becoming, in fact, males. In some cases distinct colonies may in this way arise, some composed entirely of the large well-nourished cells, and others of small hungry cells, and may be recognised as completely female or male colonies.[1]

We are now in a position to gain a clue to the difficult problem of the origin of the sexes. It would be easy as well as instructive to accumulate examples.[2] I am tempted to linger over the life-histories of these early organisms that are so full of suggestion; but the case I have selected—the *volvox*—really answers the question. Sex here is dependent on, and would seem to have arisen through, differences in environmental conditions. We find the well-nourished, larger, and usually more quiescent cell is the female, the hungrier and more mobile cell the male; the one concerned with storing energy, the other with consuming it, the one building up, the other breaking down; or expressed in biological formula, the female cell is predominantly anabolic, that of the male predominantly katabolic. Thus we find that the male, through a want of nutrition, was carried developmentally away from the well-fed female cell, which it was bound to seek and unite with to continue life. This relation between the food supply and the

[1] *Evolution of Sex*, pp. 137–138, 161.

[2] Geddes and Thomson, in *The Evolution of Sex*, pp. 117–123, 135–140, give many interesting and corroborative examples.

sexes is found persisting in higher forms, and, in this connection, the well-known experiments of Young on tadpoles and of Siebald on wasps may be cited. By increasing the nutrition of tadpoles the percentage of females was raised from the normal of about fifty per cent. to ninety, while similarly among wasps the number of females was found to depend on warmth and food supply, and to decrease as these diminished. Mention also may be made of the plant-lice, or aphides, which infest our rose-bushes and other plants, which, during the summer months, when conditions are favourable, produce generation after generation of females, but on the advent of autumn, with its cold and scarcity of food, males appear and sexual reproduction takes place. Similarly brine-shrimps when living under favourable conditions produce females, but when the environment is less favourable males as well are found. Another significant fact is the simple and well-known one that within the first eight days of larval life the additions of food will determine the striking and functional differences between the workers and queen-bee.[1] Among the higher animals the difficulties of proving the influence of environment upon sex are, of course, much greater. There are, however, many facts which point to a persistence of this fundamental differentiation. Among these it is sufficient to mention the experiments of stock-breeders, which show that good conditions tend to produce females; and the testimony of furriers that rich regions yield more furs from females, and poor regions

[1] Geddes and Thomson, *The Evolution of Sex*, pp. 40–52, 249–250, give a complete exposition of this theory with many examples. See also Thomas, *Sex and Society*, pp. 4–43.

more from males. Even when we reach the human species facts are not wanting to suggest a similar condition. It is usual in times of war and famine for more boys to be born; also more boys are born in the country than in cities, possibly because the city diet is richer, especially in meat. Similarly among poor families the percentage of boys is higher than in well-to-do families. And although such evidence is not conclusive and must be accepted with great caution, it seems safe to say that the facts—of which I have given a few only of the most common—are sufficient to suggest that the relation among the lower forms of life persists up to the human species, and that the female is the result of surplus nutrition and the male of scarcity.

This is sufficient for our present purpose; all other questions and theories brought forward regarding the determination and conditions of the sexes are outside our purpose. Those who will survey the evidence in detail will find ample confirmation of the point of view I wish to make clear. (1) All species are invented and tolerated by Nature for parenthood and its service; (2) the demands laid upon the female by the part required from her are heavier than those needed for the part fulfilled by the male. The female it is who is mainly responsible to the race. And for this reason the progress of the world of life has always rested upon and been determined by the female half of life. What I wish to establish now is that the male developed after and, as it were, from the female. The female led, and the male followed her in the evolution of life.

CONTENTS OF CHAPTER III

GROWTH AND REPRODUCTION

I.—*The Early Position of the Sexes*

A further examination into the opinion of the superiority of the male—Contradictions to the accepted view of female inferiority—A new way of stating the problem—The female as the creator of the male—Examples of the simplest types of the sexes—Predominance of the female in the animal kingdom below the invertebrates—Superiority of the female in size and often in power of function—Complemental male husbands—Illustrations of male parasites—Corroborative evidence from the sex-elements—The primary service of the male to assist the female in the race-work—Sex-parasitism among females—This explained by the conditions under which the species live—The lessons to be drawn from sex-parasitism—Structural modifications acquired for adapting the sexes to different modes of life—Care of offspring not always confined to the female—Among fishes it is the father who gives any attention to the young—The superiority of the female persists among higher forms—Examples—Sex-equality among birds—Conclusion—The sexual relationship may assume almost any form to suit the varying conditions of life.

II.—*Two Examples—The Beehive and the Spider*

The case of the beehive—The drones—The queen-mother—The sterile-workers—The sacrifice of the sexes to the Life-Force—The maternal instinct among the workers—This has persisted after the atrophy of the sexual needs—Maternal love has expanded out into social affection—Application of the lessons of the beehive—Analogy with modern society—The Intellectuals among women—Do they understand what they really want—The organic necessity of love—The price of sterility—The courtship of the Spider—Mr. Bernard Shaw's Ann—The part played by woman in courtship—Her passivity only apparent—Female superiority with which sexuality began remains in every courtship—The fierce hunger of the male—His absorption by the female—Nothing can, or should, alter this—The importance of woman's activity in love in connection with her claim for emancipation—General observations and conclusion.

CHAPTER III

GROWTH AND REPRODUCTION

"Sexually Woman is Nature's contrivance for perpetuating its highest achievement. Sexually Man is Woman's contrivance for fulfilling Nature's behest in the most economical way. She knows by instinct that far back in the evolution process she invented him, differentiated him, created him in order to produce something better than the single-cell process can produce."—Don Juan in Hell—*Man and Superman*.

I.—*The Early Position of the Sexes*

THE opinion of the superiority of the male sex has been so widely, and without question, accepted that it is necessary to emphasise the exact opposite view which was brought forward in the last chapter. From the earliest times it has been contended that woman is undeveloped man.[1] This opinion is at the root of the common estimation of woman's character to-day. Huxley, who was in favour of the emancipation of women, seems to have held this opinion. He says that "in every excellent character the average woman is inferior to the average man in the sense of having that character less in quantity or lower in quality;" and that "the female type of character is neither better nor worse than the male, only weaker." Few have maintained that the sexes are equal, still fewer

[1] So deep-rooted has been this opinion of female inferiority that it has formed the basis of many theories of sex. Thus Richarz holds that "the male sex represents a higher grade of development in the embryo." Hough thinks males are born when the female system is at its best, females in periods of growth, reparation, or disease. Tiedman and others regard females as an arrested male, while Velpau, on the other hand, believes them to be degenerated from primitive males. See Geddes and Thomson, *Evolution of Sex*, p. 39.

that women excel.[1] The general bias of opinion has always been in favour of men. Woman almost invariably has been accorded a secondary place, the male has been held to be the primary and essential half of life, all things, as it were, centering around him, while the female, though necessary to the continuance of the race, has been regarded as otherwise unimportant—in fact, a mere accessory to the male.

The causes that have given rise to such an opinion are not far to seek. The question has been approached from the wrong end; we have looked from above downwards—from the latest stages of life back to the beginning, instead of from the beginning on to the end. We find among the higher forms of life—the animals with which we are all familiar—that the males are as a rule larger and stronger, more varied in structure, and more highly ornamented and adorned than the females. And when we rise to the human species these sex differences persist and are even emphasised, though finding their expression in a greater number of less strongly marked characters, not on the physical side alone, but on the mental and psychical. It is difficult to divest the mind of facts with which it is most familiar. Thus it is easy to understand the widely-held opinion of the superiority of the male half of life, and that the female is the sex sacrificed to the reproductive process.

Now, were this true, the question of woman's place in life would indeed be settled. There can be no upward change which is not in accord with the laws of Nature.

[1] The theory of Lester Ward, to which I have already referred, supports this view.

If the female really started and had always remained secondary to the male, necessary to continue life, but otherwise unimportant, in such position she must be content to stay. Her struggles for advancement may be heroic, yet would they be doomed to failure, for no individual growth can persist which injures the growth of the race-life. Well it is for women that there need be no such fear, even among the most timid-hearted; woman's position and advancement is sure because it is founded with deepest roots in the organic scheme of life.

As once more we search backwards, tracing the differences of sex function to their earliest appearance in the humblest types of life, we find the exact opposite of this theory of the inferiority of the female to be true. The female is of more importance than the male from Nature's point of view. We have seen that life must be regarded as essentially female, since there is no choice but to look upon asexual reproduction as a female process; the single-cell being the mother-cell with the fertilising element of the father or male-cell wanting. We know further that a similar process, but much more highly developed, is possible in what is called parthenogenesis, or virgin-birth, which can only be explained as a survival of the early form. For long life continued without the assistance of the male-cell, which, when it did arise, was dependent on the ova, or female-cell, and was driven by hunger to unite with it in fatigue to continue life. We are thus forced to regard the male-cell as an auxiliary development of the female, or as Lester Ward ingenuously puts it, "an after-thought of

Nature devised for the advantage of having a second sex."

Now, if we examine the simplest types of the sexes in the lower reaches of the animal kingdom,[1] below the vertebrates we find the same conditions prevailing. The male is frequently inconspicuous in size, of use only to fertilise the female, and in some cases incapable of any other function; the female, on the other hand, remains unchanged and carries on the life of the species. So marked is this difference among some species that the male must be regarded as a fallen representative of the female, having not only greatly diminished in size, but undergone thorough degeneration in structure.[2] In certain extreme cases what have been well called "pigmy males" illustrate this contrast in an almost ridiculous degree. This is well seen among the common rotifers, where the males are much smaller than the females and

[1] I have left out of my inquiry any reference to plants, though all that has been said of the *protozoa* in the last chapter is equally true of the *protophyta*, the basis of plant life. Among plants there are many beautiful and instructive examples of the relative position of the female and the male plant. A well-known case is that of the hemp-plant, where the sexes are indistinguishable up to the period of fertility, but when the male plants have shed their pollen, and thus fulfilled their duty of fertilising the female plants, they cease to grow, turn yellow and sere, and if at all crowded wither and die. Many other examples might be cited, but the question is too wide to enter on here. See Lester Ward, *op. cit.*, pp. 318–322.

[2] *Encyclopædia Britannica*, article on "Sex," by Prof. Geddes; also *Evolution of Sex*, pp. 20, 21. Prof. Lester Ward, *Pure Sociology*, Part II, Chap. XIV, gives an ingenuous and complete view of the early superiority of the female, to which he gives the name of the Gynæcocentric theory, as opposed to the usual Androcentric theory, based on the superiority of the male. While fully appreciating the suggestiveness and value of this theory, and also acknowledging very gratefully the help I have derived from it, it must be stated that some of the facts brought forward in its support by the distinguished American cannot be accepted. Nor am I able, as will appear later, to accept the conclusion he arrives at of the passive character of the female. See also a popular article by Prof. Ward, "Our Better Halves," *The Forum*, Vol. VI., Nov. 1888, pp. 266–275.

very degenerate. Sometimes they seem to have dwindled out of existence altogether, as only females are to be seen; in other cases, though present they fail even to accomplish their proper function of fertilisation, and as reproduction is carried on by the females, they are not only minute but useless. Nor are such cases of male degeneration confined to this group. The whole family of the *Abdominalia* (cirripedes) have the sexes separate; and the males, comparatively very small, are attached to the body of each female, and are entirely passive and dependent upon her.[1] Some of these male parasites are so far degenerated as to have lost their digestive organs and are incapable of any function except fertilisation: the male *Sygami* (menatodes), for instance, being so far effaced that it is nothing but a testicle living on the female.[2] A yet more striking instance is furnished by the curious green worm *Bonellia,* where the male appears like a remote ancestor of the female, on whom it lives parasitically. Somewhat similar is the cocus insect, among whom the males are very degenerate, small, blind and wingless.

This phenomenon of minute parasitic male fertilisers in connection with normally developed females was noticed by Darwin, and his observations have been confirmed by Van Beneden, by Huxley, Haeckel, Milne Edwards, Fabre, Patrick Geddes, and many other eminent entomologists.[3] A full study of these early forms of

[1] Van Beneden, *Animal Parasites and Messmates*, p. 55.
[2] Milne Edwards, *Leçons sur la physiologie et l'anatomie comparée de l'homme et des animaux*, Vol. IX. p. 267.
[3] In addition to the works already mentioned, see Darwin, *Descent of Man*, Vol. I. p. 329; Haeckel, *Evolution of Man*, and *A Manual of the Anatomy of the Invertebrated Animals*, by T. Huxley, pp. 261–262.

sexuality should be made by all who wish to understand the problem of woman; their life-histories furnish prophecies of many large facts. I wish it were possible for me to bring forward further examples. It is the difficulty of treating so wide a subject within narrow limits that so many things that are of interest have to be hurried over and left out. But there is one delightful case that I cannot refrain from mentioning. The facts are given in a letter from Darwin to Sir Charles Lyell, dated September 14, 1849. It is quoted by Professor Lester Ward. This instance of the sexual relationship among the cirripedes illustrates very vividly the early superiority of the female.

The letter runs thus—

> "The other day I got a curious case of a unisexual, instead of hermaphrodite cirripede, in which the female had the common cirripedial character, and in two valves of her shell had two little pockets, in each of which she kept a little husband; I do not know of any other case in which the female invariably has two husbands. I have still one other fact, common to several species, namely, that though they are hermaphrodite, they have small additional, or shall I call them, complimental males, one specimen, itself hermaphrodite, had no less than seven of these complemental males attached to it. Truly the schemes and wonders of Nature are illimitable." [1]

Here, indeed, is a knock-down blow to the theory of the natural superiority of the male. These cases we have examined are certainly extreme, the difference between the sexes is, as we shall see, less marked in many early types. But the existence of these helpless little husbands serves to show the true origin of the male.

[1] *Life and Letters of Charles Darwin*, Vol. I. p. 345.

How often he lived parasitically on the female, his work to aid her in the reproductive process, useful to secure greater variation than could be had by the single-celled process. In other words, the male is of use to the life-scheme in assisting the female to produce progressively fitter forms. She, indeed, created him, his sole function being her impregnation.

Corroborative evidence appears in the contrast which persists in all the higher forms between the relatively large female-cell or germ and the microscopical male-cell or sperm, as also in the absorption of the male cellule by the female cellule. In the sexual cells there is no character in which differentiation goes so far as that of size.[1] The female cell is always much larger than the male; where the former is swollen with the reserve food, the spermatozoa may be less than a millionth of its volume. In the human species an ovum is about 3000 times as large as spermatozoa.[2] The male cellule, differentiated to enable it to reach the female, impregnates and becomes fused within her cellule, which, unlike hers, preserves its individuality and continues as the main source of life.

It is true that exceptions occur, sex-parasitism appearing in both sex forms, and in some cases it is the female who degenerates and becomes wholly passive and dependent, but this is usually under conditions which afford in themselves an explanation. Thus, in the troublesome thread-worm (*Heterodera schachtii*), which infests the turnip plant, the sexes are at first alike, then

[1] Thomson, J. A., *Heredity*, p. 39.
[2] Article by Ryder, *Science*, Vol. I., May 31, 1895, p. 603.

both become parasitic, but the adult male recovers himself, is agile and like other thread-worms, while the female remains a parasitic victim without power of function—a mere passive, distended bag of eggs. Another extreme but well-known example is that of the cochineal insect, where the female, laden with reserve products in the form of the well-known pigment, spends much of its life like a mere quiescent gall on the cactus plant; the male, on the other hand, is active, though short-lived. Among other insects—such, for example, as certain ticks—a very complete form of female parasitism prevails; and while the male remains a complex, highly active, winged creature, the female, fastening itself into the flesh of some living animal and sucking its blood, has lost wings and all activity and power of locomotion, having become a mere distended bladder, which, when filled with eggs, bursts and ends a parasitic existence that has hardly been life.[1] In many crustaceans, again, the females are parasitic, but this also is explained by their habit of seeking shelter for egg-laying purposes.[2]

The whole question of sex-parasitism as it appears in these first pages of the life-histories of sexes is one of deep suggestion; and one, moreover, that casts forward sharp side-lights on modern sex problems. In some early forms, where the conditions of life are similar for the two sexes, the male and the female are often like

[1] Schreiner, Olive, *Woman and Labour*, pp. 77–78.

[2] These examples of female parasitism have been taken from *Evolution of Sex*, p. 17; see also pp. 19–22. The authors bring them forward with many other examples to prove the main thesis of their book—that the character of the female is anabolic, that of the male katabolic. In establishing this theory they do not appear to give sufficient importance to the fact that this degeneration of the female is only found where the conditions of life are parasitic.

one another. Thus it is very difficult to distinguish a male starfish from a female starfish, or a male sea-urchin from a female sea-urchin. It becomes abundantly clear that degeneration in active function, whether it be that of the male or the female, is the inevitable nemesis of parasitism. The males and females in the cases we have examined may be said to be martyrs to their respective sexes.

A further truth of the utmost importance becomes manifest. Many differences between the relative position of the sexes, which we are apt to suppose are inherent in the female or male, are not inherent, in light of these early and varying types. We see that the sex-relationship and the character of the female and male assume different forms, changing as the conditions of life vary. Again and again when we come to examine the position of women in different periods of civilisation, we shall find that whenever the conditions of life have tended to withdraw them from the social activities of labour, restricting them, like these early sex-victims, to the passive exercise of their reproductive functions alone, that such parasitism has resulted invariably in the degeneration of woman, and through her passing on such deterioration to her sons, there has followed, after a longer or shorter period, the degeneration of society. But these questions belong to the later part of our inquiry, and cannot be entered on here. Yet it were well to fix in our minds at once the dangers, without escape, that follow sex-parasitism.

It may be thought that these cases of sex-victims are exceptions, and that, therefore, it is unsafe to draw conclusions from them. The truth would rather seem to be that they are extreme examples of conditions that were common at one stage of life. There is no doubt that up to the level of the amphibians female superiority in size, and often in power of function, prevails.[1] If, for example, we look at insects generally, the males are smaller than the females, especially in the imago state. There are many species, belonging to different orders—as, for instance, certain moths and butterflies—in which this superiority is very marked. The males are either not provided with any functional organs for eating, or have these imperfectly developed. It seems evident that their sole function is to fertilise the female. A familiar and interesting example is furnished by the common mosquitoes, among whom the female alone, with its harmful sting, is known to the unscientific world. The males, frail and weaponless little creatures, swarm with the females in the early summer, and then pass away, their work being done.

Dr. Howard, writing of the mosquito in America, says—

> "It is a well-known fact that the adult male mosquito does not necessarily take nourishment, and that the adult female does not necessarily rely on the blood of warm-blooded animals. The mouth parts of the male are so different from those of the female that it is probable that, if it feeds at all, it obtains its food in quite a different manner from the female. They are often observed sipping at drops of water, and in one instance a fondness for molasses has been recorded."[2]

[1] *Evolution of Sex*, p. 21; *Pure Sociology*, pp. 316–317.

[2] "Notes on the Mosquitoes of the United States," by L. O. Howard, *Bulletin* No. 25, New Series, U.S. Department of Agriculture, Division of Entomology, 1900, p. 12. Quoted by Lester Ward, *Pure Sociology*, p. 317.

We find many examples of such structural modifications acquired for the purpose of adapting the sexes to different modes of life. Darwin notes that the females of certain flies are blood-suckers, whilst the males, living on flowers, have mouths destitute of mandibles.[1] The females are carnivorous, the males herbivorous. It would be easy to bring forward many further examples among the invertebrates in which the differences between the sexes indicates very clearly the persistence of female superiority. But for these I must refer the reader to the works of Darwin and other entomologists, and to the many interesting cases given by Professor Lester Ward. There are, it is true, exceptions, but these may be explained by the conditions under which the species live.

Even when we ascend the scale to back-boned animals, cases are not wanting in which the early superiority in size of the female remains unaltered. The smallest known vertebrate, *Heterandria formosa*, has females very considerably larger than the males.[2] Among fishes the males are commonly smaller than the females, who are also, as a rule, considerably more numerous.[3] This is a fact that fishermen are well aware of. I may mention, as an example, that on one occasion when my husband and I caught twenty-five trout in a mountain lake in Wales there were only two males among them. It is curious to find that any care of offspring that is evident among fishes is usually paternal. This furnishes another instance of the truth so necessary to learn that

[1] *Descent of Man*, p. 208.
[2] *Science*, Vol. XV., Jan. 1902, p. 30.
[3] Fulton, Naturalist to the Scottish Fishery Board. Cited in *Evolution of Sex*, p. 22; see also pp. 25, 272, 295.

the sex-relationships may assume almost any form to suit the varying conditions of life.

There are some mammals among whom the sexes do not differ appreciably in size and strength, and very little or not at all, in coloration and ornament. Such is the case with nearly all the great family of rodents. It is also the case with the Erinaceidæ, or at least with its typical sub-family of hedgehogs.[1] Even among birds, where the sex instincts have attained to their highest and most æsthetic expression, we find some large families—as, for example, the hawks—in which the female is usually the larger and finer bird.[2] Thus the adult male of the common sparrow-hawk is much smaller than the female, the length of the male being 13 ins., wing 7·7 ins., and that of the female 15·4 ins., wing 9 ins. The male peregrine, known to hawkers as the tiercel, is greatly inferior in size to his mate. The merlin, the osprey, the falcon, the spotted eagle, the golden eagle, the gos-hawk, the harrier, the buzzard, the eagle-owl, and other species of owls are further examples where the female bird is larger than the male. Among many of these families the female birds very closely resemble the males, and where differences in colour and ornament do occur, they are slight.

A further point of the greatest importance to us requires to be made. Wherever amongst the birds the sexes are alike the habits of their lives are also alike. The female as well as the male obtains food, the nest is built together, and the young are cared for by both

[1] *Pure Sociology*, pp. 317, 318.
[2] *Birds of Britain*, by J. Lewis Bonhote, p. 208; also pp. 190–221.

parents. These beautiful examples of sex equality among the birds cannot be regarded as exceptions that have arisen by chance—a reversal of the usual rule of the sexes; rather they show the persistence of the earlier relations between the female and the male carried to a finer development under conditions of life favourable to the female. I will not here say more upon this subject, as I shall have to refer to it in greater detail when we come to consider the sexual and familial habits of birds. I will only add that in their delicacy and devotion to each other and to their offspring, birds in their unions have advanced to a much further stage than we have in our marriages. These associations of our ancestral lovers claim our attentive study.

II.—*Two Examples—The Beehive and the Spider*

"At its base the love of animals does not differ from that of man."
—DARWIN.

For vividness of argument I wish in a brief section of this chapter to make a digression from our main inquiry to bring forward two examples—extreme cases of the imperious action of the sexual instincts—in which we see the sexes driven to the performance of their functions under peculiar conditions. Both occur among the invertebrates. I have left the consideration of them until now because of the instructive light they throw upon what we are trying to prove in this first attack on the validity of the common estimate of the true position of the sexes in Nature. Let us begin with the familiar case of the bees. As every one knows, these truly wonderful insects belong to a highly evolved and complex society, which may be said to represent a very perfected and extreme socialism. In this society the vast majority of the population—the workers—are sterile females, and of the drones, or males, only a very few at the most are ever functional. Reproduction is carried on by the queen-mother. The lesson to be drawn from the beehive is that such an organisation has evolved a quite extraordinary sacrifice of the individual members, notably in the submergence of the personal needs of sex-function, to its wider racial end. It is from this line of thought that I wish to consider it. We have (1) the drones, the fussing males, useless except for their one duty of fertilisation, and this function only a few actively perform; thus, if they become at all numerous they are killed off by the workers, so that the hives may be rid of them; (2) the queen, an imprisoned mother, specialised for maternity, her sole work the laying of the eggs, and incapable of any other function; her brain and mind of the humblest order, she being unable even to feed and care for her offspring; (3) the great body of unsexed workers, the busy sisters, whose duty is to rear the young and carry out all the social activities of the hive.

What a strange, perplexing life-history! What a sacrifice of the sexes to each other and to the life-force.[1]

[1] A similar condition will be found in the even more complex societary forms of ant-hills. Among the vast population of the ants all the workers and soldiers are arrested in their sexual development, remaining, as it were, permanent children of both sexes. It seems probable that this explains the limit that has been reached in the evolution of these wonderful creatures, which in certain directions have attained to an extraordinary development, and have then become curiously and immovably arrested. See *Problems of Sex*, by J. A. Thomson and Prof. Patrick Geddes, p. 24; *Mind in Animals*, by Büchner, p. 60; and *Woman and Labour*, by Olive Schreiner, p. 78.

It seems probable that these active workers have even succeeded in getting rid of sexual needs. Yet the maternal instinct persists in them, and has survived the productive function; it may, indeed, be said to be enlarged and ennobled, for their affection is not confined to their own offspring, but goes out to all the young of the association. In this community one care takes precedence of all others, the care and rearing of the young. This is the workers' constant occupation; this is the great duty to which their lives are sacrificed. With them maternal love has expanded into social affection. The strength of this sentiment is abundantly proved. The queen-bee, the feeble mother, has the greatest possible care lavished upon her, and is publicly mourned when she dies. If through any ill-chance she happens to perish before the performance of her maternal duties, and then cannot be replaced, the sterile workers evince the most terrible grief, and in some cases themselves die. It would almost seem that they value motherhood more for being themselves deprived of it.

Now, how does this history from the bee-hive apply to us? Here you have before you, old as the world itself, one of the most urgent problems that has to be faced in our difficult modern society. I have little doubt that something which is at least analogous to the sterilisation of the female bees is present among ourselves. The complexity of our social conditions, resulting in the great disproportion between the number of the sexes, has tended to set aside a great number of women from the normal expression of their sex functions. Among these women a class appears to be arising who are turning away voluntarily from love and motherhood. Many of them are undoubtedly women of fine character. These "Intellectuals" suggest that women shall keep themselves free from the duties of maternity and devote their energies thus conserved, to their own emancipation and for work in the world which needs them so badly. But the biological objection to any such proposition is not far to seek. No one who thinks straight can countenance a plan which thus leaves maternity to the less intellectual woman—to a docile, domestic type, the parallel of the stupid parasitic queen-bee. Mind counts in the valuation of offspring as well as physical qualities. The splitting of one sex into two contrasted varieties, which we see in its completed development in the bee-hive, cannot be an ideal that can even be worth while for us. It means an end to all further progress.

There is another group of women who wish to bear children, but who seem to be anxious to reduce the father to the position of the drone-bee. He is to have no part in the child after its birth. The duty of caring for it and bringing it up is to be undertaken by the mother, aided, when necessary, by the State. This is a terrible injustice against the father and the child. It seems to me to be the great and insuperable difficulty against any scheme of State Endowment of Motherhood. I cannot enter into this question now, and will only state my belief that a child belongs by natural right to both its parents. The primitive form of the matriarchal family, which we shall study later, is realised in its most exaggerated form by the bees and ants. In human societies we find only imitations of this system. And here, again, there is a lesson necessary for us to remember. Any ideal that takes the father from the child, and the child from its father, giving it only to the mother, is a step backward and not forward.

And in case any woman is inclined still to admire the position of the female worker-bees, so free in labour, being liberated from sexual activity, it were well to consider the sacrifice at which such freedom is gained. These workers have highly-developed brains, but most of them die young. Nor must we forget that each one carries her poisoned sting—no new or strange weapon, but a transformation of a part of her very organ of maternity—the ovipositor, or egg-placer, with which the queen-mother lays each egg in its appointed place.[1]

Do "the Intellectuals" understand what they really want? Those women who are raising the cry increasingly for individual liberty, without considering the results which may follow from such a one-sided growth both to themselves and to the race—let them pause to remember the price paid by the sterile worker-bee. Is it unfair to suggest that any such shirking for the gains of personal freedom of their woman's right and need of love and child-bearing may lead in the psychical sphere to a result similar to the transformation of the sex-organ of the bee; and that, giving up the power of life, they will be left the possessor of the stinging weapon of death! Some such considerations may help women to decide whether it is better to be a mother or a sterile worker.

The second example I want to consider is that of the

[1] *Problems of Sex*, p. 34. I would recommend this admirable little book to all students.

common spider, whose curious courtship customs are described by Darwin.[1] Here we find the relatively gigantic female seizing and devouring the tiny male fertiliser, as he seeks to perform the only duty for which he exists. This is a case of female superiority carried to a savage conclusion. The male in these courtships often has to risk his life many times, and it seems only to be by an accident that he ever escapes alive from the embraces of his infuriated partner. I will give an example, taken from the *mantes*, or praying insect, where, though the difference in size between the sexes is much less than among many spiders, the ferocity of the female is extraordinary. This case is quoted by Professor Lester Ward,[2] who gives it on the authority of Dr. L. O. Howard, one of the best-known entomologists—

"A few days since I brought a male or *Mantes carolina* to a friend who had been keeping a solitary female as a pet. Placing them in the same jar, the male, in alarm, endeavoured to escape. In a few minutes the female succeeded in grasping him. She bit off his left front tarsus and consumed the tibia and femur. Next she gnawed out his left eye. At this the male seemed to realise his proximity to one of the opposite sex, and began vain endeavours to mate. The female next ate up his right front leg, and then entirely decapitated him, devouring his head and gnawing into his thorax. Not until she had eaten all his thorax, except about three millimetres did she stop to rest. All this while the male had continued in his vain attempt to obtain entrance at the valvula, and he now succeeded, and she voluntarily spread the parts open, and union took place. She remained quiet for four hours, and the remnant of the male gave occasional signs of life, by a movement of one of his remaining tarsi for three hours. The next morning she had entirely rid herself of her spouse, and nothing but his wings remained."

[1] *Descent of Man*, Vol. I. p. 329.

[2] *Pure Sociology*, p. 316; *Science*, Vol. VIII., Oct. 1886, p. 326. Letter by Dr. L. O. Howard.

You will think, perhaps, that this extreme case of female ferocity has little bearing upon our sexual passions. But consider. I have not quoted it, as is done by Professor Ward, to prove the existence of the superiority of the female in Nature. No, rather I want to suggest a lesson that may be wrested by us from these first courtships in the life histories of the sexes. I spoke at the beginning of this biological section of my book of the warnings that surely would come as we traced the evolution of our love-passions from those of our prehuman ancestors. We are too apt to ignore the tremendous force that the sex-impulse has gathered from its incalculably long history. As animals exhibit in their love-matings the analogies of the human virtue, it is not surprising to find the occurrence of parallel vices. Let us look for a moment at this in the light of the fierce love-contest of the female spider.

Of this habit there are various explanations; the prevalent one regards the spider as an anomalous exception; the ferocity and superiority of size in the female not easily to be explained. This is, I think, not so. Is it not rather a picture, with the details crudely emphasised, of the action of Life-Force of which the sexes are both the helpless victims? Whether we look backward to the beginning, where the exhausted male-cell seeks the female in incipient sexual union, or onwards through the long stages of sex-evolution to our own love-passions, this is surely true.

Let me try to make this clearer by an example. It would seem but a small step from the female spider, so ruthlessly eating up her lover, to the type of woman celebrated by Mr. Bernard Shaw's immortal Ann. I recall a woman friend saying to me once, "We may not like it, and, of course, we refuse to own to it, but there is something of Ann in every woman." I need not recall to you Ann's pursuit of her victim, Tanner, nor his futile efforts to escape. Here, as so often he has done, Mr. Shaw has presented us in comedy with a philosophy of life. You believe, perhaps, the fiction, still brought forward by many who ought to know better, that in love woman is passive and waits for man to woo her. I think no woman in her heart believes this. She knows, by instinct, that Nature has unmistakably made her the predominant partner in all that relates to the perpetuation of the race; she knows this in spite of all fictions set up by men. Have they done this, as Mr. Shaw suggests, to protect themselves against a too humiliating aggressiveness of the woman in following the driving of the Life-Force? This pretence of male superiority in the sexual relation is so shallow that it is strange how it can have imposed on any one.

I wish to state here quite definitely what I hold to be true; the condition of female superiority with which sexuality began has in this connection persisted. In every case the relation between woman and man is the same—she is the pursuer, he the pursued and disposed of. Nothing can or should alter this. The male from the very beginning has been of use from Nature's point of view by assisting the female to carry on life. It is the fierce hunger of the male, increasing in strength through the long course of time, which places him in woman's power. Man is the slave of woman, often when least he thinks so, and still woman uses her power, even like the spider, not infrequently, for his undoing.

Here, indeed, is a warning causing us to think. The touch of Nature that makes the whole world kin is nowhere more manifest than in sex; that absorption of the male by the female to which life owes its continuation, its ecstasy, and its pain. It has seemed to me it is here in the primitive relations of the sexes that we may find the clue to many of those wrongs which women have suffered at the hands of men. Man, acting instinctively, has rebelled, not so much, I think, against woman as against this driving hunger within himself, which forces him helpless into her power. Like the fish that cannot resist the fly of the fisherman, even when experience has taught him to fear the hidden barb, he struggles and fights for his life to escape as he realises too late the net into which his hunger has brought him.

But we may learn more than this; another truth of even deeper importance to us. It is because of this superiority of the female in the sexual relationship that women must be granted their claim for emancipation. Here is the reason stronger than all others. Nature has placed in women's hands so tremendous a power that the dangers are too great for such power to be left to the direction of untrained and unemancipated women. Above all it is necessary that each woman understands her own sexual nature, and also that of her lover, that she may realise in full knowledge the tremendous force of sexual-hunger which drives him to her, equalled, as I believe, by the desire within herself, which claims him to fulfil through her Nature's great central purpose of continuing the race.

To women has been granted the guardianship of the Life-Force. It is time that each woman asks herself how she is fulfilling this trust.

It is the possession of this power in the sexual sphere which lends real importance to even the feeblest attempts of women to prepare themselves to meet the duties in the new paths that are being opened to them. Women have now entered into labour. They are claiming freedom to develop themselves by active participation in that struggle with life and its conditions whereby men have gained their development. From thousands of women to-day the cry is rising, "Give us free opportunity, and the training that will fit us for freedom." Not, as so many have mistakenly thought, that women may compete with men in a senseless struggle for mastery, but in order first to learn, and afterwards to perform, that work in society which they can do better than men. What such work is it must be women's purpose to find out. But before this is possible to be decided all fields of activity must be open for them to enter. And this women must claim, not for themselves chiefly; but because they are the bearers of race-life, and also to save men from any further misuse of their power. Then working together as lovers and comrades, women and men may come to understand and direct those deep-rooted forces of sex, which have for so long driven them helpless to the wastage of life and love.

I would ask all those who deny this modern claim of women to consider in all seriousness the two cases I have brought forward—that of the bee-hives, and even more the destruction by the female spider of her male lover.

That they have their parallel in our society to-day is a fact that few will deny. I have tried to show the real danger that lurks in every form of sex-parasitism. It would lead us too far from our purpose to comment in further detail on the suggestions offered by these curious examples of sex-martyrs among our earliest ancestral lovers. Those whose eyes are not blinded will not fail to see.

CONTENTS OF CHAPTER IV

THE EARLY RELATIONSHIP OF THE SEXES

Summary of conclusions arrived at in the previous chapters—The necessity of a further examination of sexual love among our pre-human ancestors—The question approached from a different point of view—The impelling motive of love the union of two cells—Hermaphroditism—Its various forms—The first step in the ladder of sex—Reproduction among fishes—The next step—The attraction of one sex for the other—The female and the male begin to associate in pairs—Illustration of the salmon—Sexual differences become more frequent—The males distinguished by bright colours and ornamental appendages—Sexual passion and jealous combats of rival males—Examples—A further step—The note of physical fondness—The male plays with the female, wooing and caressing her—The love play often extraordinary—The case of the stickleback—The males, passionate, polygamous, and jealous—The paternal instinct of the stickleback—Nature making experiments in parenthood—Parental forethought among insects—Illustrations of male parental care—The obstetric frog—Further examples of primitive animal courtships—A psychic attraction added to the physical—The courtship of the octopus—A final step—The co-operation of the sexes in work together—The dung-rolling beetle—The significance of these early courtships—Analogy with our sex-passions—The love-process identical throughout the whole of life.

CHAPTER IV

THE EARLY RELATIONSHIP OF THE SEXES

"Great effects are everywhere produced in animated Nature, by minute causes. . . . Think of how many curious phenomena sexual relation gives rise to in animal life; think of the results of love in human life; now all this had for its *raison d'être* the union of two cellules. . . . There is no organic act which approaches this one in power and force of differentiation."—HAECKEL.

WHAT is the practical outcome to us of this early relation of the sexes in Nature's scheme?

In attempting to answer this question it will be necessary to take an apparently circuitous route, going back over some of the ground that already has been covered; to examine in further detail the process of sexual love as it presents itself among our pre-human ancestors. It is well worth while to do this. If we can find in this way an answer, we shall come very near to solving many of the most difficult of woman's problems. At the same time we shall have made clear how deep-rooted are the foundations of those passions of sex which agitate the human heart, and are still the most powerful force amongst us to-day.

In the light of the facts I have briefly summarised, we have been able in the former chapters to indicate how sexuality began, with the male element developed from the primary female organism, his sole function being her impregnation; how this was seized upon and continued through the advantage gained by the mixing of the two germ-plasms, which, on the whole, resembling one another somewhat closely, yet differ in details, and thus introduce new opportunities of progress into the life-elements; and how, in this way, differentiation of function between the male and the female was set up. We saw, further, how the development of the male, at first often living parasitically upon the female, continued; but how, under certain conditions of life, such parasitism was transferred to the female, so that it is she who is sacrificed to the sex function; and, lastly, taking the extreme cases of the bee-hive and the spider, we suggested certain warnings to be drawn from these early parasitic relations between the sexes. It is necessary now to penetrate deeper; to trace more fully the evolution of the sexual passion, which, from this line of thought, may be said to be the process which carried on the development and modification of the male, creating him—as surely we may believe—by the love-choice of the female. To do this we have once more to return to the consideration, under a somewhat new aspect, of the relative position of the female and the male in their love-courtships in some examples among the humbler types of animal life. After these have been considered, not only in themselves, but in the relation they bear to the higher forms which developed from them, we shall be in a surer position to re-ascend the ladder of life. We shall come to understand the biological significance of love—something of the complexity and beauty and force of the passions that we have inherited. We shall find also the causes, so important to us, which led to the reversal of the early superiority of the female in size and often in function, replacing it by the superiority of the male. Then, and then only, shall we be ready to approach the difficult problems of the sexual differences which have persisted, separating women from men among human races, and to estimate if these differences are to be considered as belonging essentially to the female and the male, or whether they have arisen through special environmental causes.

If we look back anew to the very start of sexuality, where two cells flow together, thereby to continue life, we find the very simplest expression of the sex-appetite. There is what may be called instinctive physical attraction, and the whole process is very much a satisfaction of protoplasmic hunger.[1] Now it was, of course, a long step from this incipient cell-union to the varied function of sex in animal life, and it was a long process from these to the yet more complex manifestation of the love-passion among men. But in reality the source of all love is the same; throughout the entire relations of the sexes we find this cell-hunger instinct; in every case, it matters not how fine and ennobling the love may be, the single, original, impelling motive is the union of two cells—the male element and the female driven to seek one another to continue life. I find it necessary to insist on this physical basis of all love. Women are so apt to go astray. It is one of the vicious tendencies of the female mind to think that the needs of sex are something to be resisted. Let us face the truth that this great force of love has its roots fastened in cell-hunger, and it dies when its roots are cut away.

[1] *Evolution of Sex*, p. 265.

It is evident that at first this sex-appetite cannot have been purposive, but acted subconsciously by a kind of interaction between the want of the organism and its power of function. Even in many complex multicellular organisms the liberation of the sex-elements continues very passive; and although the differentiation of the sexual-cells is already complete in plants and animals comparatively low in the scale, it at first makes little difference in the development of the other parts of the individual. Among many lower animals, and most plants, each individual develops within itself both kinds of cells—that is, female and male. This union of the two sex functions in one organism is known as hermaphroditism. There is little doubt that it was once common to all organisms, an intermediate stage in the sex-progress, after the differentiation of the sexes had been accomplished.

Hermaphroditism must be regarded as a temporary or transitional form.[1] It is found persisting in various degrees in many species—snails, earth-worms, and leeches, for example, can act alternately as what we call male and female. Other animals are hermaphrodite in their young stages, though the sexes are separate in adult

[1] There are some who believe that the higher animals pass through a state of embryonic hermaphroditism, but decisive proof of this is wanting. In this connection the structural resemblance of the male and female sexual organs should be noticed; in each sex there is a complete but rudimentary set of parallels to the organs of the other sex. This primitive and fundamental unity of the male and female sex organs is very significant. Indeed, the whole question of hermaphroditism is one of deep suggestion when these embryological facts are brought into relation with the abnormalities which occur in the expression of the sexual impulses. See *Evolution of Sex*, chapter on "Hermaphroditism," pp. 65–80; also Bloch, *Sexual Life of Our Times*, pp. 11–12, 551–554. Weininger's *Sex and Character*, pp. 6, 7, 13, 45, is also interesting.

life, as, for example, tadpoles, where the bisexuality of youth sometimes linger into adult life. Cases of partial hermaphroditism are very common, while in many species which are normally unisexual, a casual or abnormal hermaphroditism occurs—this may be seen in the common frog, and is frequent among certain fishes, when sometimes the fish is male on one side and female on the other, or male anteriorly and female posteriorly.[1]

There would seem to be a constant tendency to escape from these early and experimental methods of reproduction, and to secure true sexual union, with complete separation of the sexes and differences in the parents. We have noticed the many instances of tiny complemental males, in connection with hermaphrodite forms, which, as Darwin states, must have arisen from the advantage ensuring cross-fertilisation in the females who harbour them. Even among hermaphrodite slugs we find very definite evidence of the advance of love; and in certain species an elaborate process of courtship, taking the form of slow and beautiful movements, precedes the act of reproduction.[2] Some snails, again, are provided with a special organ, a slightly twisted limy dart, which is used to stimulate sexual excitement.[3]

[1] A similar condition has been noted among butterflies, where, in some cases, differences in the colouring of the wings on two sides has been found to correspond to an internal co-existence of the male and female sex-organs. It seems probable that this interesting phenomenon of abnormal hermaphroditism is of much commoner occurrence than the cases that have been recorded (*Evolution of Sex*, p. 67).

[2] "The Love of Slugs," article by James Bladon, *Zoologist*, Vol. XV., 1857, p. 6272.

[3] "Molluscs," article by Rev. L. H. Cooke, *Cambridge Natural History*, Vol. III. p. 143. Both these cases are quoted by Havelock Ellis in his illuminative "Analysis of the Sexual Impulse," the opening chapters in the third volume of the *Studies in the Psychology of Sex*.

What do such marvellous manifestations, low down in the ladder of life, go to prove, if not that there must be the closest identity between the development of life and the evolution of love?

These examples of hermaphrodite love lead us forward to a further step, where no reproduction takes place without the special activity and conjugation of two kinds of specialised cells, and these two kinds are carried about by separate individuals. In some species—fishes, for example—the two kinds of special cells meet outside the bodies of the parents. At this humble level the sexes are in many cases very like one another, and there is, as we should expect, a good deal of haphazard in the production of offspring. Among fishes, for instance, the eggs and sperms are liberated into the sea, or the shallow bed of a river, and, if the sperms (the milt of the males) are placed near to the spot where the eggs (the spawn) have been laid, fertilisation occurs, for within a short distance the sperms are attracted—in a way that is imperfectly understood—to enter the eggs. By this method there is of necessity great waste in the production of offspring, many thousands of eggs are never fertilised. The union of the sexual cells must be something more than haphazard for further development. There must be some reason inherent in the female or male inducing to the act of reproduction. In other words, there must be a psychic interest preceding the sex act. In this way a higher grade is reached when the presence of one sex attracts the other. Gradually the female and the male begin to associate in pairs.

We may illustrate this important step in the evolution of love by reference to the familiar case of the salmon.

The male courts the female and is her attendant during the breeding season, fertilising the deposited ova in her presence. He guards her from the attention of all other males, fighting all rivals fiercely, with a special weapon, developed at this time, in the form of a hooked lower jaw with teeth often more than half-an-inch long. Darwin records a case, told to him by a river-keeper, where he found three hundred dead male salmon, all killed through battle.[1] Thus even among cold-blooded fishes (though it may appear folly to use the word "love" in this connection) a very clear likeness with our human sex-passions can be traced.

Sex differences now become more frequent. The males are in some cases distinguished by bright colours and ornamental appendages. During their amours and duels certain male fishes flash with beautiful and glowing colours. Reptiles exhibit the same form of sexual-passion, and jealous combat of rival males. The rattle of certain snakes is supposed to act as a love-call. Snakes of different sexes appear to feel some affection for each other when confined together in cages. Romanes relates the interesting fact that when a cobra is killed, its mate is often found on the spot a day or two afterwards. Darwin cites an instance of the pairing in spring of a Chinese species of lizard, where the couples appear to have considerable fondness for one another. If one is captured, the other drops from the tree to the ground and allows itself to be caught, presumably from despair.[2]

A further development is reached by those animals

[1] Trout also fight during the breeding season. *Chapters on Human Love*, by Geoffrey Mortimer (W. M. Gallichan), pp. 13–14.

[2] *Evolution of Sex*, pp. 625–626. *Chapters on Human Love*, p. 14.

among whom what has well been called "the note of physical fondness" is first sounded. We find the males playing with the female, wooing and caressing her, it may be dancing with her. The love-play is often extraordinary,[1] as, for instance, in the well-known case of the stickleback. Not only does the male woo the female with passionate dances, but by means of its own secretions it builds a nest in the river weeds. The males at this season are transformed, glowing with brilliant colours, and literally putting on a wedding garment of love. The stickleback is passionate, polygamous and very jealous of rivals. His guardianship of the nest and vigilance in protecting the young cannot be observed without admiration.

It is certainly significant to find one of the earliest instances of genuine parental affection exhibited by the male. This reversal of the usual rôle of the sexes is common among fishes, among whom care of offspring is very little developed. In some species the eggs are carried about by the father—the male sea-horse, for instance, has a pouch developed for this purpose; in other cases the male incubates, or cares for the ova. Sometimes, however, it is the female who performs this duty, but the known cases are few.[2] Some exceedingly curious examples of male parental care occur among the amphibians. One of the most interesting is that of the obstetric frog, where the male helps to remove the eggs from the female, then twists them in the coils around its

[1] *Problems of Sex*, by J. A. Thomson and Prof. Patrick Geddes, p. 20.

[2] *Evolution of Sex*, pp. 270–272, 295.

hind legs and buries himself in the water, until the incubation period is over and the tadpoles escape and relieve him of his burden. In other species the croaking sacs of the males, which were previously used for amatory callings, become enlarged to form cradles for the young. There are also instances of the female cooperating with the male in this care of offspring. Thus in the Surinam toad the male spreads the ova on the back of the female, where skin cavities form in which the tadpoles develop. In other cases the eggs are carried in the dorsal pouches of the females. It would almost seem that in this early time Nature was making experiments as to which parent was the better fitted to rear and protect the young!

But let us return to our present examination of animal love-making. In many diverse forms there is a very remarkable courtship of touch, often prolonged and with beautiful refinements, before the climax is reached, when the two bodies unite. Racovitza[1] has beautifully described the courtship of the octopus, which is carried out with considerable delicacy, and not brutally as before had been believed.

> "The male gently stretches out his third arm on the right and caresses the female with its extremity, eventually passing it into the chamber formed by the mantle. The female contracts spasmodically, but does not attempt to move. They remain thus about an hour or more, and during this time the male shifts his arm from one viaduct to the other. Finally, he withdraws his arm, caresses her with it for a few moments, and then replaces it with his other arm."

[1] *Natural Science*, Nov. 1894, quoted by Havelock Ellis, *Psychology of Sex*, Vol. III. p. 30.

The various phenomena of primitive animal courtship may be illustrated further by the love-parades of butterflies and moths, the love-gambols of certain newts, the amatory serenading of frogs, the fragrant incense of reptiles, the love-lights of glow-worms, the duels of many male beetles and other insects, many of whom have special weapons for fighting with their rivals. Among insects the sexes commonly associate in pairs, and it seems certain there is some psychic attraction added to the primitive tactile courtship. In some cases the association of the sexes is maintained for a lengthened period, with many hints of what must be regarded as love. There are many examples also of parental forethought, amounting sometimes to a sort of divining prescience, as the habit of certain insects in preparing and leaving a special nourishment, different from their own food, for the sustenance of the future larvæ. We even find instances of co-operation of the sexes in work together, affording a first hint of this linking-force to the development of love in its later and full expression. Such are the activities of the dung-rolling beetle, where the two sexes assist each other in their curious occupation. The male and female of another order of beetle (*Lethrus cephalotes*) inhabit the same cavity, and the virtuous matron is said greatly to resent the intrusion of another male.[1]

In insects, as in the higher animals, and as in man, sexual association takes many different forms. But obviously I must not linger over these early types of love. My object is to bring forward examples, which

[1] *Evolution of Sex*, p. 265.

seem to me useful as preliminary studies to throw light on the origin of sex-passion, and proving that the love-process throughout the whole of life is identical. Those who are acquainted with the work of Fabre, "The Insects' Homer," will have no difficulty in accepting this. The studies he has given us of wonderful behaviour of insects, their arts and crafts, their courtships and marriages, their domestic and social relationships, opens up a new drama of animal life.

CONTENTS OF CHAPTER V

COURTSHIP, MARRIAGE AND THE FAMILY

I.—*Among the Birds and Mammals*

Courtship and marriage among birds and mammals—Every form of association similar to human marriage—A high standard of love-morality among birds—Monogamy, polygamy, and polyandry—Cases of absolute profligate promiscuity—Suggestions of all the sexual sins of humanity—The phenomena of courtship—The law of battle—Battles of mammals and male gallinaceæ—The frenzy of love—Where supremacy in love is gained by force the males become stronger and better armed than the females—Importance of this—Gentler ways of wooing—Æsthetic seductions—Courteous duels—The note of joy in love among birds—Affectionate partnerships lasting for life—Frequency of monogamy among birds—Co-operation of both sexes in forming the home and caring for the young—The amatory dances of birds—Significance of dancing—Numerous illustrations—The use of song and decorative plumage—Musical seduction—Æsthetic constructions—The extraordinary power of sex-hunger—General propositions.

II.—*Further Examples of Courtship, Marriage and the Family among Birds*

Darwin's theory of sexual-selection—Objections to this by Wallace and others—An explanation—The true object of courtship—The sexual passion the origin of social growth—A rough outline of society already established in the animal kingdom—The maternal and the paternal family—The former the most frequent—The importance of the female—Difference between the secondary sexual characters of the male and the female—Doubt of the accepted view—Need for a further examination—Cases among birds in which the female equals or even exceeds the male in size and strength—Beauty tests of brilliant plumage—Numerous examples of almost identical likeness between the sexes—This similarity in plumage occurs in some of the most brilliant of our birds—The interesting case of the phalaropes where the rôle of the sexes is reversed—These facts point to an error in the accepted opinion as to the secondary sexual characters—Sexual adornments cannot be regarded as a necessary and exclusive adjunct of the male—Prof. Lester Ward's Gynæocratic theory—Male efflorescence—Among the species in which male differentiation has gone farthest the males are bad fathers—Examples to prove this—The fathers devoid of affection belong to the less intelligent species—The conclusion—An extravagant growth of the secondary sexual characters not favourable to the highest development of the species—The most oppressed females the most faithful wives—The highest development in the beautiful cases in which the sexes are more alike, equal in capacity and co-operate together in the race-work—Individual fancies of females—The case of a female wild duck—Desire for sexual variety—Conjugal fidelity modified by the conditions of life—Civilisation depraves birds—General observations—Love the great creative force.

CHAPTER V

COURTSHIP, MARRIAGE AND THE FAMILY

I.—*Among the Birds and Mammals*

"The principle of 'divergence of character' pervades all nature, from the lowest groups to the highest, as may be well seen in the class of birds."—WALLACE.

A GREAT step in advance is taken when we come to study the courtship and sexual relationships of birds and mammals. There are many examples, in particular among birds, of a beautiful and high standard of love-morality. To the physical fondness of the sexes for one another there is now added a wealth of what must be recognised as psychical attraction, which finds its expression in many diverse ways. We shall find all forms of sexual association, very similar to marriage in the human species. There are temporary unions formed for the purpose of procreation, after which the partners separate and cease to care for one another. Polygamy is frequent, polyandry also occurs, and there are many cases of absolute profligate promiscuity. We shall, indeed, find the suggestion of all the sexual sins of humanity, every form of coquetry, of love-battles, jealousy and the like. There are as well many examples of monogamic unions lasting for the lives of the partners. This is especially the case with birds. Among the higher mammals polygamy is most common, but permanent unions are formed, especially among the anthropoid apes. Thus strictly monogamous marriages are frequent among gorillas and orang-utans, the young sometimes remaining with their parents to the age of six years, while any approach to loose behaviour on the part of the wife is severely punished by the husband.[1] We find both the matriarchate and patriarchate family; and we may observe the greatest difference in the conduct of the parents in their care of offspring. Even a rapid examination of these customs is worth while, for they cast forward many suggestions on our sexual, domestic, and social relationships.

Let us take first the phenomena of courtship.

It is possible to give only the briefest outline of this fascinating subject. We will begin with the law-of-battle. Courtship without combat is rare among mammals; it is less common in many species of birds. Special offensive and defensive weapons for use in these love-fights are found; such are the larger canine teeth of many male mammals, the antlers of stags, the tusks of elephants, the horns of antelopes, goats, oxen and other animals, while among birds the spurs of the cock and allied species are examples of sexual weapons.[2]

"The season of love is the season of battle," says Darwin. To those who understand love there will be no cause of surprise in these procreative explosions. There can be no doubt that such combats are a stimulus to mutual sexual excitement in the males who take part in them and the female who watches them. Throughout Nature love only reaches its goal after tremendous

[1] Havelock Ellis, *Psychology of Sex*, Vol. VI. p. 422.
[2] *Evolution of Sex*, p. 8.

expenditure of energy. Courtship is the prelude to love. The question is—what form it shall take? It is this that even yet we have not decided. But the importance of courtship cannot be overlooked. We must regard it as the servant of the Life-force. In the fine saying of Professor Lloyd Morgan,[1] "the purpose of courtship reveals itself as the strong and steady bending of the bow, that the arrow may find its mark in a biological end of the highest importance in the survival of a healthy and vigorous race."

Even the most timid animals will fight desperately under the stimulus of sex-passion. Hares and moles battle to the death in some cases; squirrels and beavers wound each other severely. Seals grapple with tooth and claw; bulls, deer and stallions have violent encounters, and goats use their curved horns with deadly effect.[2] The elephant, pacific by nature, assumes a terrible fury in the rutting season. Thus, the Sanskrit poems frequently use the simile of the elephant goaded by love to express the highest degree of strength, nobility, grandeur and even beauty.[3] It is hardly necessary to point out that in these love-conflicts we may find the sources of our own brute passions of jealousy, and the origin of duels, murders and all the violent crimes committed by men under the excitement of sexual emotion—the tares among the wheat of love that drive men mad and wild.

[1] *Animal Behaviour*, p. 265, quoted by Havelock Ellis, *Psychology of Sex*, Vol. III. p. 28.

[2] Geoffrey Mortimer (W. M. Gallichan), *Chapters on Human Love*, pp. 17–18.

[3] Letourneau, *Evolution of Marriage*, p. 16.

In birds it is among the gallinaceæ that love incites the male with warlike fury. The barn-door cock is the type of the jealous male—amorous, vain and courageous.[1] It must be noted that wheresoever supremacy in love is obtained by force the male has necessarily become, through the action of selection, stronger and better armed than the female. Among birds, where the law of battle largely gives place to a gentler wooing, there are many species in which the female is larger and stronger than the male, and a much greater number where there is no appreciable difference between the sexes. These prove what we have already established among the invertebrates, that there is no necessary correlation between weakness and the female sex. But to this question, so important in its bearing on the relative position of the sexes, I shall return later.

The acquisition of mates does not depend entirely upon strength and victory in battle. Many male mammals have crests and tufts of hair, and other marks of beauty, such as bright colouring, are often conspicuous. These are used to attract the females. The incense of odoriferous glands, which become specially functional during the breeding season, are another frequent means of sexual attraction.[2] Even many of the amatory duels are not really fights between rivals. They are rather parades, or tournaments, used by the males as a means of displaying their beauty and valour to the females. This is frequent among the contests of birds, as, for instance, the grouse of Florida (*Tetras cuspido*),

[1] Letourneau, *Evolution of Marriage*, p. 12.
[2] *Evolution of Sex*, pp. 7–8.

which are said to assemble at night to fight until morning with measured grace, and then to separate, having first exchanged formal courtesies.[1]

It is among birds that the notes of joy in love break out with a wonderful fascination. They are the most perfect of lovers; strength is often quite set aside, and the eye and ear of the mate alone is appealed to. The males (and also, in some cases, the females) use many æsthetic appeals to stimulate passion, such as dancing, beauty of plumage, and the art of showing it, as well as sweetness of song and diverse love-calls. There are numerous examples of affectionate partnerships between the sexes, in some cases lasting for life. The female Illinois parrot, for instance, rarely survives the death of her mate. Similarly the death of either sex of the *panurus* is said to be fatal to its companion. The affection of these birds is strong; they always perch side by side, and when they fall asleep one of them, usually the male, covers the other with its wing. The couples of the golden woodpeckers and doves live in perfect unison. Brehm records the case of a male woodpecker who, after the death of his mate, tapped day and night with his beak to recall the absent one, and when at last discouraged, he became silent and never recovered his gaiety.[2] According to some estimates monogamy prevails among ninety per cent. of birds.[3] This is explained by the steady co-operation of both sexes in forming the home and caring for the young, for it is surely the working together which causes their love to outlast the excite-

[1] Epinas, *Soc. Animales*, p. 326; Darwin, *Descent of Man*, p. 433.
[2] Letourneau, *Evolution of Marriage*, p. 27.
[3] Ellis, *Psychology of Sex*, Vol. VI. p. 422.

ment of the procreative season. Sometimes we find this affection flowing out into a wider altruism, extending beyond the family to the social group; which again is surely at once the condition and result of these beautiful and practical love-partnerships.

Those who have read the absorbing pages of Darwin devoted to the consideration of the sexual characters of birds, or know the examples given by Büchner, Audubon, Epinas, Wallace and other naturalists, or, better still, those who have watched and noted for themselves the love-habits of birds, will find it impossible to withhold admiration for the poetic character of many of these courtships and marriages, which put too often our own human matings to utter shame.

Let us look first at the love-dances. Dancing as a means of attracting the right pitch of passion in the male and the female has always been used in the service of the sexual instinct. It gives the highest and most complex expression of movement, and may be said to have been evolved by love from the more brutal courtships of battle display.[1] The characteristic features of the amatory dances of birds are well known; they may be witnessed frequently during the pairing season. The male blackbird, for instance, is full of action as he woos his mate; he flirts his tail, spreads his glossy wings, hops and turns; chases the hen, and all the time chuckles with delight. Similar antics are performed by the whitethroat. The male redwing, again, struts about before his female, sweeping the ground with his tail, and acting the dandy.[2]

[1] One of the most charming accounts of the loves of birds is given in a chapter on "Music and Dancing in Nature," in a volume entitled, *The Naturalist in La Plata*, by W. H. Hudson.

[2] Audubon, *Scènes de la Nature*, Vol. I. p. 350.

The crested duck raises his head gracefully, straightens his silky aigrette, struts and bows to his female, while his throat swells and he utters a sort of guttural note.[1] The common shield duck, geese, wood-pigeons, carrion-vultures, and many other birds have been observed to dance, spread their tails, chase one another, and perform many strange courting parades. A careful observer of birds, Mr. E. Selous, who is quoted by Havelock Ellis,[2] has found that all bird dances are not nuptial, but that some birds—the stone-curlew (or great plover), for example—have different kinds of dancing. The nuptial dances are taken part in by both the male and female, and are immediately followed by conjugation; but there are as well other dances or antics of a non-sexual character, which may be regarded as social, and these too are indulged in by both sexes.

The love-fights of swallows, linnets and kingfishers, and the curious aerial evolution of the swift are similar manifestations of vigour and delight in movement[3] as a sexual excitant to pairing. Some male doves have a remarkable habit of driving the hen for a few days before she lays the eggs. On these occasions his whole time is spent in keeping her on the move, and he never allows her to settle or rest for a minute except on the nest.[4]

[1] Audubon, *Scènes de la Nature*, Vol. II. p. 50.

[2] E. Selous, *Bird Watching*, pp. 15–20; Havelock Ellis, *Psychology of Sex*, Vol. III. p. 25.

[3] The jay is the only bird I know whose habits in this respect are different. Noisy and active during the winter the male becomes exceedingly quiet with the approach of the pairing season. This may possibly be explained by the fact that the two sexes of these beautiful birds are practically alike; thus there may be less temptation for the male to show off as the handsomer bird.

[4] J. Lewis Bonhote, *The Birds of Britain*, p. 272. It is from this work I have taken many facts relating to birds. See also A. R. Wallace, *Darwinism*, p. 287.

This last case affords a striking illustration of the real object of all these elaborate movements. The male albatross, an ugly and dull-coloured bird,[1] during courtship stands by the female on the nest, raises his wings, spreads his tail, throws up his head with the bill in the air, or stretches it straight out or forwards as far as he can, and then utters a curious cry.[2] But the most interesting example that I have been able to find recorded of dancing among birds is the habit of waltzing, common to the male, and in a lesser degree to the female ostrich. It is thus described by S. Cronwright Schreiner.[3]

"After running a few yards they (the ostriches) will stop, and with raised wings spin round rapidly for some time until quite giddy, when a broken leg occasionally occurs. . . . Vigorous cocks 'roll' when challenging to fight or when wooing a hen. The cock will suddenly bump down on his knees (ankle joints), open his wings, and then swing them alternately backwards and forwards as if on a pivot. At such a time the bird sees very imperfectly, if at all, in fact he seems so preoccupied that if pursued one may often approach unnoticed. Just before 'rolling,' a cock, especially if courting a hen, will often run slowly and daintily on the points of his toes, with neck slightly inflated, upright and erect, the tail half dropped and all his body feathers fluffed up; the wings raised and expanded, the inside edges touching the sides of the neck for nearly the whole length, and the plumes showing separately like an open fan. In no other attitude is the splendid beauty of his plumage displayed to such advantage."

In this case it is very suggestive to find that it is the

[1] Wallace states that these love-movements are more commonly performed by birds with dull plumage who have no special beauties to display to their mates, but the custom, as we have seen, is by no means confined to such birds.

[2] *Notes of a Naturalist on the "Challenger,"* quoted by Wallace, *Darwinism*, p. 287.

[3] "The Ostrich," *Zoölogist*, March 1897; quoted by Havelock Ellis, *Psychology of Sex*, Vol. III. p. 34.

male ostrich who takes upon himself the task of hatching and rearing the young. Perhaps this accounts for the female ostrich being able to dance as well as the male. There are very few examples of birds who are bad fathers. Often the male rivals the female in love for the young; he is in constant attendance in the vicinity of the nest; he guards, feeds and sings to the female, and sometimes shares with her the duty of incubation. This is done by the male wood-pigeon, missel-thrush, blue martin, the buzzard, stone-curlew, curlew, dottrel, the sandpiper, common gull, black-coated gull, kittiwake, razorbill, puffin, storm-petrel, the great blue heron and the black vulture. Among these birds it is usual for the family duties to be performed quite irrespective of sex, and the parent who is free takes the task of feeding the one who is occupied. As soon as one family is reared many birds at once burden themselves with another. Audubon records the case of the blue bird of America, who works so zealously that two or three broods are reared at the same time, the female sitting on one clutch, while the male feeds the young of the preceding brood.[1]

Next in importance to dancing and movement in the aid of courtship among birds is their use of song and display of decorative plumage. With them it would seem, even more than among the mammals or with man, sexual desire raises and intensifies all the faculties, and lifts the individual above the normal level of life. The act of singing is a pleasurable one, an expression of superabundant energy and joyous excitement. Thus love-songs, serving first probably as a call of recognition

[1] Audubon, *Scènes de la Nature*, Vol. I. p. 317.

from the male to the female, came to be used as a means of seduction. Every one is familiar with the exquisite lyrical tournaments of our nightingales; their songs during the love season do not cease by day or by night, so that one wonders when sleep can be taken; but as soon as the young are hatched the music ceases, and harsh croaks are the only sound left.[1] The song of the skylark, with its splendid note of freedom, is more melodious and more frequent in the season of love's delirium.[2] Another bird, the male of the weaver bird, builds an abode of pleasure for himself, wherein he retires to sing to his mate.[3] A very beautiful case of the use of these love-calls by the tyrant bird (*Pitangus Bolivianus*) is recorded by W. H. Hudson.[4]

> "Though the male and female are greatly attached they do not go afield to hunt in company, but separate to meet at intervals during the day. One of the couple (say the female) returns to the trees where they are accustomed to meet, and after a time becoming impatient or anxious at the delay of her consort, utters a very long, clear call-note. He is perhaps a quarter of a mile away, watching for a frog beside a pool, or beating over a thistle bed, but he hears the note and presently responds with one of equal power. Then, perhaps, for half-an-hour, at intervals of half-a-minute, the birds answer each other, though the powerful call of the one must interfere with his hunting. At length he returns: then the two birds, perched close together, with their yellow bosoms almost touching, crests elevated, and beating the branch with their wings scream their loudest notes in concert—a confused, jubilant noise that rings through the whole plantation. Their joy at meeting is patent, and their action corresponds to the warm embrace of a loving human couple."

[1] J. Lewis Bonhote, *The Birds of Britain*, p. 39.
[2] Audubon, *Scènes de la Nature*, Vol. I. p. 383.
[3] Epinas, *Sociétés Animales*, p. 299.
[4] *Argentine Ornithology*, Vol. I. p. 148; quoted by Havelock Ellis, *Psychology of Sex*, Vol. III. p. 33.

Some birds, who are ill-endowed from a musical point of view, have their wing feathers or tails peculiarly developed and stiffened, and are able to produce with them a strange snapping or cracking sound. Thus several species of snipe make drumming or "bleating" noises—something like the bleat of a goat—with their narrowed tails as they descend in flight.[1] Magpies have a still more curious method of call, by rapping on dry and sonorous branches, which they use not only to attract the female, but also to charm her. We may say that these birds perform instrumental music.[2]

The exercise of vocal power among birds seems to be complementary to the development of accessory plumes and ornaments. All our finest singing birds are plainly coloured, with no crests, neck or tail plumes to display. The gorgeously ornamented birds of the tropics have no song, and those which expend much energy in display of plumage, as the turkey and peacocks, have comparatively an insignificant development of voice.[3] The extraordinary manner in which birds display their plumage at the time of courting is well known. Let us take one example—the courtship of the Argus pheasant. This bird is noted for the extreme beauty of the male's plumage. Its courtship has been beautifully observed by H. O. Forbes—[4]

"It is the habit of this bird to make a large circus, some ten or twelve feet in diameter, in the forest, which it clears of every

[1] Wallace, *Darwinism*, p. 284; also J. Lewis Bonhote, *The Birds of Britain*, p. 319.
[2] Letourneau, *Evolution of Marriage*, pp. 14–15.
[3] Wallace, *Darwinism*, p. 287.
[4] H. O. Forbes, *A Naturalist's Wanderings*, p. 131; quoted by Havelock Ellis, *Psychology of Sex*, Vol. III. pp. 33–34.

leaf and twig and branch, till the ground is perfectly swept and garnished. On the margin of this circus there is invariably a projecting branch or high arched rest, at a few feet elevation from the ground on which the female bird takes its place, while in the ring the male—the male bird alone possesses great decoration—shows off all its magnificence for the gratification and pleasure of his consort, and to exalt himself in her eyes."

In this picture we have all the characteristic features of the display of personal beauty in which many birds delight. Any one may see such performances for themselves. The male chaffinch, for instance, will place himself in front of the female that she may admire at her ease his red throat and blue head; the bullfinch swells out his breast to display the crimson feathers, twisting his black tail from side to side; the goldfinch sways his body, and quickly turns his slightly expanded wings first to one side, then to the other, with a golden flashing effect.[1] Even birds of less ornamental plumage are accustomed to strut and show themselves off before the females. Birds often assemble in large numbers to compete in beauty before pairing. The *Tetras cuspido* of Florida and the little grouse of Germany and Scandinavia do this. The latter have daily amorous assemblies, or *cours d'amour*, of great length, which are renewed every year in the month of May.[2] It seems certain that this æsthetic display is conscious and premeditated; for while most pheasants parade before their females, two of the species—the *Crossoptilon auritum* and the *Phasianus Wallichii*—which are of dull colour,

[1] Darwin, *Descent of Man*, p. 438.
[2] Epinas, *Soc. animales*, p. 326; and Letourneau, *Evolution of Marriage*, p. 14.

refrain from doing so, being apparently conscious of their modest livery.[1]

Certain birds are not content alone with the display of natural ornament, but make use of further æsthetic appeal in the construction of their homes in a truly beautiful manner. Some species of humming-birds are said to decorate the exterior of their nests in great taste with lichens, feathers, etc. The bower-birds of Australia construct bowers on the ground, ornamented with shell, feathers, bones and leaves. Both sexes take part in the building of these abodes of love, which are used for the courting parades. But an even more delightful example of the rare sexual delicacy in courtship is recorded by M. O. Beccari of a bird of Paradise of New Guinea, the *Amblyornis inornata*.[2]

> "This wonderful and beautiful bird constructs a little conical hut to protect his amours, and in front of this he arranges a lawn, carpeted with moss, the greenness of which he relieves by scattering on it various bright coloured objects, such as berries, grains, flowers, pebbles and shells. More than this, when the flowers are faded, he takes great care to replace them, so that the eye may be always agreeably flattered. These curious constructions are solid, lasting for several years, and probably serving for several birds."

It is, I think, by such cases as these that we may come to realise the extraordinary power of sex-hunger. It seems to me that many of us are still walking in sleep; fear holds our eyes from the truth. But as we look back to the complex and often beautiful manifestations of love's actions among our animal ancestors, we begin to

[1] Darwin, *Descent of Man*, p. 438; Letourneau, *op. cit.*, p. 13.
[2] *Annali del Museo civico di storia naturale di Genova*, t. IX. fasc. 3–4, 1877, quoted by Letourneau, whose account I give; *op. cit.*, p. 14.

perceive that unanalysable something called "beauty," which is the glory that has arisen out of that first simple impelling hunger, which drove the male cell and the female cell to unite. This is how I see things—Life knows no development except through Love.

II.—*Further Examples of Courtship, Marriage, and the Family among Birds*

It is especially upon the efflorescence of male beauty among birds that Darwin founded his celebrated theory of sexual selection. The motley of display seems endless, beautiful plumes, elongated feathery tresses, neck-ruffs, breast-shields, brightly-coloured cowls and wattles occur with marvellous richness of variety.

Now, can we accept the Darwinian theory, and believe that all these appendages of beauty, as well as the sexual weapons, powers of song and movement, have been developed through the preference of the females? the stronger and more ornamental males becoming in this way the parents of each successive generation. Wallace, as is well known, opposed Darwin's view, preferring to regard sexual selection as a manifestation of natural selection. He has been followed by other naturalists, who have denied this creative power of love, being unable to credit conscious choice by the females of the most gifted males. The controversy on the question has been long and at times violent. Yet, it would seem, as so often happens in all disagreements, that the difference in opinion is more apparent than founded on the facts. There is really no difficulty if once we understand the true significance of courtship. What this is I have tried to make clear. During the excitement of pairing the male birds are in a condition of the most perfect development, and possess an enormous store of superabundant vitality; this, as may readily be understood, may well express itself in brilliant colours and superfluities of ornamental plumage, as also in song, in dancing, in love tournaments and in battles. The fact that we have to remember is that the female is most easily won by the male, who, being himself most charged with sex desire —and through this means reaching the finest development—is able to create a corresponding intoxication in her, and thus, by producing in both the most perfect condition, favours the chances of reproduction. There is no need whatever to suppose any conscious choice or special æsthetic perception on the part of the females. Great effects are everywhere produced in Nature by simple causes. The female responds to the stimulus of the right male at the right moment—that is really the whole matter.[1]

In these instances (brought forward in the previous section of this chapter) of the universal hunger of sex, which are fairly typical and are as complete as my space will allow, certain facts have become clear. In the first place we have seen something of the strong driving of the procreative function, which is the guarantee of the continuation and development of life. The importance

[1] Havelock Ellis, *Psychology of Sex*, Vol. III. pp. 18–24, has discussed this question at some length. The brief account I have given is a summary of his view. I take this opportunity of gratefully acknowledging the great help I have gained from the illuminating and valuable works of Mr. Ellis.

of the result to be gained explains the diverse and elaborate phenomena of courtship. The higher we ascend in the animal kingdom the stronger does the sex-appetite become: it vibrates in the nerve-centres, giving rise to violent emotions which intensify all the physical and psychic activities. Love is the great creative force. It awakens impressions and desires in the individual, giving rise to what may be called "experiments in creative self-expression," to the energy of which we owe the varied and marvellous phenomena in animal life.

A further cause arising from the development of love is certainly of not less importance—it is the beginning of life not wholly individualistic. It is in the sexual passions we must seek the origins of all social growth. This is evident. We have seen that sexual union induces durable association between the female and the male for the object of rearing the young. Here already we find that truth, which it is the chief purpose of this book to make plain, that the individual exists for the race. This is the new and practical morality of the biological view, which regards the individual as primarily the host and servant of the seed of life. And this is really of the greatest benefit to the individual. From this service to the future arises the family and the home. The familial instinct, more or less developed, may be traced far back in the scale of life; and as it gains in strength it extends from the family into a wider social love, which in some species results in the forming of societies grouped together for mutual protection and co-operation in communal activities. A rough outline of society is thus found established already in the animal kingdom.

Just as there were many different forms of sexual associations among our animal ancestors, so we may observe the two chief forms of human societies, the matriarchate and the patriarchate—or the maternal and paternal family. It is the former that is the most frequent. This is what we should expect. The female, the mother, as the natural centre of the family, the male, her servant, in the procreative act; but apart from this, we find him most frequently following personal interests; the female's love for the young is stronger and more developed than his. I lay stress upon this fact, for it shows how strongly planted in woman is the maternal instinct. I doubt if any woman can ever find true expression for her nature apart from motherhood. It is in these past histories of life's development that we may find the key for its purpose and meaning to us.

There is another point of special importance to us in estimating the true place of woman in society. This early position of the female proves conclusively (as we shall see more clearly later when we come to study the primitive human family) the importance of the mother and her children as the founders of society. Woman, by reason of her more intimate connection with the children and the home, became the centre of the social group, while the males, less bound by domestic ties, were able to wander, but came back to the home, driven by their sexual needs to return to the female. But without giving more time here to this question, to which I shall return later, there is a further consideration, arising from our study of the family habits among the birds and mammals, that now must claim our attention. Certain examples I have come across, in particular among birds, have forced into my mind doubt of a widely-accepted belief. I put forward my opinion with great diffidence; it is so easy to interpret facts by the bias of one's own wishes. I know that the cases I have found and studied are probably few in comparison with those I have missed; but to me they seem of such importance, by the light they throw on the whole question of the position of the sexes, that it seems necessary to bring them forward.

We must go back to the position we left, some time back, of the differences between the secondary sexual characters of the male and the female. We have followed the development of the male, under the action of love's selection, from his first insignificant position in the reproductive process; we have seen him becoming larger than the female, strong, jealous and masterful—in fact, a kind of fighting specialisation, with special weapons of defence for sex-battles. This is the general condition among mammals. Among birds another set of secondary character, that may be classed as beauty-tests, are more frequent. Now two questions must be answered. Can it be proved that all these acquired developments of strength and of beauty belong exclusively to the males—that they must be regarded as proof of the greater tendency to diversity in the male, which has carried him further in the evolution process than the female? Can it also be proved that such highly-marked differentiation between the sexes is in all cases necessary to reproduction—that this heightened male attractiveness is a progressive force in the service of the race? If so, examples will surely point in the direction of finding that among those species where the sexual characters of the male, whether of strength or of beauty, are most different from the female, sexual love will find its most perfect expression; and further, that the males in such case will be the most highly developed—the best parents and the most social in their habits. The whole question, I think it must be evident, turns upon this being proved.

But in the face of the facts before us this is just what we do not find. Among birds (who in erotic development far excel all other animals, not, indeed, excepting the human species, and thus must be accepted as affording the most perfect examples of sexual development) we have seen that the cases are not few in which the female equals, or even exceeds the male in size and in strength. This is so with the curlew, the merlin, the dunlin, the black-tailed goodwit, which is considerably larger than the male, and the osprey, where the female is also more spotted on the breast: these examples must be added to those I have already given (page 58).

If we turn now to the beauty-test of brilliancy of plumage, we may observe an even larger number of examples of almost identical likeness between the sexes. Among British birds alone there are no fewer than 382 species, or sub-species,[1] in which the female closely resembles the male. In some few of these examples, it

[1] These facts are taken from Mr. J. Lewis Bonhote's *British Birds*. I may add that in many species where the sexes are alike the young are quite different from the parents, a fact which seems to have escaped the notice of those who say that the young birds resemble the female. A very curious instance is furnished by the greater spotted woodpecker, where the sexes are similar, but the female lacks the red crown of the male; and yet the young *of both sexes* have this red crown.

is true, the colours of the female are slightly duller, and in others the female is rather smaller than the male, but the difference in each case is very slight. It is specially significant to note that this similarity of plumage occurs in some of the most beautiful of our birds, as, for instance, the kingfisher and the jay, where the brilliant dresses of the sexes are practically alike; the female robin shares the beauty of the male; in all the families of the charming tits the sexes are alike; this is also the case with the roller-bird with its gaily-coloured plumage; and there is no difference between the white elegance of the female and the male swan.

In the presence of such examples it seems to me impossible to refrain from thinking that there is a mistake somewhere, and that less importance is to be attached to the secondary sexual characters of the male than is generally imagined. Grant that these cases are exceptional; but if we once admit that among many species—and these highly developed in sex—the female shows no evidence of retarded development, we shall be forced also to break once for all with many beliefs and trite theories which have inspired on this subject of the sexual differences between the female and the male so much dogmatic statement and so many unproved assumptions.

I am not forgetting the gorgeous plumage of some male birds, and the contrast they afford with the plain females. What I wish to show is that such adornments cannot be regarded as a necessary adjunct to the male—an expression, in fact, of the male constitution. Nor are they, as we shall find later, necessary, or even beneficial in the highest degree, to the reproductive process.[1] I have an even more interesting case to bring forward, which to me seems to point very conclusively to what I am trying to prove. The phalaropes, both the grey and red-necked species, have a peculiarity unique among British birds, although shared by several other groups in different parts of the world.[2] Among these birds the rôle of the sexes is reversed. The duties of incubation and rearing the young are conducted entirely by the male bird, and in correlation with this habit the female does all the courting, is stronger and more pugnacious than the male, and is also brighter in plumage. In colour they are a pale olive very thickly spotted and streaked with black. The male is the psychical mother, the female taking no notice of the nest after laying the eggs. Frequently at the beginning of the breeding season she is accompanied by more than one male, so that it is evident that polyandry is practised.[3]

Now, if such an example of the reversal of the sexes has any meaning at all, it seems to me that we find the conclusion forced upon us that the secondary sexual characters are not necessarily different in the male and the female, but depend on the form of the union or marriage and the conditions of the family. Professor Lester Ward, in connection with his Gynæocratic theory, fully discusses this question. His conclusion is that this

[1] This seems to be the position taken by Professor Geddes and J. A. Thomson in *Evolution of Sex*, pp. 4–5.

[2] Several examples are mentioned by Wallace, *Darwinism*, p. 281. He, however, brings them forward in quite a different connection to prove his theory of the protective duller colours of the female birds.

[3] My facts of the phalaropes are taken from J. Lewis Bonhote's *British Birds*, pp. 314–315.

superiority of the males in strength and size among mammals and in beauty of plumage (which is also a symbol of force) among birds, instead of indicating an arrested development in the females indicates an over-development in the males. "Male efflorescence" is the apt term by which Professor Ward designates it. He says—

> "The whole phenomena of so-called male superiority bears a certain stamp of spuriousness and sham. It is to natural history what chivalry was to human history; . . . a sort of make-believe, play, or sport of nature of an airy unsubstantial character. The male side of nature shot up and blossomed out in an unnatural, fantastic way, cutting loose from the real business of life, and attracting a share of attention wholly disproportionate to its real importance." [1]

This may, I think, be regarded as a picturesque over-statement of what is in the main true. Male efflorescence has drawn upon itself an excessive importance, through what we may call its dramatic insistence upon our notice. It is plain, too, that the more we examine the question the more we are forced to the one conclusion. It is certainly very suggestive, as Professor Ward points out, that those mammals and birds in which the process of male differentiation has gone farthest, such as lions, buffaloes, stags and sheep among mammals, and pea-cocks, pheasants, turkey-cocks and barn-door-cocks among birds, do practically nothing for their families. Among the gallinaceæ it is the female who undertakes the whole burden of incubation, and feeding and caring for the young; during this time the male is running after adventures, in some cases he returns when his offspring

[1] *Pure Sociology*, p. 331.

are old enough to follow him and form a docile band under his government.[1] The conduct of the male turkey is much worse, and he often devours the eggs, which have to be hidden by the mother, while later the offspring are only saved from his attacks by large numbers of females and the young uniting in troops led by the mothers.[2] The polygamous families of monkeys are always subject to patriarchal rule. The father is the tyrant of the band—an egoist. Any protection he affords to the family is in his own interest, frequently he expels the young males as soon as they are old enough to give him trouble, the daughters, in some cases, he adds to his harem; only when old age has rendered him powerless are the tables turned, and the young, for so long oppressed, rebel and sometimes assassinate their tyrannous father. There is very little evidence of paternal affection among mammals. Even among monogamous species, where the male keeps with the female, he does so more as chief than as father. At times he is much inclined to commit infanticides and to destroy the offspring, which, by absorbing the attention of his partner, thwart his amours. Thus among the large felines the mother is obliged to hide her young ones from the male during the first few days after birth to prevent his devouring them.[3]

[1] Epinas, *Soc. animales*, p. 422.

[2] Audubon, *Scènes de la Nature*, t. Ier, p. 29. I may say, that at the time of writing this, while staying in the country, I have had an opportunity of watching these bands of female turkeys with their young. Their fear at the approach of the strutting noisy male is very manifest. On such occasions they at once seek shelter. I once saw them fly into a church. The females invariably keep together. I have never seen a single mother with her young.

[3] Letourneau, *Evolution of Marriage*, chapter on the "Family among Animals," pp. 29–34, from which these cases are taken.

It is important to note that among birds the fathers devoid of affection generally belong to the less intelligent species. We may, therefore, see that these violent polygamous amours of the male, which result in the development of the more extravagant of the second sexual characters, are not really favourable to the development of the species. They belong to a lower grade of sexual evolution. And a further proof, it seems to me, is furnished as we note that, in spite of this tyranny, the females show considerable affection for these tyrant males—the chimpanzee, for example, proving this by zealously plucking the lice from her master's coat, which with monkeys is a mark of very special attention.[1] The most oppressed females are, as a rule, the most faithful wives. Thus the females of the guanaco lamas, if their master chances to be wounded or killed, do not run away; they hasten to his side, bleating and offering themselves to the shots of the hunter in order to shield him, while, in sharp contrast, if a female is killed, the male makes off with all his troop—he thinks only of himself.[2] Must we say, then, that the female animal likes servitude? It is, of course, because the aggressive male, being the one to arouse her sexual passions, enables her to fulfil her work of procreation. This may be. But, granting this explanation, it must be allowed that love under such conditions evidences a deterioration, not

[1] Epinas, *Soc. animales*, p. 443. In this connection I may mention the fact that in Southern Spain, where the women are noted for their love of their children, I have often seen mothers sitting at their doors for several hours, extracting lice from the heads and bodies of their children. I once saw a beautiful *flamenca* (Sevillian gipsy) performing this task for her lover.

[2] Letourneau, *Evolution of Marriage*, p. 32.

alone in the size and strength of the female, but in mental capacity—love at a much lower level than those beautiful cases in which the sexes are more alike, equal in capacity, and co-operate together in the race work.

Yet in justice it must be added that even the most polygamous males are not always devoid of affection. I once saw on a Derbyshire high-road a cock show evident signs of sorrow over the death of one of his wives, who had been killed by a passing motor. He refused to leave the spot where her body lay, and walked round and round it, uttering sharp cries of grief. Nor are sexual lapses confined to the males; a female will take advantage of a moment when the attention of the old cocks is entirely absorbed by the anxiety of a fight, to run off with a young male.[1] Even among species noted for their conjugal fidelity this sometimes happens. Female pigeons, for example, have been known to fall violently in love with strange males, and this is especially common if the legitimate spouse is wounded or becomes weak.[2] Darwin records a very curious case of a sudden passion appearing in a female wild-duck, who, after breeding with her own mallard for a couple of seasons, deserted him for a stranger—a male pintail.

"It was evidently a case of love at first sight, for she swam about the newcomer caressingly, though he appeared evidently alarmed and averse to her overtures of affection. From that hour she forgot her old partner. Winter passed by, and the next spring the pintail seemed to have become a convert to her blandishments, for they nested and produced seven or eight young ones." [3]

[1] Darwin, *Descent of Man*, p. 399.
[2] *Ibid.*, p. 234.
[3] *Ibid.*, p. 455.

I am tempted to wait to consider the immense significance of such cases as these in the analogy they bear to our own sudden preferences in love. The question as to the moral conduct of this duck opens up suggestions of those cases of exceptional love-passions, which all our existing institutions, laws and penalties have never been able to crush. The desire for sexual variety is the ultimate cause of all sexual lapses and irrationalities. It is a mistake to think that this is a condition peculiar to mankind and the result of civilisation. If this were so it would be easier to deal with; but before these deeply-rooted instincts of sexual hunger we are often powerless. I know of no question that needs to be faced by women more than this one. I would like to say more about it. But already this first section of my book has exceeded its limits. I must, therefore, pass on, to draw attention to the fact, clearly proved by the case of this wild-duck's love, as well as by many other examples, that it is the females, who, exercising their right of selection much more than the males, introduce individual preference into their sexual relationships. The difficulty is that such preference, of profound biological importance, is often thwarted among civilised people by considerations of property and the accepted morality. From this standpoint permanent marriage may often fail to do justice to the sexual needs both of the individual and the wider needs of the race. Nature has no care for sex-morals as we understand them, any mode of sexual union is equally right so long as it serves the race-process. But men have set up a whole host of prohibitions and conventions —the "thou shalt nots" of society and religion. Which are we to follow? Which is the wheat and which the tares, that must be garnered or sifted from our loves?

It is important to notice that among mammals, as among men, conjugal fidelity is modified by the conditions of life. An animal belonging to a species habitually monogamic may easily change under the pressure of external causes and adopt polygamy, and, in some cases, polyandry. The shoveler duck, though normally monogamic, is said [1] to practise polyandry when males are in excess; two males being in constant and amicable attendance on the female, without sign of jealousy. Wild-ducks, again, which are strictly monogamous, good parents, and very highly developed in social qualities when in a wild state, become loosely polygamous and indifferent to their offspring under domestication. Civilisation, in this case, depraves the birds, as often it does men.

But enough has now been said. We shall find later how far the facts we have learnt of the position of the female and the sexual relationship, as we have studied them in these examples from the animal kingdom, will apply to us and to our loves. We have now to study marriage and the family as it exists among primitive peoples. We shall find a close resemblance in the courtship customs and the sexual and familial associations to those we have seen to be practised by our pre-human ancestors. The same resemblance will persist when, lastly, we come to investigate the same institutions among civilised races, up to our own. Indeed, we may have to admit that, in some directions, love is not even yet as

[1] J. G. Millais, *Natural History of British Ducks*, pp. 8, 13.

finely developed with us humans as it is among birds. It is in the loves of birds, as I believe, that we must seek hints to that evolution in fineness, which has still to come in our love.

One thing more. It refers to the disputed question of the differentiation of the sexes by the action of love's-selection. It is a truth that I wish as strongly as I am able to emphasise. We cannot learn to know love's selective powers by enclosing its action within the narrow circle of our preconceived ideas. Instead of limiting its power we should extend it without hindrance of any form—to the female as well as the male; to the woman as to the man. We should regard nothing as impossible, no development of either sex too great to be accomplished, knowing that all progress is possible to love's power. Exceptional cases, then, irregularities, it may be, in sexual expression will henceforth no longer surprise us; they will find their place in the infinite order of life. Such examples may come to be regarded as filling in the chain; they form intermediate stages and also mark the reappearance of earlier manifestations of the sexual hunger. The new morality of love, which is having its birth amongst us to-day, will be deeper and wider than the old morality, because it will be founded on surer knowledge.

PART II

HISTORICAL SECTION

CONTENTS OF CHAPTER VI

THE MOTHER-AGE CIVILISATION

I.—*Progress from Lower to Higher Forms of the Family Relationship*

Primitive human love—The same domination of sex-needs in man as among the animals—Different conditions of expression—Acquisition of a new element—The individuation of love—Sex uninterruptedly interesting—The human need for sexual variety—The personal end of passion—Primitive sex-customs and forms of marriage—Superabundance of evidence—An attempt to group the periods to be considered—An early period in which man developed from his ape-like ancestors—Illustrations from primitive savages—First formation of tribal groups—Second period—Mother-descent and mother-rights—The position of women—The importance of this early matriarchate—The transitional period from mother-right to father-right—The assertion of the male force in the person of the woman's brother—This alien position of the husband and father—The formation of the patriarchal family—The change a gradual one and dependent upon property—Civilisation started with the woman as the dominant partner—Traces of mother-descent found in all parts of the world—Evidence of folk-lore as legends—Examples of mother-descent in the early history of England, Scotland, and Ireland—The freedom enjoyed by women—Survival of mother-right customs among the ancient Hebrews.

II.—*The Matriarchal Family in America*

Traces of mother-descent frequent in the American continent—Mother-rule still in force in some districts—Morgan's description of the system among the Iroquois—The customs of Iroquois tribes—Communal dwellings—The authority of the women—The creeping in of changes leading to father-right—The system of government among the Wyandots—Further examples of the sexual relationships—The interesting customs of the Seri tribe—The probation of the bridegroom—His service to the bride's family—Stringent character of the conditions imposed—The freedom granted to the bride—A decisive example of the position of power held by women—The Pueblos—The customs of these tribes—Monogamic marriage—The happy family relationship—This the result of the supremacy of the wife in the home—Conclusions to be drawn from these examples of mother-rights among the Aboriginal tribes of America—Women the dominant force in this stage of civilisation—Why this early power of women has been denied—A meeting with a native Iroquois—He testifies to the high status and power of the Indian women.

III.—*Further Examples of the Matriarchal Family in Australia, India and other Countries*

The question of the position of women during the mother-age a disputed one—Bachofen's opinion—An early period of gynæocracy—This view not accepted—Need for unprejudiced opinion—Women the first owners of property—Their power dependent on this—Further examples of mother-right customs—The maternal family in Australia—Communal marriage—Mother-right in India—The influence of Brahmanism—Traces of the maternal family—Some interesting marriage customs—Polyandry—Examples of its practice—Great polyandrous centres—The freedom enjoyed by women—The causes of polyandry—Matriarchal polyandry—The interesting custom of the Nayars—The Malays of Sumatra—The *ambel-anak* marriage—Letter from a private correspondent—It proves the high status of women under the early customs of mother-descent—Traces of the maternal family among the Arabs—The custom of *beena* marriage—Position of women in the Mariana Islands—Rebellion of the husbands—Use of religious symbolism—The slave-wife—Her consecration to the Bossum or god in Guinea.

IV.—*The Transition to Father-right*

The position of women in Burma—The code of Manu—Women's activity in trade—Conditions of free-divorce—Traces of mother-descent in Japan—In China—In Madagascar—The power of royal princesses—Tyrannical authority of the princesses of Loango—In Africa descent through women the rule—Illustrations—The transition to father-right—The power passing from the mother into the hand of the maternal uncle—Proofs from the customs of the African tribes—The rise of father-right—Reasons which led to the change—Marriage by capture and marriage by purchase—The payment of a bride-price—Marriage with a slave-wife—The conflict between the old and the new system—Illustration by the curious marriage customs of the Hassanyeh Arabs of the White Nile—Father-right dependent on economic considerations—*Résumé*—General conclusions to be drawn from the mother-age—Its relation to the present revolt of women—The bright side of father-right.

CHAPTER VI

THE MOTHER-AGE CIVILISATION

I.—*Progress from Lower to Higher Forms of the Family Relationship*

"The reader who grasps that a thousand years is but a small period in the evolution of man, and yet realises how diverse were morality and customs in matters of sex in the period which this essay treats of" (*i. e. Mother-Age Civilisation*), "will hardly approach modern social problems with the notion that there is a rigid and unchangeable code of right and wrong. He will mark, in the first place, a continuous flux in all social institutions and moral standards; but in the next place, if he be a real historical student, he will appreciate the slowness of this steady secular change; he will perceive how almost insensible it is in the lifetime of individuals, and although he may work for social reforms, he will refrain from constructing social Utopias."—Professor KARL PEARSON.

OUR study of the sexual associations among animals has brought us to understand how large a part the gratification of the sex-instincts plays in animal life, equalling and, indeed, overmastering and directing the hunger instinct for food. If we now turn to man we find the same domination of sex-needs, but under different conditions of expression.[1] Man not only loves, but he knows that he loves; a new factor is added, and sex itself is lifted to a plane of clear self-consciousness.

[1] It is abundantly evident to any one who looks carefully into the past that sex occupied a large share of the consciousness of primitive races. The elaborate courtship rites and sex festivals alone give proof of this. It is, unfortunately, impossible for me to follow this question and give examples. I must refer the reader to H. Ellis's *Psychology of Sex*, Vol. III. pp. 34–44, where a number of typical cases are given of the courtship customs of the primitive peoples. See also Thomas, *Sex and Society*, chapter on "The Psychology of Exogamy," pp. 175–179.

Pathways are opened up to great heights, but also to great depths.

We must not, therefore, expect to take up our study of primitive human sexual and familial associations at the point where those of the mammals and birds leave off.[1] We have with man to some extent to begin again, so that it may appear, on a superficial view, that the first steps now taken in love's evolution were in a backward direction. But the fact is that the increased powers of recollection and heightened complexity of nervous organisation among men, led to different habits and social customs, separating man radically in his love from the animals. Man's instincts are very vague when compared, for instance, with the beautiful love-habits of birds; he is necessarily guided by conflicting forces, inborn and acquired. Thus precisely by means of his added qualities he took a new and personal, rather than an instinctive, interest in sex; and this after a time, even if not at first, aroused a state of consciousness in love which made sex uninterruptedly interesting in contrast with the fixed pairing season among animals. Hence

[1] This is the mistake that Westermark—in his valuable *History of Human Marriage*—as well as many writers have fallen into; assuming that because monogamy is found among man's nearest ancestors, the anthropoid apes, primitive human groups must have had a tendency towards monogamy. Whereas the exact opposite of this is true. There is, it would seem, a deeply rooted dislike in studying sex matters to face truth. This habit of fear explains the many elaborate efforts undertaken to establish the theory that primitive races practised a stricter sexual code than the facts prove. Letourneau, in *The Evolution of Marriage*, appears to adopt this view, and forces evidence in trying to prove the non-existence of a widespread early period of promiscuity (pp. 37–44). Mention may be made, on the other side, of Iwan Bloch, who, writing from a different standpoint and much deeper psychology, has no doubt at all of the early existence of, and even the continued tendency towards, promiscuity.—*The Sexual Life of Our Times*, pp. 188–195.

arose also a human and different need for sexual variety, much stronger than can ever have been experienced by the animals, which resulted in a constant tendency towards sexual licence, of a more or less pronounced promiscuity, in group marriage and other forms of sexual association which developed from it.

This is so essential to our understanding of human love, that I wish I could follow it further. All the elaborate phenomena of sex in the animal kingdom have for their end the reproduction of the species. But in the case of man there is another purpose, often transcending this end—the independent significance of sex emotion, both on the physical and psychical side, to the individual. It seems to me that women have special need to-day to remember this personal end of human passion. This is not, however, the place to enter upon this question.

I have now to attempt to trace as clearly as I can the history of primitive human love. To do this it will be necessary to refer to comparative ethnography.[1] We must investigate the sex customs, forms of marriage and the family, still to be found among primitive peoples, scattered about the world. These early forms of the sexual relationship were once of much wider occurrence, and they have left unmistakable traces in the history of many races. Further evidence is furnished by folk stories and legends. In peasant festivals and dances and in many religious ceremonies we may find survivals of primitive sex customs. They may be traced in our

[1] Our knowledge of the habits of primitive races has increased greatly of late years. The classical works of Bachofen, Waitz, Kulischer, Giraud-Teulon, von Hellwald, Krauss, Ploss-Bartels and other ethnologists, and the investigation of Morgan, McLennan, Muller, and many others, have opened up wide sources of information.

common language, especially in the words used for sex and kin relationships. We can also find them shadowed in certain of our marriage rites and sex habits to-day. The difficulty does not rest in paucity of material, but rather in its superabundance—far too extensive to allow anything like adequate treatment within the space of a brief and necessarily insufficient chapter. For this reason I shall limit my inquiry almost wholly to those cases which have some facts to tell us of the position occupied by women in the primitive family. I shall try to avoid falling into the error of a one-sided view. Facts are more important here than reflections, and, as far as possible, I shall let these speak for themselves.

In order to group these facts it may be well to give first a rough outline of the periods to be considered—

1. A very early period, during which man developed from his ape-like ancestors. This may be called the pre-matriarchal stage. With this absolutely primitive period we are concerned only in so far as to suggest how a second more social period developed from it. The idea of descent was so feeble that no permanent family groups existed, and the family remains in the primitive biological relation of male, female and offspring. The Botocudos, Fuegians, West Australians and Veddahs of Ceylon represent this primitive stage, more or less completely. They have apparently not reached the stage where the fact of kinship expresses itself in maternal social organisation.[1] A yet lower level may be seen among certain low tribes in the interior of Borneo—abso-

[1] Thomas, *Sex and Society*, p. 68, and Letourneau, *Evolution of Marriage*, pp. 269–270, 320.

lutely primitive savages, who are probably the remains of the negroid peoples, believed to be the first inhabitants of Malaya. These people roam the forests in hordes, like monkeys; the males carry off the females and couple with them in the thickets. The families pass the night under the trees, and the children are suspended from the branches in a sort of net. As soon as the young are capable of caring for themselves, the parents turn them adrift as the animals do.[1]

It was doubtless thus, in a way similar to the great monkeys, that man first lived. With the chimpanzee these hordes never become large, for the male leader of the tribe will not endure the rivalry of the young males, and drives them away. But man, more gregarious in his habits, would tend to form larger groups, his consciousness developing slowly, as he learnt to control his brute appetites and jealousy of rivals by that impulse towards companionship, which, rooted in the sexual needs, broadens out into the social instincts.

It is evident that the change from these scattered hordes to the organised tribal groups was dependent upon the mothers and their children. The women would be more closely bound to the family than the men. The bond between mother and child, with its long dependence on her care, made woman the centre of the family. The mother and her children, and her children's children, and so on indefinitely in the female line, constituted the group. Relationship was counted alone through them, and, at a later stage, inheritance of property passed through them. And in this way, through the woman,

[1] Lubbock, *Origin of Civilisation*, p. 9.

the low tribes passed into socially organised societies. The men, on the other hand, not yet individualised as husbands and fathers, held no rights or position in the group of the women and their children.

2. This leads us to the second period of mother-descent and mother-rights. It is this phase of primitive society that we have to investigate. Its interest to women is evident. Just as we found in our first inquiry that, in the beginnings of sexuality the female was of more importance than the male, so now we shall find society growing up around woman. It is a period whose history may well give pride to all women. Her inventive faculties, quickened by the stress of child-bearing and child-rearing, primitive woman built up, by her own activities and her own skill, a civilisation which owed its institutions and mother-right customs to her constructive genius, rather than to the destructive qualities which belonged to the fighting male.

3. But again we find, as in the animal kingdom, that step by step the forceful male asserts himself. We come to a third transitional period in which the male relatives of the woman—usually the brother, the maternal uncle—have usurped the chief power in the group. Inheritance still passes through the mother, but her influence is growing less. The right to dispose of women and the property which goes with them is now used by the male rulers of the group. The sex habits have changed; endogamous unions, or kin marriages within the clan, have given place to exogamy, where marriage only takes place between members of different groups. But at first the position of the husband and father is little changed;

he marries into the wife's group and lives with her family, where he has no property rights or control over his wife's children, who are now under the rule of the uncle.

4. It is plain that this condition would not be permanent. The male power had yet to advance further; the child had to gain a father. We reach the patriarchal period, in which descent through the male line has replaced the earlier custom. Woman's power, first passing to her brother or other male relative, has been transferred to the husband and father. This change of power did not, of course, take place at once, and even under fully developed father-right systems many traces of the old mother-rights persist.

What it is necessary to fasten deeply in our minds is this: the father as the head of the woman and her children, the ruler of the house, was not the natural order of the primitive human family. Civilisation started with the woman being dominant—the home-maker, the owner of her children, the transmitter of property. It was—as will be made abundantly clear from the cases we shall examine—a much later economic question which led to a reversal of this plan, and brought the rise of father-right, with the father as the dominant partner; while the woman sank back into an unnatural and secondary position of economic dependence upon the man who was her owner—a position from which she has not even yet succeeded in freeing herself.

The maternal system of descent is found in all parts of the world where social advance stands at a certain level. This fact, added to the widespread traces the custom has left in every civilisation, warrants the assumption that mother-right in all cases preceded father-right, and has been, indeed, a stage of social growth for all branches of the human race.[1]

I shall not attempt to give the numerous traces of mother-descent that are to be found in the early histories of existing civilised nations, for to do this would entail the writing of the whole chapter on this subject. For the same reason I must reluctantly pass over the abundant evidence of mother-right that is furnished in folk-lore, in heroic legends, and in the fairy stories of our children. These stories date back to a time long before written history; they are known to all of us, and belong to all countries in slightly different forms. We have regarded them as fables; they are really survivals of customs and practices once common to all society. Wherever we find a king ruling as the son of a queen, because he is the queen's husband, or because he marries a princess, we have proof of mother-descent. The influence of the mother over her son's marriage, the winning of a bride by a task done by the wooer, the brother-sister marriage so frequent in ancient mythologies, the interference of a wise woman, and the many stories of virgin-births—all are survivals of mother-right customs. Similar evidence is furnished by mother-goddesses, so often converted into Christian local saints. I wish it were possible to follow this subject,[2] whose interest offers rich rewards. Perhaps

[1] This opinion is founded on the anthropological investigations during the past half century. See Hartland, *Primitive Paternity*, Vol. I. pp. 256–257; H. Ellis, *Psychology of Sex*, Vol. VI. pp. 390–392, and "The Changing Status of Women," *Westminster Review*, October 1886; Thomas, *Sex and Society*, p. 58, and Bloch, *Sexual History of our Times*, pp. 190–196.

[2] For a full and illuminative treatment of this subject I would refer my readers to the essays of Professor Karl Pearson, *The Chances of*

nowhere else can we gain so clear and vivid a picture as in these ancient stories and legends of the early powerful position of woman as the transmitter of inheritance and guardian of property.

It may interest my readers to know that mother-descent must once have prevailed in Britain. Among the Picts of Scotland kingship was transmitted through women. Bede tells us that down to his own time—the early part of the eighth century—whenever a doubt arose as to the succession, the Picts chose their king from the female rather than from the male line.[1] Similar traces are found in England: Canute, the Dane, when acknowledged King of England, married Emma, the widow of his predecessor Ethelred. Ethelbald, King of Kent, married his stepmother, after the death of his father Ethelbert; and, as late as the ninth century, Ethelbald, King of the West Saxons, wedded Judith, the widow of his father. Such marriages are intelligible only if we suppose that the queen had the power of conferring the kingdom upon her consort, which could only happen where matrilineal descent was, or had been, recognised.[2]

Death, Vol. II.—"Woman as Witch: Evidences of Mother-Right in the Customs of Mediæval Witchcraft"; "Ashiepattle, or Hans Seeks his Luck"; "Kindred Group Marriage," Part I.; "The Mother-Age Civilisation," Part II.; "General Words for Sex and Kinship," Part III.; "Special Words for Sex and Relationship." In these suggestive essays Professor Pearson has brought together a great number of facts which give a new and charming significance to the early position of women. Perhaps the most interesting essay is that of "Woman as Witch," in which he shows that the beliefs and practices connected with mediæval witchcraft were really perverted rites, survivals of mother-age customs.

[1] Bede, II. 1–7.

[2] F. Frazer, *Golden Bough*, Pt. I. *The Magic Art*, Vol. II. pp. 282–283. Canute's marriage was clearly one of policy: Emma was much older than he was, she was then living in Normandy, and it is doubtful

In Ireland (where mother-right must have been firmly established, if Strabo's account of the free sexual relations of the people [1] is accepted) women retained a very high position and much freedom, both before and after marriage, to a late period. "Every woman," it was said, "is to go the way she willeth freely," and after marriage "she enjoyed a better position and greater freedom of divorce than was afforded either by the Christian Church or English common law." [2]

Similar survivals of mother-right customs among the ancient Hebrews are made familiar to us in Bible history. To mention a few examples only: when Abraham sought a wife for Isaac, presents were taken by the messenger to induce the bride to leave her home; and these presents were given to her mother and brothers. Jacob had to serve Laban for fourteen years before he was permitted to marry Leah and Rachel,[3] and six further years of service were given for his cattle. Afterwards when he wished to depart with his children and his wives, Laban made the objection, "these daughters are my daughters, and

---

if the Danish king had ever seen her. Such marriages with the widow of a king were common. The familiar example of Hamlet's uncle is one, who, after murdering his brother, married his wife, and became king. His acceptance by the people, in spite of his crime, is explained if it was the old Danish custom for marriage with the king's widow to carry the kingdom with it. In Hamlet's position as avenger, and his curious hesitancy, we have really an indication of the conflict between the old and new ways of reckoning descent.

[1] Strabo, IV. 5, 4. Hartland, *Primitive Paternity*, Vol. II. p. 132. It must not be thought that mother-descent was always accompanied by promiscuity, or even with what we should call laxity of morals. We shall find that it was not. But the early custom of group marriages was frequent, in which women often changed their mates at will, and perhaps retained none of them long. We shall see that this freedom, whatever were its evils, carried with it many privileges for women.

[2] H. Ellis, citing Rhys and Brynmor-Jones, *The Welsh People*, p. 214.

[3] Gen. xxiv. 5-53.

these children are my children."[1] Such acts point to the subordinate position held by Jacob, which is clearly a survival of the servitude required from the bridegroom by the relatives of the woman, who retain control over her and her children, and even over the property of the man, as was usual under the later matriarchal custom. The injunction in Gen. ii. 24, "Therefore shall a man leave his father and mother, and shall cleave unto his wife," refers without any doubt to the early marriage under mother-right, when the husband left his own kindred and went to live with his wife and among her people. We find Samson visiting his Philistine wife, who remained with her kindred.[2] Even the obligation to blood vengeance rested apparently on the maternal kinsmen (Judges viii. 19). The Hebrew father did not inherit from his son, nor the grandfather from the grandson,[3] which points back to an ancient epoch when the children did not belong to the clan of the father.[4] Among the Hebrews individual property was instituted in very early times (Gen. xxiii. 13); but various customs show clearly the ancient existence of communal clans. Thus the inheritance, especially the paternal inheritance, must remain in the clan. Marriage in the tribe is obligatory for daughters. "Let them marry to whom they think best; only to the family of the tribe of their father shall they marry. So shall not the inheritance of the children of Israel remove from tribe to tribe."[5] We have here an indication of the close relation between father-right and property.

[1] Gen. xxxi. 41, 43. [2] Judges xv. 1. [3] Num. xxxii. 8–11.
[4] Letourneau, *Evolution of Marriage*, p. 326. [5] Num. xxxvi. 4–8.

Under mother-descent there is naturally no prohibition against marriage with a half-sister upon the father's side. This explains the marriage of Abraham with Sara, his half-sister by the same father. When reproached for having passed his wife off as his sister to the King of Egypt and to Abimelech, the patriarch replies: "For indeed she is my sister; she is the daughter of my father, but not the daughter of my mother, and she became my wife."[1] In the same way Tamar could have married her half-brother Amnon, though they were both the children of David.[2] The father of Moses and Aaron married his father's sister, who was not legally his relation.[3] Nahor, the brother of Abraham, took to wife his fraternal niece, the daughter of his brother.[4] It was only later that paternal kinship became recognised among the Hebrews by the same title as the natural kinship through the mother.[5]

Other examples might be added. All these survivals of mother-descent (and they may be discovered in the early history of every people) have their value; they are, however, only survivals, and their interest rests mainly in comparing them with similar facts among other peoples among whom the presence of mother-right customs is undisputed. To these existing examples of the primitive family clan grouped around the mother we will now turn our attention.

[1] Gen. xii. [2] 2 Sam. xiii. 16. [3] Exod. vi. 20.
[4] Gen. xi. 26–29. [5] See Thomas, *Sex and Society*, pp. 63–64.

II.—*The Matriarchal Family in America*

Traces of mother-descent are common everywhere in the American continent; and in some districts mother-rule is still in force. Morgan, who was commissioned by the American Government to report on the customs of the aboriginal inhabitants, gives a description of the system as it existed among the Iroquois—

> "Each household was made up on the principle of kin. The married women, usually sisters, own or collateral, were of the same *gens* or clan, the symbol or *totem* of which was often painted upon the house, while their husbands and the wives of their sons belonged to several other *gentes*. The children were of the *gens* of their mother. As a rule the sons brought home their wives, and in some cases the husbands of the daughters were admitted to the maternal household. Thus each household was composed of persons of different *gentes*, but the predominating number in each household would be of the same *gens*, namely that of the mother." [1]

There are many interesting customs belonging to the Iroquois; I can notice a few only. The *gens* was ruled by chiefs of two grades, distinguished by Morgan as *sachem* and common chiefs. The *sachem* was the official head of the *gens*. The actual occupant of the office was elected by the adult members of the *gens*, male and female, the own brother or son of a sister being most likely to be preferred.[2] The wife never left the parental home, because she was considered the mistress, or, at least, the heiress; her husband lived with her. In

[1] Morgan, *House and House-life of the American Aborigines*, p. 64. This example of mother-descent may be taken as typical of Indian life in all parts of America at the epoch of European discovery.

[2] Morgan, *Anc. Soc.*, 62, 71, 76; Hartland, *Primitive Paternity*, Vol. I. p. 298, Vol. II. p. 65.

the house all the duties and the honour as the head of the household fell on her. She was required in case of need to look after her parents. The Iroquois recognised no right in the father to the custody of his children; such power was in the hands of the maternal uncle.[1] Marriages were negotiated by the uncles or the mothers; sometimes the father was consulted, but this was little more than a compliment, as his approbation or opposition was usually disregarded.[2] The suitor was required to make presents to the bride's family. It was the custom for him to seek private interviews at night with his betrothed. In some instances, it was enough if he went and sat by her side in her cabin; if she permitted this, and remained where she was, it was taken for consent, and the act would suffice for marriage. If a husband and wife could not agree, they parted, or two pairs would exchange husbands and wives. An early French missionary remonstrated with a couple on such a transaction, and was told: "My wife and I could not agree. My neighbour was in the same case. So we exchanged wives, and all four are content. What can be more reasonable than to render one another mutually happy, when it costs so little and does nobody any harm?"[3] It would seem that these primitive people have solved some difficulties better than we ourselves have!

[1] McLennan, *Studies*, I. p. 271. Thus among the Choctas, if a boy is to be placed at school, his uncle, instead of his father, takes him to the mission and makes arrangements.

[2] Report of an Official for Indian Affairs on two of the Iroquoian tribes, cited by Hartland, *op. cit.*, Vol. I. p. 298. McLennan attributes the arrangement of the marriages to the mothers (*Studies*, ii. p. 339). This would be the earlier custom and is still practised among several tribes.

[3] Charlevoix, V. p. 418, quoted by Hartland, *op. cit.*, Vol. II. p. 66.

Among the Senecas,[1] an Iroquoian tribe with a less organised social life, the authority remained in the hands of the women. These people led a communal life, dwelling in long houses, which accommodated as many as twenty families, each in its own apartments.[2]

"As to their family system, it is probable that some one clan predominated (in the houses), the women taking in husbands, however, from the other clans, and sometimes for novelty, some of their sons bringing in their young wives until they felt brave enough to leave their mothers. Usually the female portion ruled the house, and were doubtless clannish enough about it. The stores were in common, but woe to the luckless husband or lover who was too shiftless to do his share of the providing. No matter how many children or whatever goods he might have in the house, he might at any time be ordered to pack up his blanket and budge, and after such orders it would not be healthful for him to attempt to disobey; the house would be too hot for him, and, unless saved by the intercession of some aunt or grandmother, he must retreat to his own clan, or, as was often done, go and start a new matrimonial alliance in some other. The women were the great power among the clans as everywhere else. They did not hesitate, when occasion required, to 'knock off the horns,' as it was technically called, from the head of a chief and send him back to the ranks of the warrior. The original nomination of the chiefs also always rested with them."

This last detail is very interesting; we find the woman's authority extending even over warfare, the special province of men.

[1] The customs of the Senecas have been noted by the Rev. A. Wright, who was a missionary for many years amongst them, and was familiar with their language and habits. His account is quoted by Morgan, *House and House-life of the American Aborigines*.

[2] We seem here to have a suggestion of the modern plan of co-operative dwelling-houses. It is extraordinary how many of our new (!) ideas seem to have been common in the mother-age. Was it because women, who are certainly more practical and careful of detail than men are, had part in the social arrangements? This would explain the revival of the same ideas to-day, when women are again taking up their part in the ordering of domestic and social life.

The Wyandots, another Iroquoian tribe, camp in the form of a horse-shoe, every clan together in regular order. Marriage between members of the same clan is forbidden; the children belong to the clan of the mother. The husbands retain all their rights and privileges in their own *gentes*, though they live in the *gentes* of their wives. After marriage the pair live for a time, at least, with the wife's mother, but afterwards they set up house-keeping for themselves.[1]

We may note here the creeping in of changes which led to father-right. This is illustrated further by the Musquakies, also belonging to the Algonquian stock. Though still organised in clans, descent is no longer reckoned through the mother. The bridegroom, however, serves his wife's mother, and he lives with her people. This does not make him of her clan; she belongs to his, till his death or divorce separates her from him. As for the children, the minors at the termination of the marriage belong to the mother's clan, but those who have had the puberty feast are counted to the father's clan.[2]

The male authority is chiefly felt in periods of war. This may be illustrated by the Wyandots, who have an elaborate system of government. In each *gens* there is a small council composed of four women, called *yu-wai-yu-wá-na;* chosen by the women heads of the household. These women councillors select a chief of the *gens* from its male members, that is from their brothers and sons.

[1] Powell, *Rep. Bur. Ethn.*, I, p. 63.
[2] Owen, *Musquakies*, p. 72, quoted by Hartland, *op. cit.*, Vol. II. pp. 68–69.

He is the head of the *gentile* council. The council of the tribe is composed of the aggregated *gentile* councils, and is thus composed of four-fifths of women and one-fifth of men. The *sachem* of tribes, or tribal-chief is chosen by chiefs of the *gentes*. All civil government of the *gens* and of the tribe is carried on by these councils, and as the women so largely outnumber the men, who are also—with the exception of the tribal chief chosen by them—it is surely fair to assume that the social government of the *gens* and *tribe* is largely directed by them. In military affairs, however, the men have sole authority; there is a military council of all the able-bodied men of the tribe, with a military chief chosen by the council.[1] This seems a very wise adjustment of civic duties; the constructive civil work directed by the women; the destructive work of war in the hands of men.

Some interesting marriage customs of the Seri, on the south-west coast, now reduced to a single tribe, are described by McGee.[2] The matriarchal system exists here in its early form, it is, therefore, an instructive example by which to estimate the position held by the women—

"The tribe is divided into exogamous *totem* clans. Marriage is arranged exclusively by the women. The elder woman of the suitor's family carries the proposal to the girl's clan-mother. If this is entertained, the question of the marriage is discussed at length by the matrons of the two clans. The girl herself is consulted; a *jacal* is erected for her, and after many deliberations, the

[1] I have summarised the account of the Wyandot government as given by Hartland, who quotes from Powell's "Wyandot Government," *First Annual Report of the Bureau of American Ethnology*, 1879–1880, pp. 61 ff.

[2] "The Beginning of Marriage," *American Anthropologist*, Vol. IX. p. 376. *Rep. Bur. Ethn.*, XVII. p. 275.

bridegroom is provisionally received into his wife's clan for a year, under conditions of the most exacting character. He is expected to prove his worthiness of a permanent relation by demonstrating his ability as a provider, and by showing himself an implacable foe to aliens. He is compelled to support all the female relatives of his bride's family by the products of his skill and industry in hunting and fishing for one year. There is also another provision of a very curious nature. The lover is permitted to share the *jacal* and sleeping robe, provided for the prospective matron by her kinswomen, not as a privileged spouse, but merely as a protective companion; and throughout this probationary term he is compelled to maintain continence—he must display the most indubitable proof of moral force."

This is the more extraordinary if we compare the freedom granted to the bride. "During this period the always dignified position occupied by the daughters of the house culminates." Among other privileges she is allowed to receive "the most intimate attentions from the clan-fellows of the group."[1] "She is the receiver of the supplies furnished by her lover, measuring his competence as would-be husband. Through his energy she is enabled to dispense largess with lavish hand, and thus to dignify her clan and honour her spouse in the most effective way known to primitive life; and at the same time she enjoys the immeasurable moral stimulus of realising she is the arbiter of the fate of a man who becomes a warrior or an outcast at her bidding, and through him of the future of two clans—she is raised to a responsibility in both personal and tribal affairs which, albeit temporary, is hardly lower than that of the warrior chief." At the close of the year, if all goes well, the probation ends in a feast provided by the lover, who

[1] This is supposed by McGee to suggest a survival of a vestigial polyandry.

now becomes husband, and finally enters his wife's *jacal* as "consort-guest." His position is wholly subordinate, and without any authority whatever, either over his children or over the property. In his mother's hut he has rights, which seem to continue after his marriage, but in his wife's hut he has none.

The customs of the Pueblo peoples of the south-west of the United States are almost equally interesting. They live in communal dwellings, and are divided into exogamous *totem* clans. Kinship is reckoned through the women, and the husband on marriage goes to live with the wife's kin and becomes an inmate of her family. If the house is not large enough, additional rooms are built adjoining and connected with those already occupied. Hence a family with many daughters increases, while one consisting of sons dies out. The women are the builders of the houses, the men supplying the material. The marriage customs are instructive. As is the case among the Seri, the lover has to serve his wife's family, but the conditions are much less exacting. Unlike most maternal peoples, these, the Zuñi Indians, are monogamists. Divorce is, however, frequent, and a husband and wife would "rather separate than live together unharmoniously."[1] Their domestic life "might well serve as an example for the civilised world." They do not have large families. The husband and wife are deeply attached to one another and to their children. "The keynote of this harmony is the supremacy of the wife in the home. The house, with all that is in it, is

[1] Mrs. Stevenson, *Rep. Bur. Ethn.*, XXIII. pp. 290, 293. Cushing, *Zuñi Folk Tales*, p. 368, cited by Hartland, *op. cit.*, Vol. II. pp. 73, 74.

hers, descending to her through her mother from a long line of ancestresses; and her husband is merely her permanent guest. The children—at least the female children—have their share in the common home; the father has none." Outside the house the husband has some property in the fields, though probably in earlier times he had no possessory rights. "Modern influences have reached the Zuñi, and mother-right seems to have begun its inevitable decay."

The Hopis, another Pueblo tribe, are more conservative, and with them the women own all the property, except the horses and donkeys, which belong to the men. Like the Zuñis, the Hopis are monogamists. Sexual licence is, however, often permitted to a woman before marriage. This in no way detracts from her good repute; even if she has given birth to a child "she will be sure to marry later on, unless she happens to be shockingly ugly." Nor does the child suffer, for among these matriarchal people the bastard takes an equal place with the child born in wedlock. The bride lives for the first few weeks with her husband's family, during which time the marriage takes place, the ceremony being performed by the bridegroom's mother, whose family also provides the bride with her wedding outfit. The couple then return to the home of the wife's parents, where they remain, either permanently, or for some years, until they can obtain a separate dwelling. The husband is always a stranger, and is so treated by his wife's kin. The dwelling of his mother remains his true home, in sickness he returns to her to be nursed, and stays with her until he is well again. Often his position in his wife's home is so irksome that he severs his relation with her and her family and returns to his old home. On the other hand, it is not uncommon for the wife, should her husband be absent, to place his goods outside the door: an intimation which he well understands, and does not intrude himself upon her again.[1]

Lastly, among the Pueblo peoples we may consider the Sai. Like the other tribes they are divided into exogamous *totem* clans; descent is traced only through the women. The tribe through various reasons has been greatly reduced in numbers, and whole clans have died out, and under these circumstances exogamy has ceased to be strictly enforced. This has led to other changes. The Sai are still at least normally monogamous. When a young man wishes to marry a girl he speaks first to her parents; if they are willing, he addresses himself to her. On the day of the marriage he goes alone to her home, carrying his presents wrapped in a blanket, his father and mother having preceded him thither. When the young people are seated together the parents address them in turn enjoining unity and forbearance. This constitutes the ceremony. Tribal custom requires the bridegroom to reside with the wife's family.[2]

Now I submit to the judgment of my readers—what do these examples of mother-right among the aboriginal tribes of America show, if not that, speaking broadly, women were the dominant force in this early stage of

[1] *Rep. Bur. Ethn.*, XIII. p. 340. Solberg, *Zeits. f. Ethnol.*, XXXVII. p. 269. Voth, *Traditions of the Hopi*, pp. 67, 96, 133. Hartland, *op. cit.*, Vol. II. pp. 74–76.

[2] *Rep. Bur. Ethn.*, IX. p. 19. Hartland, *Ibid.*, pp. 76–77. It would seem in some cases, the husband, after a period of residence with his wife's family, provides a separate house.

civilisation? In some instances, it is true, their power was shared, or even taken from them, by their brothers or other male relatives. This I believe to have been a later development—a first step in the assertion of male-force. In all cases the alien position of the father, without tribal rights in his wife's clan and with no recognised authority over her children, is evident. If this is denied, the only conclusion that suggests itself to me is, that those who seek to diminish the importance of mother-rule have done so in reinforcement of their preconceived idea of male superiority as the natural and unchanging order in the relationship between the sexes. I have no hesitation as the result of very considerable study, in believing that it is the exact opposite of this that is true. The mother, and not the father, was the important partner in the early stages of civilisation; father-right, the form we find in our sexual relationships, is a later reversal of this natural arrangement, based, not upon kinship, but upon property. This we shall see more clearly later.

Thomas[1] suggests another reason for the general tendency among many investigators to lessen the importance of the mother-age civilisations. He thinks it due to dislike in acknowledging the theory of promiscuity (notably Westermark in his *History of Human Marriage*). This view would seem to be connected with the mistaken opinion that womb-kinship arose through the uncertainty of paternity. But this was not the sole reason, or indeed the chief one, of descent being traced through the mother. We have found mother-rule in very active existence

[1] *Sex and Society*, pp. 65–66.

among the Pueblo peoples, who are monogamists, and where the paternity of the child must be known. The modern civilised man cannot easily accustom himself to the idea that in the old matriarchal family the dominion of the mother was accepted as the natural, and, therefore, the right order of society. It is very difficult for us to accept a relationship of the sexes that is so exactly opposite to that to which we are accustomed.

After I had written the foregoing account of mother-rule as it exists in the continent of America, I had the exceeding good fortune to attend a lecture given by a native Iroquois. I wish it were possible for me to write here those things that I heard; but I could not do this, I know, without spoiling it all. This would destroy for me what is a very beautiful and happy memory. For to hear of a people who live gladly and without any of those problems that are rotting away our civilisation brings a new courage to those of us who sometimes grow hopeless at this needless wastage of life.

The lecturer told us much of the high status and power of women among the Iroquoian tribes. What he said, not only corroborated all I have written, but gave a picture of mother-rule and mother-rights far more complete than anything I had found in the records of investigators and travellers. The lecturer was a cultured gentleman, and I learnt how false had been my view that the race to which he belonged was uncivilised. I learnt, too, that the Iroquoian tribes were now increasing in numbers, and must not be looked upon as a diminishing people. They have kept, against terrible difficulties, and are determined to keep, their own civilisation and customs, knowing these to be better for them than those of other races. The lecturer astonished me by his familiarity with, and understanding of, our social problems. He spoke, in particular, of the present revolution among women. This, in his opinion, was due wholly to the unnatural arrangement of our family relationship, with the father at the head instead of the mother. There seem to be no sex-problems, no difficulties in marriage, no celibacy, no prostitution among the Iroquoians. All the power in the domestic relationship is in the hands of women. I questioned the lecturer on this point. I asked him if the women did not at times misuse their rights of authority, and if men did not rebel? He seemed surprised. His answer was: "Of course the men follow the wishes of the women; they are our mothers." To him there seemed no more to be said.

III.—*Further Examples of the Matriarchal Family in Australia, India, and other countries*

It is only fair to state that the question of the position of women during the mother-age is a disputed one. Bachofen[1] was the first to build up in his classical works of Matriarchy, the gynæcocratic theory which places the chief social power under the system of mother-descent in the hands of women. This view has been disputed,

[1] Bachofen's work was foreshadowed by an earlier writer, Father Lafiteau, who published his *Mœurs des sauvages americains* in 1721. *Das Mutterrecht* was published in 1861. McLennan, ignorant of Bachofen's work, followed immediately after with his account of the Indian Hill Tribes. He was followed by Morgan, with his knowledge of Iroquois, and many other investigators.

especially in recent years, and many writers who acknowledge the widespread existence of maternal descent deny that it carries with it, except in exceptional cases, mother-rights of special advantage to women; even when these seem to be present they believe such rights to be more apparent than real.[1]

One suspects prejudice here. To approach this question with any fairness it is absolutely essential to clear the mind from our current theories regarding the family. The order is not sacred in the sense that it has always had the same form. It is this belief in the immutability of our form of the sexual relationship which accounts for the prejudice with which this question is so often approached. I fully admit the dark side of the mother-age among many peoples; its sexual licence, often brutal in practice, its cruelties and sacrifice of life. But these are evils common to barbarism, and are found existing under father-right quite as frequently as under mother-right. I concede, too, that mother-descent was not necessarily or universally a period of mother-rule. It was not. But that it did in many cases—and these no exceptional ones—carry with it power for women, as the transmitters of inheritance and property I am certain that the known facts prove.[2] Nor do I forget that cruel treatment of women was not uncommon in matriarchal societies. I have shown how in many tribes the power rested in the

[1] Lord Avebury, for example, says: "I believe that communities in which women have exercised supreme power were quite exceptional," *Marriage, Totemism and Religion*, p. 51. See also Letourneau, *Evolution of Marriage*, pp. 281–282.

[2] In this opinion I am glad to have the support of so high an authority as Mr. Havelock Ellis. See his admirable summary of this question, *Psychology of Sex*, Vol. VI. pp. 390–393; also the essay already referred to, "Changing Status of Women," *Westminster Review*, Oct. 1886.

woman's brother or male relations, and in all such cases mother-descent was really combined with a patriarchal system, the earlier authority of the mother persisting only as a habit. But to argue from the cases of male cruelty that mother-descent did not confer special advantages upon women is, I think, as absurd as it would be to state that under the fully developed patriarchal rule (as also in our society to-day) the authority was not in the hands of men, because cases are not infrequent in which women ill-treat their husbands. And, indeed, when we consider the position of the husband and father under this early system, without rights of property and with no authority over his children, and subject to the rule either of his wife or of her relatives, no surprise can be felt if sometimes he resorted to cruelties, asserting his power in whatever direction opportunity permitted. I may admit that for a long time I found it difficult to believe in this mother-power. The finding of such authority held by primitive woman is strange, indeed, to women to-day. Reverse the sexes, and in broad statement the conditions of the mother-age would be true of our present domestic and social relationship. Little wonder, then, that primitive men rebelled, disliking the inconveniences arising from their insecure and dependent position as perpetual guests in their wives' homes. It is strange how history repeats itself.

Women, from their association with the home, were the first organisers of all industrial labour. A glance back at the mother-age civilisation should teach men modesty. They will see that woman was the equal, if not superior, to man in productive activity. It was not until a much later period that men supplanted women and monopolised the work they had started. Through their identification with the early industrial processes women were the first property owners; they were almost the sole creators of ownership in land, and held in respect of this a position of great advantage. In the transactions of North American tribes with the colonial government many deeds of assignment bear female signatures.[1] A form of divorce used by a husband in ancient Arabia was: "Begone, for I will no longer drive thy flocks to pasture."[2] In almost all cases the household goods belonged to the woman. The stores of roots and berries laid up for a time of scarcity were the property of the wife, and the husband would not touch them without her permission. In many cases such property was very extensive. Among the Menomini Indians, for instance, a woman of good circumstances would own as many as from 1200 to 1500 birch-bark vessels.[3] In the New Mexican *pueblo* what comes from outside the house, as soon as it is inside is put under the immediate control of the women. Bandelier, in his report of his tour in Mexico, tells us that "his host at Cochiti, New Mexico, could not sell an ear of corn or a string of chilli without the consent of his fourteen-year-old daughter Ignacia, who kept house for her widowed father."[4]

The point we have now reached is this: while mother-

[1] Ratzel, *History of Mankind*, Vol. II. p. 130; see Thomas, *op. cit.*, chapter on "Sex and Primitive Industry."

[2] Robertson Smith, *Kinship and Marriage in Early Arabia*, p. 65.

[3] Hoffman, "The Menomini Indians," *Fourteenth Rep. of the Bur. of Am. Ethon.*, p. 288.

[4] Papers of the *Arch. Inst. of Am.*, Vol. II. p. 138.

descent did not constitute or make necessary rule by women, under this system they enjoyed considerable power as the result (1) of their position as property-holders, (2) of their freedom in marriage and the social habits arising from it. This conclusion will be strengthened if we return to our examination of mother-right customs, as we shall find them in all parts of the world. I must select a few examples from as various countries as is possible, and describe them very briefly; not because these cases offer less interest than the matrilenial tribes of America, but because of the length to which this part of my inquiry is rapidly growing.

Let us begin with Australia, where the aboriginal population is in a more primitive condition than any other race whose institutions have been investigated. In certain tribes the family has hardly begun to be distinguished from kin in general. The group is divided into male and female classes, in addition to the division into clans.[1] This is so among the tribes of Mount Gambier, of Darling River, and of Queensland. Marriage within the clan is strictly forbidden, and the male and female classes of each clan are regarded as brothers and sisters. But as every man is brother to all the sisters of his clan, he is husband to all the women of the other clans of his tribe. Marriage is not an individual act, it is a social condition. The custom is not always carried out in practice, but any man of one clan has the right, if he wishes to exercise it, to call any woman belonging to another clan of his tribe his wife, and to treat her

[1] Fison and Howitt, *Native Tribes of Australia*; also *Kamilaroi* and *Kurnai*, pp. 33, 65, 66. See also Hartland, *op. cit.*, Vol. I. p. 294.

as such.[1] The children of each group belong naturally to the clan of the mother, and there is no legal parenthood between them and their father. In the case of war the son must join the maternal tribe. But this is not the universal rule, and in many tribes the children now belong to the paternal clan. The paternal family is beginning to be established in Australia, and varied artifices are used to escape from the tribal marriage and to form unions on an individual basis.

Mother-right is still in force in parts of India, though owing to the influence of Brahmanism on the aboriginal tribes the examples are fewer than might be expected. This change has brought descent through the fathers, and has involved, besides, the more or less complete subjugation of women, with insistence on female chastity, abolition of divorce, infant marriage, and perpetuation of widowhood.[2] Not every tribe is yet thus revolutionised. Among the Kasias of south-east India the husband lives with the wife or visits her occasionally.

> "Laws of rank and property follow the strictest maternal rule; when a couple separate the children remain with the mother, the son does not succeed his father, but a raja's neglected offspring may become a common peasant or a labourer; the sister's son succeeds to rank and is heir to the property." [3]

This may be taken as an extreme example of the conditions among the unchanged tribes. The Garos tribe have an interesting marriage custom.[4] The girl

[1] Letourneau, *op. cit.*, pp. 44, 271–274. Thomas, *op. cit.*, p. 61.

[2] Hartland, *Primitive Paternity*, Vol. II. pp. 155–156, 39–41.

[3] Dalton, *Ethnology of Bengal*, p. 54; also Tylor, "The Matriarchal System," *Nineteenth Century*, July 1896, p. 89.

[4] Dalton, *op. cit.*, p. 63, cited by Hartland. I would suggest that Mr. Bernard Shaw may have had this marriage custom in his mind when he created Ann. See p. 66.

chooses her lover and invites him to follow her; any advance made on his side is regarded as an insult to the woman's clan, and has to be expiated by presents. This marriage is very similar to the ceremony of capture, only the actors change parts; it is here the bridegroom who runs away, and is conducted by force to his future wife amidst the lamentations of his relations.

Even tribes that have adopted paternal descent preserve numerous customs of the earlier system. The husband still remains in the wife's home for a probationary period, working for her family.[1] Women retain rights which are inconsistent with father-rule. The choice of her lover often remains with the girl. If a girl fancies a young man, all she has to do is to give him a kick on the leg at the tribal dance of the *Karama*, and then the parents think it well to hasten on a wedding. Among Ghasiyas in United Provinces a wife is permitted to leave her husband if he intrigues with another woman, or if he become insane, impotent, blind or leprous, while these bodily evils do not allow him to put her away.[2] We find relics of the early freedom enjoyed by women in the licence frequently permitted to girls before marriage. Even after marriage adultery within the tribal rules is not regarded as a serious offence. Divorce is often easy, at the wish of either the woman or the man.[3] This is the case among the Santál tribes, which are

[1] This custom prevails, for instance, among the Kharwârs and Parahiya tribes, and is common among the Ghasiyas, and is also practised among the Tipperah of Bengal. Among the Santâls this service-marriage is used when a girl is ugly or deformed and cannot be married otherwise, while the Badagas of the Nil'giri Hills offer their daughters when in want of labourers.

[2] Crooke, *Tribes and Castes*, iii. p. 242.

[3] Hartland, *op. cit.*, Vol. II. pp. 156, 157.

found in Western Bengal, Northern Orissa, Bhágulpur and the Santál Párganas.[1] It seems probable that fraternal polyandry must formerly have been practised.

Polyandry must have been common at one time in southern India. It will be sufficient to give a few examples. The interesting Todas tribe of the Nil'giri Hills practise fraternal polyandry. The husbands of the women are usually real brothers, but sometimes they are clan brothers. The children belong to the eldest brother, who performs the ceremony of giving the mother a miniature bow and arrow; all offspring, even if born after his death, are counted as his until one of the other brothers performs this ceremony. It is also allowed sometimes for the wife to be mistress to another man besides her husbands, and any children born of such unions are counted as the children of the regular marriage. There is little restriction in love of any kind. In the Toda language there is no word for adultery. It would even seem that "immorality attaches rather to him who grudges his wife to another man."[2]

Similarly among a fine tribe of Hindu mountaineers at the source of the Djemmah fraternal polyandry has been proved to have existed. A woman of this tribe, when asked how many husbands she had, answered, "Only four!" "And all living?" "Why not?" This tribe had a high standard of social conduct; they held lying in horror, and to deviate from the truth even quite innocently was almost a sacrilege.[3] To-day the Kammalaus

[1] Risley, *The Tribes and Castes of Bengal*, Vol. I. pp. 228, 231.
[2] Rivers, *The Todas*; Schrott, *Tras. Ethno. Soc.* (New Series), Vol. VIII. p. 261.
[3] Letourneau, quoting Skinner, *Evolution of Marriage*, p. 78.

(artisans) of Malabar practise fraternal polyandry. The wives are said to greatly appreciate the custom; the more husbands they have the greater will be their happiness.[1]

At another extremity of India, in Ceylon, the polyandric rule is still common,[2] but it is particularly in lamaic Thibet that fraternal polyandry is in full vigour, for in this country religion sanctions the custom, and it is practised by the ruling classes.[3] Its customs are too well known to need description. "The tyranny of man is hardly known among the happy women of Thibet; the boot is perhaps upon the other leg," writes Hartland.[4]

Polyandry is a survival of the group-marriage of the mother-age.[5] It is not really dependent on, though in many cases it occurs in connection with, the economic causes of poverty and a scarcity of women, due to the practice of female infanticide. This form of sexual association has evident advantages for women when compared with polygamy. That freedom in love carried

[1] Thurston, *Ethnographic Notes in Southern India*, p. 114. Polyandry has flourished not only among the primitive races of India. The Hindoo populations also adopted it, and traces of the custom may be found in their sacred literature. Thus in the *Mahâbhârata* the five Pándava brothers marry all together the beautiful Drûaupadi, with eyes of lotus blue (*Mahâbhârata*, trad. Fauche, t. II. p. 148). For an account of polyandry in ancient India the reader should consult Jolly, *Gundriss der Indo-Arischen Philologie und Altertumskunde*.

[2] Davy, *Ceylon*, p. 286; Sachot, *L'Île de Ceylon*, p. 25.

[3] Turner, *Thibet*, p. 348, and *Hist. Univ. des. Voy.*, Vol. XXXI. p. 434; Dalton, *Descriptive Ethnology of Bengal*, p. 36.

[4] Hartland, *op. cit.*, Vol. II. p. 164.

[5] This is the opinion of Bernhöft, quoted by Iwan Bloch. Marshall points out that among the Todas group-marriages occur side by side with polyandry. Bloch also notes that in the common cases where the husband has a claim on his wife's sister, and even her cousins and aunts, we find polygamy developed out of group-marriage. The practice of wife lending and wife exchange is also connected with the early communal marriage (*Sexual History of Our Times*, pp. 193–194). It is possible that prostitution may be a relic of this early sexual freedom. What is moral in one stage of civilisation often becomes immoral in another, when the reasons for its existing have changed.

with it domestic and social rights and privileges to women I have no longer to prove.[1]

The case of the Nâyars of Malabar, where polyandry exists with the early system of maternal filiation, is specially instructive. It is impossible to give the details of their curious customs. The young girls are married when children by a rite known as tying the *tali;* but this marriage serves only the purpose of initiation, and is often performed by a stranger. On the fourth day the fictitious husband is required to divorce the girl. Afterwards any number of marriages may be entered upon[2] without any other restrictions than the prohibitions relative to caste and tribe. These later unions, unlike the solemn initial rite, have no ceremony connected with them, and are entered into freely at the will of the women and their families. As a husband the man of the Nâyars cannot be said to exist; he does not as a rule live with his wife.[3] It is said that he has not the right to sit down by her side or that of her children, he is merely a passing guest, almost a stranger. He is, in fact, reduced to the primitive rôle of the male, and is simply progenitor. " No Nâyar knows his father, and every man looks upon

[1] Havelock Ellis writing on this subject ("Changing Status of Women," *Nineteenth Century*, Oct. 1886) says: "It seems that in the dawn of the race an elaborate social organisation permitted a more or less restricted communal marriage, every man in the tribe being at the outset the husband of every woman, first practically, then theoretically, and that the social organisation which had this point of departure was particularly favourable to women."

[2] It is a matter of dispute whether a woman may have more than one husband at a time. The older accounts state this, while later it has been denied. The probability is that this was the custom, but that it is dying out under modern influences. Hartland, *op. cit.*, Vol. I. p. 267.

[3] In north Malabar a custom has arisen by which after a special ceremony the bridgroom is allowed to take the bride to live in his house, but in the case of his death she must at once return to her own family.

his sister's children as his heirs. A man's mother manages his family; and after her death his eldest sister assumes the direction." The property belongs to the family and is enjoyed by all in common (though personal division is coming into practice under modern influences). It is directed and administered by the maternal uncle or the eldest brother.[1]

The Malays of the Pedang Highlands of Sumatra have institutions bearing many points of similarity with the Nâyars. On marriage neither husband nor wife changes abode, the husband merely visits the wife, coming at first by day to help her work in the rice-fields. Later the visits are paid by night to the wife's house. The husband has no rights over his children, who belong wholly to the wife's *suku*, or clan. Her eldest brother is the head of the family and exercises the rights and duties of a father to her children.[2] The marriage, based on the *ambel-anak*, in which the husband lives with the wife, paying nothing, and occupying a subordinate position, may be taken as typical of the former conditions.[3]

[1] *J. A. I.*, XII. p. 292; Hartland, *op. cit.*, p. 288. Letourneau, apparently quoting Bachofen, says that the women control property. This was probably an earlier custom, when the power was more truly in the hands of women, and had not passed to their male relatives.

[2] Wilken, *Verwantschap*, p. 678; *Bijdragen*, XXXI. p. 40.

[3] Havelock Ellis, *Psychology of Sex*, Vol. VI. p. 291. A second form of marriage, known as Jujur, was also practised. It was much more elaborate, and shows very instructively the rise of father-right. By it the authority of the husband over his wife is asserted by a very complicated system of payments; his right to take her to his home, and his absolute property in her depending wholly on these payments. If the final sum is paid (but this is not commonly claimed except in the case of a quarrel between the families) the woman becomes to all intents the slave of the man; but if on the other hand, as is not at all uncommon, the husband fails or has difficulty in making the main payment, he becomes the debtor of his wife's family and is practically a slave, all his labour being due to his creditor without any reduction in the debt, which must be paid in full, before he regains liberty. (See Marsden, *History of Sumatra*, pp. 225, 235, 257, 262, for an account of both marriages.)

But among other tribes who have come in contact with outside influences this custom of the husband visiting the wife, or residing in her house, is modified.

From a private correspondent, a resident in the Malay States, I have received some interesting notes about the present condition of the native tribes and the position of the women. In most of the Malay States exogamous matriarchy has in comparatively modern times been superseded by feudalism (*i. e.* father-right). But where the old custom survives the women are still to a large extent in control. The husband goes to live in the wife's village; thus the women in each group are a compact unity, while the men are strangers to each other and enter as unorganised individuals. This is the real basis of the woman's power. In other tribes where the old custom has changed women occupy a distinctly inferior position, and under the influence of Islam the idea of secluding adult women has been for centuries spreading and increasing in force.

Male kinship prevails among the Arabs, but the late Professor Robertson Smith discovered abundant evidence that mother-right was practised in ancient Arabia.[1] We find a decisive example of its favourable influence on the position of women in the custom of *beena*[2] marriage. Under such a system the wife was not only freed from any subjection involved by the payment of a bride-price (which always places her more or less under the authority of her husband), but she was the owner of the tent and household property, and thus enjoyed the liberty which ownership always entails. This explains how she

[1] *Kinship and Marriage in Early Arabia.*
[2] Havelock Ellis, *op. cit.*, pp. 391–392, quoting Robertson Smith.

was able to free herself at pleasure from her husband, who was really nothing but a temporary lover.[1] Ibn Batua in the fourteenth century found that the women of Zebid were perfectly ready to marry strangers. The husband might depart when he pleased, but his wife in that case could never be induced to follow him. She bade him a friendly adieu and took upon herself the whole charge of any child of the marriage. The women in the Jâhilîya[2] had the right to dismiss their husbands, and the form of dismissal was this: "If they lived in a tent they turned it round, so that if the door faced east it now faced west, and when the man saw this he knew that he was dismissed and did not enter." The tent belonged to the woman; the husband was received there and at her good pleasure.[3]

A further striking example of mother-right is furnished by the Mariana Islands, where the position of women was distinctly superior.

"Even when the man had contributed an equal share of property on marriage, the wife dictated everything and the man could undertake nothing without her approval; but if the woman committed an offence, the man was held responsible and suffered the punishment. The women could speak in the assembly, they held property, and if a woman asked anything of a man, he gave it up

[1] Barlow, *Semitic Origins*, p. 45.

[2] Robertson Smith, *op. cit.*, p. 65.

[3] This kind of union for a term is said to have been recognised by Mahommed, though it is irregular by Moslem law. The cases of *beena* marriage are very frequent among widely different peoples. (See Hartland, *Primitive Paternity*, Vol. II. pp. 11, 13, 14, 19, 20, 24, 27, 30–36, 38, 41–43, 51, 53, 55, 60–63, 67–72, 76, 77.) Frazer (*Academy*, March 27, 1886) cites an interesting example among the tribes on the north frontier of Abyssinia, partially Semitic peoples, not yet under the influence of Islam, who preserve a system of marriage closely resembling the *beena* marriage, but have as well a purchase marriage, by which a wife is acquired by payment of a bride-price and becomes the property of her husband. (Quoted by Ellis, *op. cit.*, p. 392 *note*.)

without a murmur. If a wife was unfaithful, the husband could send her home, keep her property and kill the adulterer; but if the man was guilty, or even suspected of the same offence, the women of the neighbourhood destroyed his house and all his visible property, and the owner was fortunate if he escaped with a whole skin; and if the wife was not pleased with her husband, she withdrew and a similar attack followed. On this account many men were not married, preferring to live with paid women."[1]

A similar case of the rebellion of men against their position is recorded in Guinea, where religious symbolism was used by the husband as a way of escape. The maternal system held with respect to the chief wife.

"It was customary, however, for a man to buy and take to wife a slave, a friendless person with whom he could deal at pleasure, who had no kindred that could interfere for her, and to consecrate her to his Bossum or god. The Bossum wife, slave as she had been, ranked next to the chief wife, and was exceptionally treated. She alone was very jealously guarded, she alone was sacrificed at her husband's death. She was, in fact, wife in a peculiar sense. And having, by consecration, been made of the kindred and worship of her husband, her children could be born of his kindred and worship." [2]

This practice of having a slave-wife who was the property of the husband became more and more common; and was one of the causes that led to the establishment of father-right. How this came we have now to see.

IV.—*The Transition to Father-right*

In the preceding sections of this chapter I have collected together, with as much exactitude as I could, many

[1] Thomas, *Sex and Society*, pp. 73–74. Quoting Waitz-Gerland, *Anthropologie der Naturvölker*, Vol. V. p. 107.
[2] McLennan, *The Patriarchal Theory*, p. 235.

examples of the maternal family. I want now to refer briefly to a few further cases, which will make clearer the causes which led to the adoption of father-right.

Many countries where the patriarchal system is firmly established retain practices which can only be explained as survivals of the earlier custom of mother-descent.[1] It must suffice to mention one or two examples. In Burma, which offers in this respect a curious contrast to India, the women have preserved under father-right most of the privileges of mother-right. This is the more remarkable as the law of marriage and the relationship of the sexes is founded on the code of Manu, which proclaims aloud the inferiority of woman. It is interesting, however, to note that the code recognises only three kinds of men: the good man, the indifferent man, and the bad man. Women, though recognised solely in their relation as wives, are placed in seven classes: the mother-wife, the sister-wife, the daughter-wife, the friend-wife, the master-wife, the servant-wife, and the slave-wife. Manu holds that the last of these, the slave-wife, is the best wife. It is, however, certain that the interpretation of the code in Burma was entirely opposed to any subjection of the wife. That mother-right must have been once practised and was very firmly established is proved by the occurrence of brother-sister marriages. The queens of the last rulers of the country, Minden-Min and Thebaw, were either their own or their half-sisters, and the power of government seems to have been almost wholly in the

[1] Thomas, *op. cit.*, p. 75, points out that this survival of woman's power after the rise of father-right is similar to the assertion of male-power under mother-right in the person of the woman's brother or male relative.

hands of these queens. The patriarchal custom, so far as the position of women was concerned, is but a thread, binding them in their marriage, but leaving them entirely free in other respects. The Burmese wife is much more the master than the slave of her husband, though she is clever enough as a rule not to let him feel any inconvenience from her power, which, therefore, he accepts. The exceptional position of the women is clearly indicated by the fact that they enter freely into trade, and, indeed, carry out most of the business of the country. Nearly all the shops are kept by women. In the markets, where everything that any one could posibly want is sold, almost all the dealers are women. All classes of the Burmese girls receive their training in these markets; the daughters of the rich sell the costly and beautiful stuffs, the poorer girls sell the cheaper wares. It is this training which accounts for the business capacity shown by the women. The boys are trained by the priests, as every boy is required, "in order to purify his soul, to acquire a knowledge of sacred things." This explains a great deal. It would seem that religion enforces the same penalties on men that in most countries fall upon women. The Burmese women are very attractive, as is testified by all who know them. The streets of the towns are thronged with women at all hours of the day, and they show the greatest delight in everything that is lively and gay.

Given such complete freedom of women, it is self-evident that the sexual relationships will also be free. Very striking are the conditions of divorce. The marriage contract can be dissolved freely at the wish of both, or even of one, of the partners. In the first case the family property is divided equally between the wife and the husband, while if only one partner desires to be freed the property goes to the partner who is left. The children of the marriage remain with the mother while they are young; but the boys belong to the father. I wish it were possible for me to give a fuller account of the Burmese family. The freedom and active work of the women offer many points of special interest. One thing further must be noted. The Burmese women would seem not to be wholly satisfied with their power, disliking the work and responsibility which their freedom entails. For this reason many of them prefer to marry a Chinese husband; he works for them, while with a husband of their own country they have to work for him. This is very instructive. It points to what I believe to be the truth. The loss of her freedom by woman is often the result of her own desire for protection and her dislike of work, and is not caused by man's tyranny. Woman's own action in this matter is not sufficiently recognised. I must not enter upon this here, as I shall return to the subject later in this chapter. We must now consider the traces left by mother-descent in Japan and China.

In Japan, as among the Basques, filiation is subordinated to the transmission of property. It is to the first-born, whether a boy or a girl, that the inheritance is transmitted, and he or she is forbidden to abandon it. At the time of marriage the husband or wife must take the name of the heir or heiress who marries and personifies the property. Filiation is thus sometimes paternal and sometimes maternal. The maternal uncle still bears the name of "second little father."[1] The children of the same father, but not of the same mother, were formerly allowed to marry, a decisive proof of mother-descent. The wife remained with her own relatives, and the husband had the right of visiting her by night. The word commonly used for marriage signified *to slip by night into the house.* It was not until the fourteenth century that the husband's residence was the home of the wife, and marriage became a continued living together by the married pair. Even now when a man marries an only daughter he frequently lives with her family, and the children take her name. There is also a custom by which a man with daughters, but no son, adopts a stranger, giving him one of his daughters in marriage; the children are counted as the heirs of the maternal grandfather.[2] Similar survivals are frequent in China. The patriarchate is rigidly established, but there is evidence to show that the family in this ancient civilisation has passed through the usual stages of development, having for its starting-point the familial clan, and passing from this through the stage of mother-right.[3] The Chinese language itself attests the ancient existence of the earliest form of marriage, contracted by a group of brothers having their wives in common, but not marrying their sisters. Thus a Chinaman calls the sons of his brothers "his sons," but he considers those of his sisters as his nephews.[4] Certain of the aboriginal

[1] Letourneau, *op. cit.*, p. 323, who quotes Lubbock, *Orig. Civil.*, p. 177.

[2] Hartland, *op. cit.*, Vol. II, p. 14, citing Morgan, *Systems of Consanguinity*.

[3] Letourneau, *op. cit.*, p. 323.

[4] Morgan, *Systems of Consanguinity* ("Smithsonian Contributions"), Vol. XVII. pp. 416–417.

tribes still require the husband to live with his wife's family for a period of seven or ten years before he is allowed to take her to his home. The eldest child is given to the husband, the second belongs to the family of the wife.[1] The authority which the Chinese mother exercises over her son's marriage and over his wife can only be explained by mother-right customs. There are many other examples which I must pass over.

In the Island of Madagascar, with whose interesting civilisation, as it existed before the unfortunate conquest of the country by the French, I am personally acquainted, mother-right has left much more than traces.[2] Great freedom in sexual relations was permitted to the men, and in certain cases to women also. There was no word in the native language for virgin; the word *mpitòvo*, commonly used, means only an unmarried woman. On certain festive ceremonies the licence was very great. The hindrances to marriage were much more stringent with the mother's relations than with the father's. Divorce was frequent and easy; the power to exercise it rested with the husband; but the wife could, and often did, run away, and thus compel a divorce. A Malagasy proverb compared marriage to a knot so lightly tied that it could be undone by a touch. Such freedom was due to the great desire for children; every child was welcome in the family, whatever its origin.[3] The children

[1] Hartland, Vol. II. p. 45, quoting Gray, *China*, Vol. II. p. 304.

[2] This is the opinion of Hartland. He quotes Ellis, *History of Madagascar*, and Sibree, *The Great African Island*. I am able to speak as to the truths of the facts given in their books from my knowledge of the Malagasy before the French occupation of the island. Madagascar is my birth-place, and my father was a missionary in the country at the same time as Mr. Ellis and Mr. Sibree.

[3] As an instance of the importance attached to children, I may

belonged to the husband, and so complete was this possession, that in the case of a divorce not only the children previously born, but any the wife might afterwards bear, were counted as his.

Among the ruling classes mother-right remained in its early force. The royal family and nobility traced their descent, contrary to the general practice, through the mother, and not through the father. The rights of an unmarried queen were great. She was permitted to have a family by whomsoever she wished, and her children were recognised as legitimately royal through her. Among the Hovas not only wealth, but political dignities, and even sacerdotal functions, were transmitted to the nephew, in preference to the son.

In the adjacent continent of Africa we find similar privileges enjoyed by royal women. A delightful example is given by Frazer[1] in Central Africa, where a small state, near to the Chambezi river, is governed by a queen, who belongs to the reigning family of Ubemba. She bears the title *Mamfumer*, "Mother of Kings." The privileges attached to this dignity are numerous; the husbands may be chosen at will and from among the common people.

"The chosen man becomes prince consort, without sharing in the government of affairs. He is bound to leave everything to follow his royal and often little accommodating spouse. To show that in these households the rights are inverted and that a man may be changed into a woman, the queen takes the title of *Mon-*

---

mention the fact that, after my birth my father was not announced to preach under his own name, but as "the father of Kéteka," the Malagasy equivalent of my name.

[1] Frazer, *Golden Bough*, Pt. I. *The Magical Art*, Vol. II. p. 277.

sieur and the husband that of *Madame*." A visitor to this state,[1] who had an interview with the queen, reports that, "she was a woman of gigantic stature, wearing many amulets."

Battle reported that "Loango was ruled by four princes, the sons of a former king's sister, since the sons of a king never succeed.[2] Frazer gives an account of the tyrannical authority of the princesses in this state.[3]

"The princesses are free to choose and divorce their husbands at pleasure, and to cohabit at the same time with other men. The husbands are nearly always plebeians. The lot of a prince consort is not a happy one, for he is rather the slave and prisoner than the mate of his imperious princess. In marrying her he engages never more to look at a woman; when he goes out he is preceded by guards whose duty it is to drive all females from the road where he is to pass. If, in spite of these precautions, he should by ill-luck cast his eyes on a woman, the princess may have his head chopped off, and commonly exercised, or used to exercise, the right. This sort of libertinism, sustained by power, often carries the princesses to the greatest excesses, and nothing is so much dreaded as their anger."

In Africa descent through women is the rule,[4] though there are exceptions, and these are increasing. The amusing account given by Miss Kingsley[5] of Joseph, a member of the Batu tribe in French Congo, strikingly illustrates the prevalence of the custom. When asked by a French official to furnish his own name and the name of his father, Joseph was wholly nonplussed. "My fader?" he said. "Who my fader?" Then he gave the name of his mother.

[1] Father Guillemé, Missiones Catholiques, XXXIV. (1902), p. 16.
[2] Lubbock, *Origin of Civilisation*, p. 151.
[3] Frazer, *Ibid.*, p. 276.
[4] "Birth," we are told by a keen observer, who has lived for many years in intimate converse with the natives, "sanctifies the child; birth alone gives him status as a member of his mother's family" (Dennett, *Jour. Afr. Soc.*, I. p. 265).
[5] *Travels*, p. 109.

The case is the same among the Negroes. The Fanti of the Gold Coast may be taken as an example. Among them an intensity of affection (accounted for partly by the fact that the mothers have exclusive care of the children) is felt for the mother, while the father is hardly known, or disregarded, notwithstanding that he may be a wealthy and powerful man and the legal husband of the mother.[1] The practice of the Wamoima, where the son of a sister is preferred in legacies, "because a man's own son is only the son of his wife," is typical.[2] The Bush husband does not live with his wife, and often has wives in different places. The maternal uncle supplies his place in the family.

Wherever mother-right has progressed towards father-right, as is the condition, broadly speaking, in the African continent, the supreme authority is vested in the maternal uncle. The tribal duty of blood-revenge falls to him, even against the father. Thus, in some cases, if a woman is murdered, the duty of revenge is undertaken by her kinsman.[3] In the state of Loango among the common people the uncle is addressed as *tate* (father). He has even the power to sell his sister's children.[4] The child is so entirely the property of the kin that he may be given in pledge for their debts. Among the Bavili the mother has the right to pawn the child, but she must first consult the father, so that he may have a chance of giving her

[1] Hartland, quoting Mr. Sarbah, a native barrister, *op. cit.*, Vol. I. p. 286.

[2] Lippert, *Kulturgeschichte*, Vol. II. p. 57.

[3] This is done among the Beni Amer on the shores of the Red Sea and in the Barka valley, which is the more remarkable as mother-descent has fallen into desuetude under the influence of Islamism. (Hartland, Vol. I. p. 274, quoting Munzinger, *Ostafrikanische studien*.)

[4] Bastian, *Loango-Küste*, I. p. 166.

goods to save the pledging.[1] This is very plainly a step towards father-right. There is no distinction between legitimate and illegitimate children. Similar conditions prevail among the Alladians of the Ivory Coast, but here the mother cannot pledge her children without the consent of her brother or other male head of the family. The father has the right to ransom the child.[2] An even stronger example of the property value of children is furnished by the custom found among many tribes, by which the father has to make a present to the wife's kin when a child dies: this is called "buying the child."[3]

These cases, with the inferences they suggest, show that though mother-descent may be strongly established in Africa, this does not confer (except to the royal princesses) any special distinction upon women. This is explained if we recognise that a transitional period has been reached, when, under the pressure of social, and particularly of military activities, the government of the tribe has passed to the male kindred of the women. It wants but a step further for the establishment of father-right.

There are many cases pointing to this new father-force asserting itself and pushing aside the earlier order. Again I can give one or two examples only. Among

[1] Dennett, *Jour. Afr. Soc.*, I. p. 266.
[2] *Jour. Afr. Soc.*, I. p. 412. See Hartland, *op. cit.*, Vol. I, pp. 275–288.
[3] A similar custom prevails among Maori people of New Zealand. When a child dies, or even meets with an accident, the mother's relations, headed by her brother, turn out in force against the father. He must defend himself until wounded. Blood once drawn the combat ceases; but the attacking party plunders his house and appropriates the husband's property, and finally sits down to a feast provided by him (*Old New Zealand*, p. 110). This case is the more extraordinary as the Maori reckon descent through the father; it is doubtless a custom persisting from an earlier time.

Wayao and Mang'anja of the Shire highlands, south of Lake Nyassa, a man on marrying leaves his own village and goes to live in that of his wife; but, as an alternative, he is allowed to pay a bride-price, in which case he takes his wife away to his home.[1] Whenever we find the payment of a bride-price, there is sure indication of the decay of mother-right: woman has become property. Among the Bassa Komo of Nigeria marriage is usually effected by an exchange of sisters or other female relatives. The women are supposed to be faithful to their husbands. If, however, as frequently happens, there is a preliminary courtship period, during which the marriage is considered as provisional, considerable licence is granted to the woman. Chastity is only regarded as a virtue when the woman has become the property of the husband. The men may marry as many wives as they have sisters or female relatives to give in exchange. In this tribe the women look after the children, but the boys, when four years old, go to work and live with their fathers.[2] The husbands of the Bambala tribe (inhabiting the Congo states between the rivers Inzia and Kwilu) have to abstain from visiting their wives for a year after the birth of each child, but they are allowed to return to her on the payment to her father of two goats.[3] Among the Basanga on the south-west of Lake Moeru the children of the wife belong to the mother's kin, but the children of slaves are the property of the father.[4]

[1] Macdonald, *Africana*, Vol. I. p. 136.

[2] *Jour. Afr. Soc.*, VIII. pp. 15–17. This tribe now traces descent through the father.

[3] Torday and Joyce, *J. A. I.*, XXXV. p. 410.

[4] Arnot, *Garenganze*, p. 242.

It is rendered clear by such cases as these, that the rise of father-right was dependent on property and had nothing to do with blood relationship. The payment of a bride-price, the giving of a sister in exchange, as also marriage with a slave, gained for the husband the control over his wife and ownership of her children. I could bring forward much more evidence in proof of this fact did the limits of my space allow me to do this; such cases are common in all parts of the world where the transitional stage from mother-right to father-right has been reached. But I believe that the causes by which the father gained his position as the dominant partner in marriage must be clear to every one from the examples I have given. I will, therefore, quote only one final and most instructive case. It illustrates in a curious way the conflict between the old rights of the woman and the rising power of the male force in connection with marriage. It occurs among the Hassanyeh Arabs of the White Nile, where the wife passes by contract for only a portion of her time under the authority of her husband.

"When the parents of the man and the woman meet to settle the price of the woman, the price depends on how many days in the week the marriage tie is to be strictly observed. The woman's mother first of all proposes that, taking everything into consideration, with due regard to the feelings of the family, she could not think of binding her daughter to a due observance of that chastity which matrimony is expected to command for more than two days in the week. After a great deal of apparently angry discussion, and the promise on the part of the relations of the man to pay more, it is arranged that the marriage shall hold good as is customary among the first families of the tribe, for four days in the week, viz. Monday, Tuesday, Wednesday and Thursday, and in compliance with old established custom, the marriage rites during the three remaining days shall not be insisted on, during which days the bride shall be perfectly free to act as she may think proper, either by adhering to her husband and home, or by enjoying her freedom and independence from all observance of matrimonial obligation." [1]

We have at length concluded our investigation of this first period of organised society, and have ascertained many facts that we can use as a touchstone to try the truth of the various theories that are put forward with regard to woman and her position in the family and in the State. The importance of the mother-age to women is evident. Thus I offer no apology for the length at which I have treated the subject. It has seemed to me after careful revision that no one of the examples given can be omitted. Facts are of so much more importance than opinions if we are to come to the truth.

Without attempting to trace exhaustively the history or even to enumerate the peoples living, or who have lived, under mother-right customs, we have examined many and varied cases of the actual working of this system, with special reference to the position held by women. The examples have been chosen from all parts of the world, so as to prove (what is sometimes denied) that mother-right has not been confined to any one race, that it is not a local custom under special conditions, but that it has been a necessary stage of growth of human societies. My aim has been to illustrate the stages through which society passed from mother-right to father-right. It has not been possible to arrange the evidence in any exact progressive sequence, but I hope the cases

[1] Spencer, *Descriptive Sociology*, Vol. V. p. 8, citing Petherick, *Egypt, the Soudan, and Central Africa*, pp. 140–144. This case is quoted by Thomas, *op. cit.*, pp. 85, 86.

given will make clear what I believe to have been the general trend of growth: at first the power in the hands of the women, but this giving way to the slow but steady usurping of the mother's authority by the ever-assertive male.

I shall now conclude this study of the mother-age by attempting to formulate the general truths, which, it seems to me, may be drawn from the examples we have examined.

I. The first effort of primitive society was to establish some form of order, and in that order the women of the group were the more stable and predominant partners in the family relationship.

II. Impelled by the conditions of motherhood to a more settled life than the men of the tribe, women were the first agriculturists, weavers, dyers and dressers of skins, potters, the domesticators of animals, the first architects, and sometimes the primitive doctors—in a word, the inventors and organisers of the peaceful art of life.[1] Primitive women were strong in body[2] and capable

[1] For fuller information on this important subject the reader is referred to Professor Otis Mason, who gives a picturesque summary of the work done by women among the primitive tribes of America (*American Antiquarian*, January 1889, "The Ulu, or Woman's Knife of the Eskimo," *Report of the United States National Museum*, 1890). H. Ellis, *Man and Woman*, pp. 1–17, and Thomas, *Sex and Society*, pp. 123–146, give interesting accounts of the division of labour among primitive people, showing the important part women took in the start of industrialism. For direct examples from primitive peoples, the works of Fison and Howit, James Macdonald, Professor Haddow, Hearn, Morgan, Bancroft, Lubbock, Ratzel, Schoolcroft and other anthropologists should be consulted.

[2] It is an entirely mistaken view, founded on insufficient knowledge, that in early civilisations women were a source of weakness to the men of the tribe or group, and, thus, liable to oppression. The very reverse is the truth. Fison and Howit, who discuss the question, say of the Australian women, "In time of peace they are the hardest workers and the most useful members of the community." In time of war, "they

in work. The power they enjoyed as well as their manifold activities were a result of their position as mothers, this function being to them a source of strength and not a plea of weakness.

III. Moral ideas, as we understand them, hardly existed. The oldest form of marriage was what is known as "group marriage," which was the union of two tribal groups or clans, the men of one *totem* group marrying the women of another, and *vice versa*, but no man or woman having one particular wife or husband.

IV. The individual relationship between the sexes began with the reception of temporary lovers by the woman in her own home. But as society progressed, a relationship thus formed would tend under favourable circumstances to be continued, and, in some cases, perpetuated. The lover thus became the husband, but he was still without property right, with no—or very little—control over the woman, and none over her children, occupying, indeed, the position of a more or less permanent guest in her hut or tent.

V. The social organisation which followed this custom was in most cases—and always, I believe, in their primitive form—favourable to women. Kinship was recognised through the mother, and the continuity of the

---

are perfectly capable of taking care of themselves at all times, and so far from being an encumbrance on the warriors, they will fight, if need be, as bravely as the men, and with even greater ferocity" (*Kamilaroi and Kurnai*, pp. 133–147, 358). This is no exceptional case, and is confirmed by the reports of investigators of widely different peoples. I may mention the ancient Iberian women of Northern Spain, whose bravery in battle is testified to by Strabo: the descendants of these women still carry on the greater part of the active labour connected with agriculture (*Spain Revisited*, pp. 191–292). In our own day we have the witness to the same truth in the heroic part taken by women in the Balkan army.

family thus depending solely on the woman, it followed she was the holder of all property. Her position and that of her children was, by this means, assured, and in the case of a separation it was the man who departed, leaving her in possession. The woman was the head of the household, and in some instances held the position of tribal chief.

VI. This early power of women, arising from the recognition alone of womb-kinship, with the resulting freedom in sexual relationships permitted to women, could not continue. It was no more possible for society to be built up on mother-right alone than it is possible for it to remain permanently based on father-right.

VII. It is important to note that the causes which led to the change in the position of the sexes had no direct connection with moral development; it was not due, as many have held, to the recognition of fatherhood. The cause was quite different and was founded on property. It arose, in the first instance, through a property value being connected with women themselves. As soon as the women's kin began to see in their women a means by exchange of obtaining wives for themselves, and also the possibility of gaining worldly goods, both in the property held by women, and by means of the service and presents that could be claimed from their lovers, we find them exercising more or less strict supervision over the alliances of their female relatives.

VIII. At first, and for a long time, the early freedom of women persisted in the widely spread custom of a preliminary period before marriage of unrestricted sexual relationships. But permanent unions became subject to the consent of the woman's kindred.

It was in this way, I am certain, and for no moral considerations that the stringency of the sexual code was first tightened for women.

IX. At a much later date virginity came to have a special market-value, from which time a jealous watch began to be kept upon maidenhood.

It seems to me of very great importance that women should grasp firmly this truth : the virtue of chastity owes its origin to property. Our minds fall so readily under the spell of such ideas as chastity and purity. There is a mass of real superstition on this question—a belief in a kind of magic in purity. But, indeed, chastity had at first no connection with morals. The sense of ownership has been the seed-plot of our moral code. To it we are indebted for the first germs of the sexual inhibitions which, sanctified by religion and supported by custom, have, under the unreasoned idealism of the common mind, filled life with cruelties and jealous exclusions, with suicides and murders and secret shames.

X. This intrusion of economics into the sexual relationships brought about the revolution in the status of women. As soon as women became sexually marketable, their early power was doomed. First came what I hold to have been the transitional stage of the mother-age. This will explain how it is that, even where matrilineal descent is in full force, we may find the patriarchal subjection of women. The mother's authority has been usurped by her male kindred, usually her brother.

XI. We have noted the alien position of the father

even among peoples at a stage of development where paternity was fully established. This subjection, which, perhaps, would not be felt in the earlier stage of mother-right, must have been increased by the intrusion of the authority of the wife's male kindred. The impulse to dominate by virtue of strength or of property possessions has manifested itself in every age. As society advanced property would increase in value, and the social and political significance of its possession would also increase. It is clear that such a position of insecurity for the husband and father would tend to become impossible.

XII. One way of escape—which doubtless took place at a very early stage—was by the capture of women. Side by side with the customary marriages in which the husband resided in the home of the wife, without rights and subject to her clan-kindred, we find the practice of a man keeping one or more captive wives in his own home for his use and service. It will be readily seen that the special rights in the home over these owned wives (rights, moreover, that were recognised by the tribe) would come to be desired by other men. But the capture of wives was always difficult as it frequently led to a quarrel and even warfare with the woman's tribe, and for this reason was never widely practised. It would, therefore, be necessary for another way of escape to be found. This was done by changing the conditions of the customary marriage. Nor do I think it unlikely that such change may have been received favourably by women. The captive wives may even have been envied by the regular wife. An arrangement that would give a more individual relationship to marriage and the protection of a husband for herself and the children of their union may well have been preferred by woman to her position of subjection that had now arisen to the authority of her brother or other male relative. The alteration from the old custom may thus be said to have been due, in part, to the interests of the husband, but also, in part, to the inclination of the wife.

XIII. The change was gained by elopement, by simulated capture, by the gift or exchange of women, and by the payment of a bride-price. The bride-price came to be the most usual custom, gradually displacing the others. As we have seen, it was often regarded as a condition, not of the marriage itself, but of the transfer of the wife to the home of the husband and of the children to his kin.

XIV. It was in this way, for economic reasons, and the personal needs of both the woman and the man, and not, I believe, specially through the fighting propensities of the males, and certainly not by any unfair domination or tyranny on the part of the husband that the position of the sexes was reversed.

XV. But be this as it may, to woman the result was no less far-reaching and disastrous. She had become the property of one master, residing in her husband's tribe, which had no rights or duties in regard to her, where she was a stranger, perhaps speaking a different language. And her children kept her bound to this alien home in a much closer way than the husband could ever have been bound to her home under the earlier custom. Woman's early power rested in her organised position among her own kin: this was now lost.

XVI. The change was not brought about quickly. For long the mother's influence persisted as a matter of habit. We have its rather empty shadow with us to-day.

XVII. But, under the pressure of the new conditions, the old custom of tracing descent and the inheritance of property in the female line (so favourable to women) died. Mother-right passed away, remaining only as a tradition, or practised in isolated cases among primitive peoples. The patriarchal age, which still endures, succeeded. Women became slaves, who of old had been dominant.

One final word more.

The opinion that the subjection of women arose from male mastery, or was due to any special cruelty, must be set aside. To me the history of the mother-age does not teach this. I believe this charge could not have arisen, at all events it would not have persisted, if women, with the power they then enjoyed, had not desired the gaining of a closer relationship with the father of their children. With all the evils that father-right has brought to woman, we have got to remember that woman owes the individual relation of the man to herself and her children to the patriarchal system. The father's right in his children (which, unlike the right of the mother, was not founded on kinship, but rested on the quite different and insecure basis of property) had to be established. Without this being done, the family in its full and perfect development was impossible. We women need to remember this, lest bitterness stains our sense of justice. It may be that progress social and moral could not have been accomplished otherwise; that the cost of love's development has been the enslavement of woman. If so, then women will not, in the long account of Nature, have lost in the payment of the price. They may be (when they come at last to understand the truth) better fitted for their refound freedom.

Neither mother-right alone, nor father-right alone, can satisfy the new ideals of the true relationship of the sexes. The spiritual force, slowly unfolding, that has uplifted, and is still uplifting, womanhood, is the foundation of woman's claim that the further progress of humanity is bound up with her restoration to a position of freedom and human equality. But this position she must not take from man—that, indeed, would be a step backwards. No, she is to share it with him, and this for her own sake and for his, and, more than all, for the sake of their children and all the children of the race.

This replacement of the mother side by side with the father in the home and in the larger home of the State is the true work of the Woman's Movement.

CONTENTS OF CHAPTER VII

WOMAN'S POSITION IN THE GREAT CIVILISATIONS OF ANTIQUITY

I.—*In Egypt*

The importance of estimating woman's position in the great civilisations of the ancient world—The Egyptian civilisation—Women more free and more honoured than in any country to-day—The account given by Herodotus—The Egyptian woman never confined to the home—No restraint upon her actions—She entered into commerce in her own right and made contracts for her own benefit—Abundant material in proof of the high status of Egyptian women—Marriage contracts—Their importance and interest—Numerous examples—The proprietary rights of the wife—An early period of mother-rule—Property originally in the hands of women—The marriage contracts a development of the early system—The Egyptians solved the difficult problem of the fusion of mother-right with father-right—The statement of Dioderus that among the Egyptians the woman rules over the man—The conditions of marriage dependent on the birth of children—M. Paturet's view the Egyptian woman the equal of man—The high status of woman proved by the fact that her child was never illegitimate—The position of the mother secure in every relationship between the sexes—This made possible by the free conditions of the marriage contracts—Polygamy allowed—This practice in Egypt very different from polygamy in a patriarchal society—The husband a privileged guest in the home of the wife—The high ideal of the domestic relationship—Illustrations from the inscriptions of the monuments—Reasons which explain this civilised and human organisation—The Egyptians an agricultural and a conservative people—They were also a pacific race—The significance of the Maxims of the Moralists—Honour to the wife and the mother strongly insisted on—The health and character of the Egyptian mother—Some reflections in the Egyptian Galleries of the British Museum.

II.—*In Babylon*

Traces of mother-right in primitive Babylon—The honour paid to women—The position of women in later Babylonian history, though still at an early period—Their rights more circumscribed—The marriage code of Hammurabi—Polygamy permitted, though restricted, by the code—The exacting conditions of divorce—The position of the wife as subject to her husband—The later Neo-Babylonian periods—The position of women continuously improving—They obtain a position equal in law with their husbands—Their freedom in all social relations—They conduct business transactions in their own right—Illustrations from the contract tablets—Remarks and conclusion.

III.—*In Greece*

Traces of mother-right traditions in Greek literature and history—The women of the Homeric period—Dangers arising from the patriarchal subjection of women—Illustrations and various reflections—Historic Greece—The social organisation of Sparta—Their marriage system—The laws of Lycurgus—The freedom of the Spartan girls—The wise care for the health of the race—Plato's criticism of the Spartan system—He accuses the women of ruling their husbands—The Athenian women—Their subjection under the strict patriarchal rule—The insistence on chastity—Reasons for this—The degraded position of the wife—The *hetairæ*—They the only educated women in Athens—Aspasia—She leads the movement to raise the position of the Athenian women—Plato's estimate of women—Remarks on the sexual penalties for women that are always found under a strict patriarchal regime—The ideal relationship between the wife and the husband—Euripides voices the sorrows of women—He foreshadows their coming triumph.

IV.—*In Rome*

Little known of the position of women in Rome in prehistoric times—Indications of an early period of mother-rule—The patriarchal system formerly established when Roman history opens—The Roman marriage law—The woman regarded as the property first of her father and afterwards of her husband—The patrician marriage of *confarreatio*—The form known as *coemptio*—Marriage by *usus*—The inequality of divorce—The subjection of the woman—The terrible right of the husband's *manus*—The way of escape—The development of the early marriage by *usus*—The new free marriage by consent—Free divorce—A revolution in the position of women—The patriarchal rule of women dwindled to a mere thread—They gained increasingly greater liberty until at last they gained complete freedom—The public entry of women into the affairs of State—Illustrations to show the fine use made by the Roman matrons of their freedom—An examination into the supposed licentiousness of Roman women—This opinion cannot be accepted—The effect of Christianity—The view of Sir Henry Maine—Some concluding remarks on the position of women in the four great civilisations examined in this chapter.

CHAPTER VII

WOMAN'S POSITION IN THE GREAT CIVILISATIONS OF ANTIQUITY

I.—*In Egypt*

" If we consider the status of woman in the great empires of antiquity, we find on the whole that in their early stage, the stage of growth, as well as in their final stage, the stage of fruition, women tend to occupy a favourable position, while in their middle stage, usually the stage of predominating military organisation on a patriarchal basis, women usually occupy a less favourable position. This cyclic movement seems to be almost a natural law of development of great social groups."—HAVELOCK ELLIS.

THE civilisations through which I am now going to follow the history of woman, in so far as they offer any special features of interest to our inquiry into woman's character and her true place in the social order, belong to the great civilisations of the ancient world, civilisations, moreover, that have deeply influenced human culture. It forms the second part of our historical investigation. There can be no doubt of its interest to us, for if we can prove that women have exercised unquestioned and direct authority in the family and in the State, not only among primitive peoples, but in stable civilisations of vital culture, we shall be in a position to answer those who wish to set limits to women's present activities.

It is necessary to enter into this inquiry with caution: the difficulties before me are very great. Again, it is not in any scarcity of evidence, but in its superabundance that the trouble rests. It is hard to condense the social habits of peoples into a few dozen pages. Nothing would be easier than from the mass of material available to pile up facts in furnishing a picture of the high status of woman that would unnerve any upholders of female subordination. It is just possible, on the other hand, to interpret these facts from a fixed point of thought, and then to argue that, in spite of her power, woman was still regarded as the inferior of man.[1] I wish to do neither. It is my purpose to outline the domestic relationships and the family law and customs as they existed in Egypt and in Babylon, in Greece and in Rome; to touch the features of social life only in so far as they illustrate this, and so to discover to what extent the mother was still regarded as the natural transmitter of property and head of the household. The subject is an immensely complicated and seductive one, so that I must keep strictly to the path set by this inquiry.

Let us turn first to Egypt.

We have so rich a collection of the remains of the ancient Egyptian civilisation, and so careful and industrious a scholarship has been given to interpret them, that we can with confidence reconstruct in outline the legal status and proprietary rights enjoyed by women, which gave them a position more free and more honoured than they have in any country of the world to-day. This is not an overestimate of the facts. The security of her proprietary rights made the Egyptian woman the legal

[1] This is the position taken up, for instance, by Letourneau, *Evolution of Marriage*, p. 176.

head of the household, she inherited equally with her brothers, and had full control of her own property. She was juridically the equal of man, having the same rights, with the same freedom of action, and being honoured in the same way.

The position of woman in Egypt is, indeed, full of surprises to the modern believer in woman's subjection. Herodotus, who was a keen observer, was the first to record his astonishment. He writes—

> "They have established laws and customs opposite for the most part to those of the rest of mankind. With them the women go to market and traffic; the men stay at home and weave. . . . The men carry burdens on their heads, the women on their shoulders. . . . The boys are never forced to maintain their parents unless they wish to do so, the girls are obliged to, even if they do not wish it." [1]

There is probably some exaggeration in this account, but it is certain that the wide activities of the free Egyptian women were never confined to the home. An important part was taken by her in industrial and commercial life. In these relations and in social intercourse it is allowed on all hands woman's position was remarkably free.[2] The records of the monuments show her to have been as actively concerned in all the affairs of her day, war alone excepted, as her father, her husband, or her sons.[3] No restraint was placed upon her actions, she appears eating and also drinking freely, and taking her part in equal enjoyment with men in social scenes and religious ceremonies. She was able to enter into

[1] *Herodotus*, Bk. II. p. 35.
[2] Hobhouse, *Morals in Evolution*, Vol. I. p. 189.
[3] Maspero, Preface to *Queens of Egypt*, by J. R. Buttles, q. v.

commerce in her own right and to make contracts for her own benefit. She could bring actions, and even plead in the courts. She practised the art of medicine. As priestess she had authority in the temples. Frequently as queen she was the highest in the land. One of the greatest monarchs of Egypt was Hatschepsut,[1] B.C. 1550. "The mighty one!" "Conqueror of all Lands!" Queen in her own right by the will of her father, Thothmes I.

The material in proof of this high status of Egyptian women is abundant. It consists partly of the descriptions of Greek travellers, partly of the numerous and interesting marriage contracts, and partly of inscriptions and passages in the writings of the moralists, all of which testify to the beautiful and happy family relationships and usual honour in which women were held, which is further illustrated by incidents in the ancient stories. Of these the marriage contracts are the most important for our purpose.

The fullest information relates to the latest period of independent Egyptian history, when the position of women stood highest, but some of the contracts reach back to the time of King Bocchoris, and there are a few of an even earlier date. I wish that I had space to quote some of these marriage contracts in full: they are very instructive, and open out many paths of new suggestion.[2]

[1] For an account of the reign of Hatschepsut, as well as of the other queens who ruled in Egypt, I must refer the reader to the excellent and careful work of Miss Buttles. It is worth noting that the temple built by Queen Hatschepsut is one of the most famous and beautiful monuments of ancient Egypt. On the walls are recorded the history of her prosperous reign, also the private events of her life: "Ra hath selected her for protecting Egypt and for rousing bravery among men."

[2] We owe our knowledge of the Egyptian marriage contracts chiefly

I would commend their study to all those who are questioning the institution of marriage as it stands to-day on the rights of the patriarchal family system, by which the woman is considered the inferior, and submits herself and is subordinate to the man as the ruler of the family. The issue really rests at its root upon this—is the mother or the father to be regarded as the natural transmitter of property and head of the family. Our decision here will affect our outlook on the entire relation of the sexes. The Egyptians decided on the right of the mother. Their marriage contracts seem to have been entirely in favour of women. There was no sale of the bride by her parents, but the bride-price went to her; her own property also remained in her own charge and was at her own disposal. The husband stipulates in the contracts how much he will give as a yearly allowance for her support, and the entire property of the husband is pledged as security for these payments, whilst the wife is further protected by a dowry[1] or charge on the husband, to be paid to her in the event of his sending her away.

It will readily be seen how advantageous these proprietary rights must have been to the wife. She was

to M. Revillout, whose works should be consulted. See also Paturet (the pupil of Revillout), *La Condition juridique de la femme dans l'ancienne Égypte*; Nietzold, *Die Ehe in Aegypten*; Greenfel, *Greek Papyri*; Améliheau, *La Morale Égyptienne*; Müller, *Liebespoesie der alten Aegypten*, and the numerous works of M. Maspero and Flinders Petrie. Simcox, writing on "Ownership in Egypt," gives a good summary of the subject, *Primitive Civilisations*, Vol. I. pp. 204–211; also Hobhouse, *Morals in Evolution*, Vol. I. p. 182, *et seq.*

[1] Hobhouse regards this dowry as being the original property of the wife in the forms of the bride-price. Revillout and Müller accept the much more probable view, that the dowry was fictitious, and was really a charge on the property of the husband to be paid to the wife if he sent her away.

able to claim either the fidelity of her husband or freedom for herself to leave him—and in some cases for both together, her property being secured to her and her children. In one contract by which the husband gives his wife one-third of all his property, present and to come, he values the movables she brought with her, and promises her the equivalent in silver. "If thou stayest, thou stayest with them, if thou goest away, thou goest away with them."[1] The importance of this right of free separation to women can hardly be over-estimated. Nietzold says the wife has absolutely nothing to lose, even when she is the guilty party.[2] Some of the marriage contracts are even more favourable to women; in these the husband literally endows his wife with all his worldly goods, "stipulating only that she is to maintain him while living, and provide for his burial when dead."[3] M. Paturet distinguishes two forms of marriage settlements, one which secures to the wife an annual pension of specified amount—usually one-third of the property of the husband—and the other, probably the older custom, which established a complete community of goods. The earlier contracts are much less detailed, due probably to the fact that the position of the established wife was then fixed by custom; but there seems no doubt that the equal lawful wife, she whose proper title is "lady of the house," was also joint ruler and mistress of the family heritage.[4] There is a very

[1] Paturet, *La Condition juridique de la femme dans l'ancienne Égypte*, p. 69.

[2] Nietzold, *Die Ehe in Aegypten*, p. 79.

[3] *Études égyptologiques*, livre XIII. pp. 230, 294; quoted by Simcox, *op. cit.*, Vol. I. p. 210.

[4] Simcox, *op. cit.*, Vol. I. p. 204.

curious early contract of the time of Darius I, in which the usual stipulation of latter contracts are reversed, the wife speaking of the man being established as her husband, acknowledging the receipt of a sum of money as dowry, and undertaking that if she deserts or disposes of him, a third part of all her goods, present and to come, shall be forfeited to him.[1]

The high honour, freedom and proprietary rights enjoyed by the Egyptian wife can only be explained as being traceable to an early period of mother-right. Here the ancient privileges of women have persisted, not as an empty form, but would seem to have been adopted because of their advantage in the family relationship, and been incorporated with father-right. This would account for the last-named contract. Its very ancient date seems clearly to point to this. It is unlikely that, if it were an exceptional form, it should have chanced to be one of the very few early contracts that have been preserved.[2] It would rather seem that property was originally entirely in the hands of women, as is usual under the matriarchal system. The Egyptian marriage law was simply a development of this, enforcing by agreement what would occur naturally under the earlier custom. The interests of the children's inheritance was the chief object of the settlement of property on the wife. In the earlier stage, the daughter inheriting property from her parents, would marry—the husband would then become its joint administrator, but not its owner; it would

[1] Simcox, *op. cit.*, Vol. I. pp. 210–211, citing Revillout, *Cours de droit*, p. 285.

[2] This is the view of Simcox, *op. cit.*, pp. 210–211.

pass by custom to the children with the eldest as administrator, but if the wife dismissed the husband, as under this system she could and often did, she would of right retain the family property in control for the children.[1] As society advanced this older custom would tend to break up in favour of individual ownership, property would come to belong to the husband and father, and it would then be necessary to ensure the position of the wife and children by contract. The Egyptian marriage may thus be regarded as a development of the individual relationship arising from father-right modified to conform with the mother-right custom of transmitting property through the woman. Under the earlier system the inheritance of the husband would pass to the children of his sister, and not to his own children. The contract was, therefore, made to prevent this. The husband's property was passed over to the wife (at first entirely and later in part) to secure its inheritance by the children of the marriage. Hence the formula common to these contracts by which the husband declares to the wife, "My eldest son, thy eldest son, shall be the heir to all my property present and to come." The only difference to the earlier custom was the prominence given to the eldest child (a son) in the contract.

This gift by the husband of his property to the wife, which made her a joint partner with him in all the family transactions, while at the same time she retained complete control over her own property, clearly placed the woman and her children in the same position of security as she had held during the mother-age; and added to this

[1] Hobhouse, Vol. I. p. 185 (*Note*).

she gained the individual protection and support of the father in the family relationship. Doubtless it was this freedom and right over property, which explains the frequent cases in which the Egyptian women conducted business transactions, and also their active participation in the administration of the social organisation. Equal partners with their husbands in the administration of the home, they became partners with men in the wider administration of the State. It was in such wise way that the Egyptians arranged the difficult problem of the fusion of mother-right with father-right.

One result of these marriage contracts, giving apparently great power to the wife, arose out of the mortgage on the husband's property as security for the wife's settlement; her consent became necessary to all his acts. Thus it is usual for the husband's deeds to be endorsed by the wife, while he did not endorse hers. In some cases the wife's consent seems to have been necessary even in the case of the initial mortgage, when the only possible explanation is that the wife was regarded as co-proprietor with the husband, and therefore had to be party to any act disposing of the joint estate.[1]

Such a custom was apparently so wholly in favour of the wife, reversing the customary position of the man and the woman in the marriage partnership, that in the light of these contracts we understand the statement of Diodorus, when he says that "among the Egyptians the woman rules over the man"; though plainly he has not understood their true significance, when he goes on to

[1] *Les obligations en droit égyptien*, p. 82; quoted by Simcox, *op. cit.*, Vol. I. pp. 209–210.

say that "it is stipulated between married couples, by the terms of the dowry-contract that "the man shall obey the woman."[1]

If the view is accepted, as I think it must be, that these contracts were made to add the advantages of father-right to the natural privileges of mother-right, and thus to secure the enjoyment of the family property to all its members, it will become evident that, however surprising such an agreement might seem from the one-sided patriarchal view (which always accepts the subjection of the woman), it was entirely a wise and just arrangement. It was certainly one that was entered into voluntarily by both partners of the marriage; there was no compulsion of law. All the evidence that has come down to us is witness to the success in practice of these marriage contracts. No other nation has yet developed a family relationship so perfect in its working as the Egyptians. The reason is not far to seek. It was based on the equal freedom and responsibility of the mother with the father. There was no question, it seems to me, of one sex ruling or obeying the other, rather it was the co-operation of the two for the welfare of both and of the children.

[1] Diodorus, bk. i. p. 27. The whole passage is: "Contrary to the received usage of other nations the laws permit the Egyptians to marry their sisters, after the example of Osiris and Isis. The latter, in fact, having cohabited with her brother Osiris, swore, after his death, never to suffer the approach of any man, pursued the murderer, governed according to the laws, and loaded men with benefits. All this explains why the queen receives more power and respect than the king, and why, among private individuals, the woman rules over the man, and that it is stipulated between married couples by the terms of the dowry-contract that the man shall obey the woman." The brother-sister marriages, referred to by Diodorus, which were common, especially in early Egyptian history, are further witness to the persistence among them of the customs of the mother-age.

So far we have dealt only with the position of the established wife. All the written marriage contracts refer to the "taking" and "establishing" a wife as two distinct steps, and in some cases the second stage, which seems to have conveyed the proprietary rights, was not taken until after the birth of children. There would thus be wives not necessarily holding the position of "lady of the house," but capable of being raised to such rank by later contract.[1] It is probable, as M. Revillout suggests,[2] that "the taking to wife" was a comparatively informal matter, but needing ratification by contract for any lasting establishment, which commonly would be done after the birth of a child to ensure the rights of the father's inheritance, passing through the mother to the children. All the evidence is in favour of this wise arrangement. There are many examples of contracts being entered into by the husband for the benefit of a woman, who had been "with him as a wife to him." Relations between the sexes of an even less binding character than this were not ignored.[3] It seems clear that little regard was paid to pre-nuptial chastity for women, and in no marriage contract is any stress laid on virginity, which, as Havelock Ellis[4] says, clearly indicates the absence of any idea of women as property. "It is the glory of Egyptian morality to have been the first to express the dignity of woman."[5]

M. Paturet takes the view that it was not so much as the mother, but as woman, and being the equal of man,

[1] Simcox, *op. cit.*, Vol. I. p. 205. [2] *Revue égyptologique*, I. p. 110.
[3] Revillout, *Cours de droit*, Vol. I. p. 222.
[4] *Psychology of Sex*, Vol. VI. p. 393.
[5] Amélineau, *La morale égyptienne*, p. 194.

that the Egyptians honoured their women. Perhaps the truth rather is that there was no separation between the woman and the mother. This is the view that I would take; to me it is the right and natural one. But be this as it may, Egyptian morality placed first the rights of the mother. No religious or moral superiority seems to have attached to the established wife. Even when there had been no betrothal, and no intention of marriage, law or custom recognises the claim of any mother of children to some kind of provision at their father's expense. "Nothing proves the high status of woman so clearly as this: her child was never illegitimate; illegitimacy was not recognised even in the case of a slave woman's child."[1]

There is a curious deed of the Ptolemaic period by which a man cedes to a woman a number of slaves; and —in the same breath—recognises her as his lawful wife, and declares her free *not* to consider him as her husband.[2] A byssus worker at the factory of Amon promises to the wife he is about to establish, one-third of all his acquisitions thenceforward: "my eldest son, thy eldest son, *among the children born to thee previously* and those thou shalt bear to me in future shall be master of all I possess now or shall hereafter acquire." Even when such arrangements were not entered into voluntarily, public opinion seems always to have been in favour of the woman. A case is recorded where four villagers of the town of Arsinöe pledged themselves to the priest, scribe, and mayor that a fellow villager of theirs will

[1] Ellis, citing Donaldson, *Woman*, p. 196. This is also the opinion of Müller.

[2] Revillout, *Revue égyptologique*, Vol. I. p. 113.

become the friend of the woman who has been as his wife, and will love her as a woman ought to be loved.[1]

Most significant of all is the well-known precept of Petah Hotep, which refers to the expected conduct of a man to a prostitute or outcast—

> "If thou makest a woman ashamed, wanton of heart, whom her fellow townspeople know to be under two laws" (*i. e.* in an ambiguous position), "be kind to her for a season, send her not away, let her have food to eat. The wantonness of her heart appreciateth guidance."

I know of nothing finer than this wide understanding of the ties of sex. It is an essential part of morality, as I understand it, that it accepts responsibility, not alone in the regular and permanent relationships between one man and one woman, but also in those that are temporary and are even considered base. Only in this way can the human passions be unified with love.

The freedom of the Egyptian marriage made this possible. Law, at least as we understand it, did not interfere with the domestic relationships; there was no one fixed rule that must be followed. Marriage was a matter of mutual agreement by contract. All that was required (and this was enforced by custom and by public opinion) was that the position of the woman and the children was made secure. Each party entered on the marriage without any constraint, and each party could cancel the contract and thereby the marriage. No legal judgment was required for divorce. It is a significant fact that in all the documents cancelling the marriage contracts that have come down to us, no mention is made

[1] Simcox, *op. cit.*, Vol. I. p. 207.

of the reason which led to the annulling of the contract, only in one case it is suggested that "some evil daimon" may be at the bottom of it.[1]

Polygamy was allowed in Egypt, though, as in all polygamous countries, its practice was confined to the rich. This has been thought by some to exclude the idea of the woman's power in the family.[2] But such an opinion seems to me to arise from a want of understanding of the Egyptian conception of the sexual tie. Under polygamy each wife had a house, her proprietary rights and those of her children were established, the husband visiting her there as a privileged guest on equal footing.[3] This is very different from polygamy in a patriarchal society, and would carry with it no social dishonour to the woman. It would seem, too, in later Egyptian history that polygamy, though legal in theory, in practice died out, the fidelity of the husband, as we have seen, being claimed by the wife in the conditions of the marriage contract.[4]

That the Egyptians had a high ideal of the domestic relations—and had this, let it be remembered, more than four thousand years ago—is abundantly illustrated by their inscriptions. In one epitaph of the Hykos period, the speaker, who boasts a family of sixty children, says of himself, "I loved my father, I honoured my mother, my brothers and my sisters loved me."[5] The commonest formula, which continued in use as long as

[1] Donaldson, *Woman*, pp. 244–245, citing Nietzold, p. 79.
[2] Letourneau (*Evolution of Marriage*, p. 176) takes this view.
[3] This is, of course, a survival of the old matriarchal custom.
[4] Hobhouse, *op. cit.*, Vol. L. pp. 5–186. Herodotus (Bk. II. p. 42) states that many Egyptians, like the Greeks, had adopted monogamy.
[5] Burgsch, *Hist.*, Vol. I. p. 262, quoted by Simcox.

Egyptian civilisation survived, was one describing the deceased as "loving his father, reverencing his mother, and being beloved by his brothers," and there can be no doubt that this sentiment represented the maturest convictions of the Egyptians as to the sentiments necessary for the felicitous working of the family relationships.[1] It is, indeed, significant to find this reversal of the usual sentiments towards the father and the mother—the former to be loved and the latter to be reverenced. It would seem as if "they assumed that fathers would be sufficiently reverenced if they were loved, and mothers loved if they were honoured." How true here is the understanding of affection and of the sexes!

If we pause for a moment to seek the reason why the Egyptians had, as Herodotus so strikingly states, established in their domestic relationships laws and customs different from the rest of mankind—the answer is easy to find. The Egyptians were an agricultural and a conservative people. They were also a pacific race. They would seem not to have believed in that illusion of younger races—the glory of warfare. I have seen it stated that in battle they were known for the habit of running away. This may, of course, be thought to count against them as a people. It depends entirely on the point of view that is taken. But if, as I believe, the fighting activities belong to an early and truly primitive stage of social development, then the view would be very different. Races begin with the building up of

[1] Simcox, Vol. I. p. 198–199. I take this opportunity of acknowledging the help I have received from this writer's careful and interesting chapter on "Domestic Relationships and Family Law" among the Egyptians.

society, then there follows the period of warfare—the patriarchal period which leads on to a later stage, much nearer in its working to the first—a final period, as Havelock Ellis says, "the stage of fruition." Woman's place and opportunity for the true expression of the powers that are hers belong to the first and last of these stages; in the middle stage she must tend to fall into a position of more or less complete dependence on the fighting male. Here is, I think, the explanation of the power and privilege of the Egyptian women. The Egyptians, due to their pacific and conservative temperament, seem to have escaped the patriarchal stage, and passed on from the first to final stage. Through the long centuries of their civilisation they devoted their energies to the building up and preserving of their social organisation. Thus, it may be, came about that solving of the problem of the sexes, which they among all races seem to have accomplished. The relationships of their family life and domestic administration were entirely civilised and humane.

Nowhere, except in Egypt, is so much stress laid upon the truth, that authority is sustained by affection. Their monuments and the inscriptions that have come down to us abundantly testify the value set upon affection: it is always the love of the husband for the wife, the wife for the husband, or the parent for the child, that is recorded. The frequency and detail with which such affections are described, prove the high estimation in which the purely domestic virtues were held, as forming the best and chief title of the dead to remembrance and honour. It is clear, moreover, that these affectionate relations between the members of a family are counted among the pleasures and joy of life. The inscriptions urge and warn the survivors to miss none of the joys of life, since the disembodied dead sleep in darkness, and this is the worst of their grief, "they know neither father nor mother, they do not awake to behold their brethren, their heart yearns no longer after wife and child."[1] There is a delightful inscription on the sepulchral tablet of the wife of a high priest of Memphis,[2] in which she urges the duty of happiness for her husband. It says—

> "Hail, my brother, husband, friend, . . . let not thy heart cease to drink water, to eat bread, to drink wine, to love women, to make a happy day, and to suit thy heart's desire by day and by night. And set no care whatsoever in thy heart: are the years which (we pass) upon the earth so many (that we need do this)?"

Such a conception, with its clear idea of the right of happiness, stands as witness to the high ideal of love which regulated the Egyptian family relationships.

It is necessary to remember, in this connection, that the domestic ties of the Egyptians were firmly based on proprietary considerations. No surprise need be felt that this was so, when we recall the wise arrangements of the marriage contracts, whereby both parties of the union secured equal freedom and an equal share in the family property. The antagonism between ownership and affection which so frequently destroys domestic happiness must thus have been unknown. "There was no marriage without money or money's worth, but to marry *for* money, in the modern sense, was impossible

[1] Maspero, *Hist.* (German tr.), p. 41; see Simcox, *op. cit.*, p. 199.
[2] This tablet is in the British Museum, London. S. Egyptian Gallery, Bay 29, No. 1027.

where individual ownership was abolished by the act of marriage itself."[1]

This in itself explains the fact, proved by these inscriptions, that the Egyptian woman remained to the end of life, "the beloved of her husband and the mistress of the house." "Make glad her heart during the time that thou hast," was the traditional advice given to the husband. To this effect runs the precept of Petah Hotep[2]—

> "If thou wouldst be a wise man, rule thy house and love thy wife wholly and constantly. Feed her and clothe her, love her tenderly and fulfil her desires as long as thou livest, for she is an estate which conferreth great reward upon her lord.[3] Be not hard to her, for she will be more easily moved by persuasion than by force. Observe what she wisheth, and that on which her mind runneth, thereby shalt thou make her to stay in thy house. If thou resisteth her will it is ruin."

The maxims of Ani,[4] written six dynasties later, give the same advice with fuller detail—

> "Do not treat rudely a woman in her house when you know her perfectly; do not say to her, 'Where is that? bring it to me!' when she has set it in its place where your eye sees it, and when you are silent you know her qualities. It is a joy that your hand should be with her. The man who is fond of heart is quickly master in his house."

[1] Simcox, Vol. I. pp. 218, 219.

[2] Petah Hotep was a high official in the reign of Assa, a king of the IVth Dynasty, about 3360 B.C. His precepts consist of aphorisms of high moral worth; there is a late copy in the British Museum. I have followed the translation given in the *Guide to the Egyptian Collection* p. 77.

[3] This passage in other translations reads: "she is a field profitable to its owner."

[4] The Maxims of Ani are preserved in the Egyptian Museum at Cairo. The work inculcates the highest standard of practical morality and gives a lofty ideal of the duty of the Egyptians in all the relations of life.

Honour to the mother was strongly insisted on. The sage Kneusu-Hetep [1] thus counsels his son—

> "Thou shalt never forget thy mother and what she has done for thee. From the beginning she has borne a heavy burden with thee in which I have been unable to help her. Wert thou to forget her, then she might blame thee, lifting up her arms unto God, and he would hearken to her. For she carried thee long beneath her heart as a heavy burden, and after thy months were accomplished she bore thee. Three long years she carried thee upon her shoulder and gave thee her breast to thy mouth, and as thy size increased her heart never once allowed her to say, 'Why should I do this?'. And when thou didst go to school and wast instructed in the writings, daily she stood by thy master with bread and beer from the house."

I would note in passing that in this passage we have a conclusive testimony to health and character of the Egyptian mother. The importance of this is undoubted, when we remember the active part taken by women in business and in social life. It is, I am sure, an entirely mistaken view to hold that motherhood is a cause of weakness to women. In a wisely ordered society this is not so. It is the withdrawal of one class of women from labour—the parasitic wives and daughters of the rich (which of these women could feed and carry her child for three years?), as the forcing of other women into work under intolerable conditions that injures motherhood. But on these questions I shall speak in the final part of my inquiry.

When I had written thus far in this chapter, I went from the reading-room of the British Museum, where

[1] From the Boulak Papyrus (1500 B.C.). I have followed in part the translation given by Griffiths, *The World's Literature*, p. 5340, and in part that of Maspero given in *Life in Ancient Egypt and Assyria* (trans. by Alice Morton, p. 16).

all day I had been working, to spend a last quiet hour in the Egyptian Galleries. I knew one at least of these galleries well, but as a rule I had hurried through it, as so many of the reading-room students do, to reach the refreshment-room which is placed there. I found I had never really seen anything. This time it was different, for my thoughts were aflame with the life of this people, whose wonderful civilisation speaks in all these sculptured remains through the silence of the centuries. Some fresh thought came to me as I waited to look at first one statue and then another. I sought for those which represented women. There is a small statue in green basalt of Isis holding a figure of Osiris Un-nefer, her son.[1] The goddess is represented as much larger than the young god, who stands at her feet. The marriage of Isis with her brother Osiris did not blot out her independent position, her importance as a deity remained to the end greater than his. Think for a moment what this placing of the goddess, rather than the god, in the forefront of Egyptian worship signifies; very clearly it reflects the honour in which the sex to whom the supreme deity belongs was held. In the third Egyptian room is a seated statuette of Queen Teta-Khart, a wife of Aāhmes I (1600 B.C.), whose title was "Royal Mother," and another figure of Queen Amenártās of the XXVth Dynasty 700 B.C.; near by is a beautiful head of the stone figure of a priestess.[2] There is something enigmatic and strangely seductive in the Egyptian faces; a joy and calmness which are

[1] Southern Egyptian Gallery, Bay 28, No. 964. This statue belongs to later Egyptian history. It was dedicated by Shashanq, a high official of the Ptolemaic period.

[2] Wall case 102, Nos. 187, 38, and 430.

implicit in freedom. And the impression is helped by the fixed attitudes, usually seated and always facing the spectator, and also by the great size of many of the figures; one seems to realise something of the simplicity and strength of the tireless enduring power of these women and men.

But I think what interested me most of all was the little difference manifested in the representations of the two sexes. The dress which each wears is very much the same; the attitudes are alike, and so often are the faces, even in the figures there seems no accentuation of the sexual characters. Often I did not know whether it was at a man or a woman, a god or a goddess, I was looking, until the title of the statue told me. How strange this seemed to me, and yet how significant of the beautiful equality of partnership between the woman and the man. It is in the statues which represent a husband and wife together, seated side by side, that this likeness is most evident. There are several of these domestic groups. One very interesting one is of early date, and belongs to the IVth Dynasty 3750 B.C.[1] It is in painted limestone, and shows the portrait figures of Ka-tep, "a royal kinsman" and priestly official, and his wife Hetep-Heres, "a royal kinswoman." The figures are small and of the same size; the faces are clearly portraits. The one, which I take to be the woman, though I am uncertain whether I am right, has her arm around the man, embracing him. There is another group[2] in white limestone of very fine work, portraits of a high official and his wife. The figures resemble each other closely, but that of the

[1] Vestibule of North Egyptian Gallery, East doorway, No. 14.
[2] South Gallery, No. 565.

man is a little larger, showing his rank. The man holds the hand of the woman. This statue belongs to the XIXth Dynasty. On the right-hand side of the North Gallery is a second group of an earlier period.[1] The husband and wife are seated, and the figures are of the same size, showing that their rank was equal; their arms are intertwined, and between them, standing at their feet, is a small figure of their son. It was before this family group I waited longest: it pleased me by its completeness and its sincerity. Once more I should have had difficulty in identifying which figure was the father and which the mother, but the man wears a small beard. In all these statue groups there is this great resemblance between the sexes.

Were the sexes, then, really alike in Egypt? I do not know. Such a conception opens up biological considerations of the deepest significance. It is so difficult to be certain here. Is the great boundary line which divides the two halves of life, with the intimate woman's problems that depend upon it, to remain for ever fixed? In sex are we always to be faced with an irresolvable tangle of disharmonies? Again, I do not know. Yet, looking at these seated figures of the Egyptian husband and wife, I felt that the answer might be with them. Do they not seem to have solved that secret which we are so painful in our search of? The statues thus took on a kind of symbolic character, which eloquently spoke of a union of the woman and the man that in freedom

[1] No. 375. This group belongs to the XVIIIth Dynasty: the husband was a warden of the palace and overseer of the Treasury; the wife a priestess of the god Amen.

had broken down the boundaries of sex, and, therefore, of life that was in harmony with love and joy. And the beautiful words of the Egyptian *Song of the Harper* came to my memory, and now I understood them—

> "Make (thy) day glad! Let there be perfumes and sweet odours for thy nostrils, and let there be flowers and lilies for thy beloved sister (*i. e.* wife) who shall be seated by thy side. Let there be songs and music of the harp before thee, and setting behind thy back unpleasant things of every kind, remember only gladness, until the day cometh wherein thou must travel to the land which loveth silence."

II.—*In Babylon*

> "The modern view of marriage recognises a relation that love has known from the outset. But this is a relation only possible between free self-governing persons."—HOBHOUSE.

If we turn now to the very ancient civilisation of Babylon we shall find women in a position of honour similar in many ways to what we have seen already in Egypt: there are ever indications that the earliest customs may have gone beyond those of the Egyptians in exalting women. The most archaic texts in the primitive language are remarkable for the precedence given to the female sex in all formulas of address: "Goddess" and gods, women and men, are mentioned always in that order, which is in itself a decisive indication of the high status of women in this early period.[1]

There are other traces all pointing to the conclusion that in the civilisation of primitive Babylon mother-right was still very much alive. It is significant that the first

[1] Simcox, *Primitive Civilisation*, Vol. I. pp. 9, 271.

rulers of Sumer and Akkad—the oldest Babylonian cities —frequently made boast of their unknown parentage, which can only be explained by the assumption that descent through the father was not recognised. Thus Sargon,[1] one of the earlier rulers, says: "My mother was a princess, my father I know not . . . my mother, the princess, conceived me, in a secret place she brought me forth." A little monument in the Hague museum has an inscription which has been translated thus: "Gudea patesi of Sirgulla dedicates thus to Gin-dung-nadda-addu, his wife." The wife's name is interpreted "maid of the god Nebo." It is thought that Gudea reigned in her right. The inscription goes on to say: "Mother I had not, my mother was the water deep. A father I had not, my father was the water deep." The passage is obscure, but it is explained if we regard this as one of the legends of miraculous birth so frequent in primitive societies under mother-descent.[2] Another relic of some interest is an ancient statue of a Babylonian woman, not a goddess or a queen, who is presented alone and not with her husband, as was common in Egypt; such a monument may suggest, as is pointed out by Simcox, that women at this period possessed wealth in their own right.

As in Egypt, the mother, the father, and the eldest son seem to have been the essential members of the family. We find that the compound substantive translated "family" means literally "children household." This is very interesting and may betoken a conception of

[1] Hommel, *Geschichte Babyloniens und Assyriens*, p. 271.
[2] Simcox, who quotes Hommel, *op. cit.*, p. 320.

marriage and the family like that of the Egyptians, in which the union of the wife and the husband is only fully established by the birth of children.[1] In the house the wife is "set in honour," "glad and gladdening like the mid-day sun." The sun-god Merodach is thus addressed: "Like a wife thou behavest thyself, cheerful and rejoicing." The sun-god himself is made to say, "May the wife whom thou lovest come before thee with joy." These examples, and also many others, such, for instance, as the phrase, "As a woman fashioned for a mother made beautiful," show that the Babylonians shared the Egyptian idealism in their conception of the wife and mother and her relation to the family. Many of the Summerian expressions throw beautiful light on the happiness of the domestic relationships. The union of the wife and husband is spoken of as "the undivided half," the idiogram for the mother signifies the elements "god" and "the house," she is "the enlarger of the family," the father is "one who is looked up to."

The information that has come down to us is not so full as our knowledge of the Egyptian family, or, at least, the facts which relate to women have not yet been so firmly established. We may, however, accept the statement of Havelock Ellis when he says that "in the earliest times a Babylonian woman enjoyed complete independence and equal rights with her brothers and husband."[2]

Later in Babylonian history—though still at an early

[1] Simcox, Vol. I. p. 361.
[2] *Psychology of Sex*, Vol. VI. p. 393. Ellis quotes Revillout, "La femme dans l'antiquité," *Journal Asiatique*, 1906, Vol. VII. p. 57.

period—women's rights were more circumscribed, and we find them in a position of some subordination. How the change arose is not clear, but it is probable that in Babylon civilisation followed the usual order of social development, and that with the rise of military activities, bringing the male force into prominence, women fell to a position of inferior power in the family and in the State.

That this was the condition of society in Babylon in the time of Hammurabi (*i. e.* probably between 2250 B.C. and 1950 B.C.) is proved by the marriage code of this ruler, which in certain of its regulations affords a marked contrast with the Egyptian marriage contracts, always so favourable to the wife. Marriage, instead of an agreement made between the wife and the husband, was now arranged between the parents of the woman and the bridegroom and without reference to her wishes. The terms of the marriage were a modified form of purchase, very similar to the exchange of gifts common among primitive peoples. It appears from the code that a sum of money or present was given by the bridegroom to the woman's father as well as to the bride herself, but this payment was not universal; and, on the other side of the account, the father made over to his daughter on her marriage a dowry, which remained her own property in so far that it was returned to her in the case of divorce or on the death of her husband, and that it passed to her children and, failing them, to her father.[1]

Polygamy, though permitted, was definitely restricted

[1] I quote these facts from Hobhouse, *Morals in Evolution*, Vol. I. p. 179.

by the code. Thus a man might marry a second wife if "a sickness has seized" his first wife, but the first wife was not to be put away. This is the only case in which two equal wives are recognised by the code. But it was also possible—as the contracts prove—for a man to take one or more secondary wives or concubines, who were subordinate to the chief wife. In some cases this appears to have been done to enable the first wife to adopt the children of the concubine "as her children." [1]

It is worth while to note the exact conditions of divorce in the reference to women as given in the clauses of Hammurabi's code—

> "137. If a man has set his face to put away his concubine, who has granted him children, to that woman he shall return his marriage portion, and shall give her the *usufruct* of field, garden, and goods, and shall bring up her children. From the time that her children are grown up, from whatever is given to her children, they shall give her a share like that of one son, and she shall marry the husband of her choice."
>
> "138. If a man shall put away his bride, who has not borne him children, he shall give her money as much as her bride-price."
>
> "139. If there was no bride-price he shall give her one mina of silver."
>
> "140. If he is a poor man he shall give one third of a mina of silver."

So far the position of the wife is secured in the case of the infidelity of the husband. But if we turn to the other side, when it is the woman who is the unfaithful partner it is evident how strongly the patriarchal idea of woman as property has crept into the family relations. We find that a woman "who has set her face to go out and has acted the fool, has wasted her house or has

[1] Hobhouse, *op. cit.*, Vol. I. p. 181.

belittled her husband," may either be divorced without compensation or retained in the house as the slave of a new wife.

I would ask you to contrast this treatment with the free right of separation granted to the Egyptian wife, whose position, as also that of her children, in all circumstances was secure, and to remember that this difference in the moral code for the two sexes is always present, in greater or lesser force, against woman wherever the property considerations of father-right have usurped the natural law of mother-right. Conventional morality has doubtless from the first been on the side of the supremacy of the male. To me it seems that this alone must discredit any society formed on the patriarchal basis.

The Babylonian wife was permitted to claim a divorce under certain conditions, namely, "if she had been economical and had no vice," and if she could prove that "her husband had gone out and greatly belittled her." But the proof of this carried with it grave danger to herself, for if on investigation it turned out that "she has been uneconomical or a gad-about, that woman one shall throw into the water." Probably such penalty was not really carried out, but even if the expression be taken figuratively its significance in the degradation of woman is hardly less great. The position of the wife as subject to her husband is clearly marked by the manner in which infidelity is treated. The law provides that both partners may be put to death for an act of unfaithfulness, but while the king may pardon "his servant" (the man), the wife has to receive pardon from "her owner" (*i.e.* the husband). The lordship of the husband is seen also in his power to dispose of his wife as well as his children for debt.[1] The period for debt slavery was, however, confined to the years of Hammurabi.[2]

From this time onwards we find the position of the wife continuously improving, and in the later Neo-Babylonian periods she again acquired equal rights with her husband. The marriage law was improved in the woman's favour. Contracts of marriage by purchase became very rare. It appears from the later contracts that a wife could protect herself from divorce or the taking of another wife by special penalties imposed on the husband by the conditions of the deed, thus giving her a position of security similar to that of the Egyptian wife.

In all social relations the Babylonian women had remarkable freedom. They could conduct business in their own right. Their power to dispose of property is proved by numerous contract tablets, and, at any rate in later periods, they were held to possess a full legal personality equal in all points with their husbands. In many contracts husband and wife are conjoined as debtors, creditors, and as together taking pledges. The wife, as in Egypt, is made a party to any action of the husband in which her dowry is involved. The wife could also act independently; women appear by themselves as creditors, and in some contracts we find a wife standing in that relation to her husband. In one case a woman acts as security for a man's debts to another woman. In a suit about a slave a woman, who was

[1] Hobhouse, *op. cit.*, Vol. I. p. 180.

[2] There is one case as late as the thirteenth year of Nebuchadnezzar in which a wife is bought for a slave for one and a half gold minas.

proved by witnesses to have made a wrongful claim, was compelled to pay a sum of money equivalent to the value of the slave. We find, too, a married woman joining with a man to sell a house. In another case, in which a mother and son had a sum of money owing to them, the debt was cancelled by giving a bill on the mother. The rich woman, by name Gugua, disposes her property among her children, but she reserves the right of taking it back into her own hands if she should so wish, and stipulates that it may not be mortgaged to any one without her consent.[1] There is another interesting deed[2] by which a father who, it is suggested, was a spendthrift, assigns the remnant of his property to his daughter under the stipulation "thou shalt measure to me, and as long as thou livest give me maintenance, food, ointment and clothing."

It would be easy to multiply such cases.[3] All these contract tablets have interest for us. The active participation of the Babylonian women in property transactions is the more instructive when we consider that in the development of commercial enterprise the Babylonians were in advance of all the rest of the world. One is tempted to suggest that the assistance of women may have brought an element into commerce beneficial to its growth. There is ample evidence to show the administrative and financial ability of women. This quality is noted by Lecky in the chapter on "Woman

[1] Simcox, *op. cit.*, Vol. I. p. 374, citing *Les Obligations*, p. 346; also *Revue d'Assyriologie*.

[2] This deed was translated by Dr. Peiser, *Keilinschriftliche Aktenstücke aus babylonischen Städte*, p. 19.

[3] See Simcox, Chapters, "Commercial Law and Contract Tablets" and "Domestic Relations and Family Law," *op. cit.*, Vol. I. pp. 320–379.

Questions" in his *Democracy and Liberty*. He says:

> "How many fortunes wasted by negligence or extravagance have been restored by a long minority under female management?"

He notes, too, the financial ability of the French women.

> "Where can we find in a large class a higher level of business habits and capacity than that which all competent observers have recognised in French women of the middle classes?"

The estimate of J. S. Mill on this question is too well known to call for quotation. We may recall also the superior ability in trade of the women of Burma. It is not necessary, however, to seek for proof of women's ability in finance. Against one woman who mismanages her income at least six men may be placed who mismanage theirs, not from any special extravagance, but from sheer male inability to adapt expenditure to income. A woman who has had any business training will discriminate better than a man between the essential and the non-essential in expenditure.

The civilisation of a people is necessarily determined to a large extent by the ideas of the relations of the sexes, and by the institutions and conventions that arise through such ideas. One of the most important and debatable of these questions is whether women are to be considered as citizens and independently responsible, or as beings differing in all their capacities from men, and, therefore, to be set in positions of at least material dependence to an individual man. It is the answer to this question we are seeking. The Babylonians decided for the civic equality of their women, and this decision must have affected all their actions from the larger matters of the State down to the smallest points of family conduct. The wisdom which, by giving a woman full control over her own property, recognised her right and responsibility to act for herself, was not, as we have seen, at once established. This recognition of the equality and fellowship between women and men as the finest working idea for the family relationship was only developed slowly through the long centuries of their civilisation.

III.—*In Greece*

"Of all things upon earth that breathe and grow
A herb most bruised is woman. We must pay
Our store of gold, hoarded for that one day
To buy us some man's love, and lo, they bring
A master of our flesh. There comes the sting
Of the whole shame, and then the jeopardy
For good or ill, what shall that master be?
Reject she cannot, and if she but stays
His suit, 'tis shame on all that woman's days.
So thrown amid new laws, new places, why,
'Tis magic she must have to prophesy.
Home never taught her that—how best to guide
Towards peace this thing that sleepeth at her side,
And she, who, labouring long, shall find some way
Whereby her lord may bear with her, nor fray
His yoke too fiercely, blessed is the breath
That woman draws! Else let her pray for death.
Her lord, if he be wearied of her face
Within doors, gets him forth; some merrier place
Will ease his heart; but she waits on, her whole
Vision enchained on a single soul.
And then, forsooth, 'tis they that face the call
Of war, while we sit sheltered, hid from all
Peril. False mocking. Sooner would I stand
Three times to face their battles, shield in hand,
Than bear our child."—EURIPIDES.

If we turn now from eastern civilisation to ancient Greece, the picture there presented to us is in many ways in sharp contrast to anything we have yet examined. The Greeks founded western civilisation, but their rapid advance in general culture was by no means accompanied by a corresponding improvement in the position of women. The fineness of their civilisation and their exquisite achievement in so many directions makes it the more necessary to remember this.

At one time there would seem to have been in prehistoric Greece a period of fully developed mother-rights, as is proved by numerous survivals of the older system so frequently met with in Greek literature and history. This was at an earlier stage of civilisation, before the establishment of the patriarchal system. There is little doubt, however, that the influence of mother-right remained as a tradition for long after the actual rights had been lost by women.[1] It will be remembered how great was the astonishment of the Greek travellers at the free position of the Egyptian women, in particular the apparent subjection of the husband to his wife. Now, such surprise is in itself sufficient to prove a different conception of the relation of the sexes.

[1] To give a few examples, Plutarch mentions that the relations between husband and wife in Sparta were at first secret (Plutarch, *Lycurgas*). The story told by Pausanias about Ulysses' marriage points to the custom of the husband going to live with his wife's family (*Pausanias*, III. 20 (10), Frazer's translation). The legend of the establishment of monogamy by Cecrops, because, before his time, "men had their wives in common and did not know their fathers," points clearly to a confused tradition of a period of mother-descent. (*Athenæus*, XIII. 2). Herodotus reports that mother-descent was practised by the Lycians, and states that "if a free woman marry a man who is a slave their children are free citizens; but if a free man marry a foreign woman or cohabit with a concubine, even though he be the first person in the state, the children forfeit all rights of citizenship (*Herodotus*, Bk. I. 173). The wife of Intaphernes, when granted by Darius permission to claim the life of a single man of her kindred, chose her brother, saying that both husband and brother and children could be replaced (*Herodotus*, Bk. III. 119). Similarly the declaration of Antigone in Sophocles (line 905 ff.) that neither for husband nor children would she have performed the toil she undertook for Polynices clearly shows that the tie of the common womb was held as closer than the tie of marriage.

The patriarchal view whereby the woman is placed under the protection and authority of the man was already clearly established in the Hellenic belief. Yet, in spite of this fact, the position of the woman was striking and peculiar, and in some directions remarkably free, and thus offering many points of interest not less important in their significance to us than what we have seen already in Egypt and in Babylon.

In speaking of the Hellenic woman I can select only a few facts; to deal at all adequately with so large a subject in briefest outline is, indeed, impossible. I shall not even try to picture the marriage and family relationships, which offer in many and varied ways a wide and fascinating study; all that I can do is to point to some of the conditions and suggest the conclusions which seem to arise from them. Glancing first at the women of the Homeric [1] period we find them represented as holding a position of entire dependence, without rights or any direct control over property; under the rule of the father, and afterwards of the husband, and even in some cases humbly submissive to their sons. Telemachus thus rebukes his mother: "Go to thy chamber; attend to thy work; turn the spinning wheel; weave the linen; see that thy servants do their tasks. Speech belongs to men, and especially to me, who am the master here." And Penelope allows herself to be silenced and obeys, "bearing in mind the sage discourse of her son." [2]

[1] For a full account of the Homeric woman the reader is referred to Lenz, *Geschichte des Weiber im Heroischen Zeitalter*, an admirable work. The fullest English account will be found in Mr. Gladstone's *Homeric Studies*, Vol. II. See also Donaldson, *Woman*, pp. 11–23, where an excellent summary of the subject is given.

[2] *Odyssey*, I. 2.

This is the fully developed patriarchal idea of the duties of the woman and her patient submission to the man.

Now, if we look only at the outside of such a case as this it would appear that the position of the Homeric woman was one of almost complete subjection. Whereas, as every one knows, the facts are far different. The protection of the woman was a condition made necessary in an unstable society of predominating military activity. Apart from this wardship, women very clearly were not in a subordinate position and, moreover, never regarded as property. The very reverse is the case. Nowhere in the whole range of literature are women held in deeper affection or receive greater honour. To take one instance. Andromache relates how her father's house has been destroyed with all who were in it, and then she says: "But now, Hector, thou art my father and gracious mother, thou art my brother, nay, thou art my valiant husband."[1] It is easy to see in this speech how the early ideas of relationships under mother-right had been transferred to the husband, as the protector of the woman, conditioned by father-right.

Again and again we meet with traces of the older customs of the mother-age. The influence of woman persists as a matter of habit; even the formal elevation of woman to positions of authority is not uncommon, with an accompanying freedom in action, which is wholly at variance with the patriarchal ideal. Thus it is common for the husband to consult his wife in all important concerns, though it was her special work to look after the affairs of the house. "There is nothing," says Homer,

[1] *Iliad*, VI. 429–430.

"better and nobler than when husband and wife, being of one mind, rule a household."[1] Penelope and Clytemnestra are left in charge of the realms of their husbands during their absence in Troy; the beautiful Chloris ruled as queen in Pylos.[2] Arete, the beloved wife of Alcinous, played an important part as peacemaker in the kingdom of her husband. It is to her Nausicäa brings Ulysses on his return, bidding him kneel to her mother if he would gain a welcome and succour from her father.[3]

We find the Homeric women moving freely among men. They might go where they liked, and do what they liked.[4] As girls they were educated with their brothers and friends, attending together the classes of the bards and dancing with them in the public dancing-places which every town possessed. Homer pictures the youths and the maidens pressing the vines together. They mingled together at marriage feasts and at religious festivals. Women took part with men in offering the sacrifices to the gods; they also went alone to the temples to present their offerings.[5] Nor did marriage restrict their freedom. Helen appears on the battlements of Troy, watching the conflict, accompanied only by her maidens.

This freedom insured to the Homeric women that vigour of body and beauty of person for which they are renowned. Health was the first condition of beauty. The Greeks wanted strong men, therefore the mothers

[1] *Odyssey*, VI. 182.
[2] Gladstone, *Homeric Studies*, Vol. II. p. 507.
[3] *Odyssey*, VII. 142 ff.
[4] Donaldson, *Woman*, p. 18–19.
[5] *Odyssey*, III. 450; *Iliad*, VI. 301.

must be strong, and this, as among all peoples who have understood the valuation of life more clearly than others, made necessary a high physical development of woman. Yet, I think, that an even more prominent reason was the need by the woman herself for the protection of the male, which made it her first duty to charm the man whom destiny brought to be her companion. This is a point that must not be overlooked. To me it is very significant that in all the records of the Egyptians, showing so clearly the love and honour in which woman was held, we find no insistence on, and, indeed, hardly a reference to, the physical beauty of woman. It is love itself that is exalted; a husband wishing to honour his lost wife says: "she was sweet as a palm tree in her love," he does not tell us if she were beautiful.[1] I cannot follow this question further. Yet it is clear that danger lurks for woman and her freedom, when to safeguard her independence, she has no other resources than the seduction of her beauty to gain and to hold the love she is able to inspire. Sex becomes a defensive weapon, and one she must use for self-protection, if she is to live. It seems clear to me that this economic use of sex is the real cancer at the very root of the sexual relationship. It is but a step further and a perfectly logical one, that leads to prostitution. At a later period of Hellenic civilisation we find Aristotle warning the young men of Athens against "the excess of conjugal tenderness and feminine tyranny which enchains a man to his wife."[2]

[1] Simcox, *Primitive Civilisation*, Vol. I. p. 199. Reference may also be made to the love-charm translated by M. Revillout in his version of the *Tales of Selna*, p. 37.

[2] 2 *Nic. Ethics*, VIII. 14; *Econom*. I. p. 94.

Can any surprise be felt; does one not wonder rather at the blindness of man's understanding? That such warning against women should have been spoken in Egypt is incredible. Woman's position and liberty of action was in no way dependent on her power of sex-fascination, not even directly on her position as mother, and this really explains the happy working of their domestic relationships. Nature's supreme gifts of the sexual differences among them were freed from economic necessities, and woman as well as man was permitted to turn them to their true biological ends—the mutual joy of each other and the service of the race. For this is what I want to make clear; it is men who suffer in quite as great a degree as women, wherever the female has to use her sexual gifts to gain support and protection from the male. It is so plain—one thing makes the relations of the sexes free, that both partners shall themselves be free, knowing no bondage that is outside the love-passion itself. Then, and then only, can the woman and the man—the mother and father, really love in freedom and together carry out love's joys and its high and holy duties.

The conditions that meet us when we come to examine the position of women in historic Greece are explained in the light of this valuation of the sexual relationship. We are faced at once by a curious contrast; on one hand, we find in Sparta, under a male social organisation, the women of Æolian and Dorian race carrying on and developing the Homeric traditions of freedom, while the Athenian women, on the contrary, are condemned to an almost Oriental seclusion. How these conditions arose becomes clear, when we remember that the prominent idea regulating all the legislation of the Greeks was to maintain the permanence and purity of the State. In Sparta the first of these motives ruled. The conditions in which the State was placed made it necessary for the Spartans to be a race of soldiers, and to ensure this a race of vigorous mothers was essential. They had the wisdom to understand that their women could only effectively discharge the functions assigned to them by Nature by the free development of their bodies, and full cultivation of their mental faculties. Sappho, whose "lofty and subtle genius" places her as the one woman for whose achievement in poetry no apology on the grounds of her sex ever needs to be made, was of Æolian race. The Spartan woman was a huntress and an athlete and also a scholar, for her training was as much a care of the State as that of her brothers. Her education was deliberately planned to fit her to be a mother of men.

It was the sentiment of strict and zealous patriotism which inspired the marriage regulations that are attributed to Lycurgus. The obligation of marriage was legal, like military service.[1] All celibates were placed under the ban of society.[2] The young men were attracted to love by the privilege of watching (and it is also said assisting in) the gymnastic exercise of naked young girls, who from their earliest youth entered into contests with each other in wrestling and racing and in throwing the quoit and javelin.[3] The age of marriage was also fixed, special care being taken that the Spartan girls

[1] Letourneau, *Evolution of Marriage*, p. 195.
[2] *Lycurgus*, XXXVII. [3] *Ibid.*, XXVI.

should not marry too soon; no sickly girl was permitted to marry.[1] In the supreme interest of the race love was regulated. The young couple were not allowed to meet except in secret until after a child was born.[2] Brothers might share a wife in common, and wife lending was practised. It was a praiseworthy act for an old man to give his wife to a strong man by whom she might have a child.[3] The State claimed a right over all children born; each child had to be examined soon after birth by a committee appointed, and only if healthy was it allowed to live.[4]

Such a system is no doubt open to objections, yet no other could have served as well the purpose of raising and maintaining a race of efficient warriors. The Spartans held their supremacy in Greece through sheer force and bravery and obedience to law; and the women had equal share with the men in this high position. Necessarily they were remarkable for vigour of character and the beauty of their bodies, for beauty rests ultimately on a biological basis.

Women took an active interest in all that concerned the State, and were allowed a freedom of action even in sexual conduct equal and, in some directions, greater than that of men. The law restricted women only in their function as mothers. Plato has criticised this as a marked defect of the Spartan system. Men were under

[1] Donaldson, *Woman*, pp. 28–29.
[2] Plutarch, *Apophthegms of the Lacedemonians.—Demandes Romaines*, LXV.
[3] Lycurgus, Polybius, XII. 6. Xenophon, *Rep. Laced.* I. Aristotle, *Pol.* II. 9. Aristotle notes especially the sexual liberty allowed to women.
[4] Donaldson, *op. cit.*, p. 28.

strict regulation to the end of their days; they dined together on the fare determined by the State; no licence was permitted to them; almost their whole time was occupied in military service. No such regulations were made for women, they might live as they liked. One result was that many wives were better educated than their husbands. We find, too, that a great portion of land passed into the hands of women. Aristotle states that they possessed two-fifths of it. He deplores the Spartan system, and affirms that in his day the women were "incorrigible and luxurious"; he accuses them of ruling their husbands. "What difference," he says, "does it make whether the women rule or the rulers are ruled by women, for the result is the same?"[1] This gynæcocracy was noticed by others. "You of Lacedæmon," said a strange lady to Gorgo, wife of Leonidas, "are the only women in the world that rule the men." "We," she answered, "are the only women who bring forth men."[2] Such were the Spartan women.

In Athens the position of women stands out in sharp contrast. Athens was the largest of the city-states of Greece, and, for its stability, it was ruled that no stranger might enter into the rights of its citizens. Restrictions of the most stringent nature and punishments the most terrible were employed to keep the citizenship pure. As is usual, the restrictions fell most heavily upon women. It would seem that the sexual virtue of the Athenian women was not trusted—it was natural to women to love. Doubtless there were many traces of the earlier sexual

[1] *Polit.* II. 9.
[2] Plutarch, *Life of Agis*; Donaldson, *Woman*, pp. 34, 35.

freedom under mother-right. Women must be kept in guard to ensure that no spurious offspring should be brought into the State. This explains the Athenian marriage code with its unusually strict subordination of the woman to her father first, and then to her husband. It explains also the unequal law of divorce. In early times the father might sell his daughters and barter his sisters. This was abolished by Solon, except in the case of unchastity. There could, however, be no legitimate marriage without the assignment of the bride by her guardian.[1] The father was even able to bequeath his unmarried daughters by will.[2] The part assigned by the Athenian law to the wife in relation to her husband was very similar to that of the married women under ancient Jewish law.

Women were secluded from all civic life and from all intellectual culture. There were no regular schools for girls in Athens, and no care was taken by the State, as in Sparta, for the young girls' physical well-being. The one quality required from them was chastity, and to ensure this women were kept even from the light of the sun, confined in special apartments in the upper part of the house. One husband, indeed, Ischomachus, recommends his wife to take active bodily exercise as an aid to her beauty; but she is to do this "not in the fresh air, for that would not be suitable for an Athenian matron, but in baking bread and looking after her linen."[3] So strictly was the seclusion of the wife adhered to that she

[1] Hobhouse, *Morals in Evolution*, Vol. I. p. 208.

[2] Thus Demosthenes bequeathed his two daughters, aged seven and five years, and also their mother, to his nephews, classing them with his property in the significant phrase "all these things" (Letourneau, *op. cit.*, p. 196).

[3] Xenophon, *Economicus*, VII.–IX.

was never permitted to show herself when her husband received guests. It was even regarded as evidence of the non-existence of a regular marriage if the wife had been in the habit of attending the feasts [1] given by the man whom she claimed as husband.

The deterioration of the Athenian citizen-women followed as the inevitable result. It is also impossible to avoid connecting the swift decline of the fine civilisation of Athens with this cause. Had the political power of her citizens been based on healthier social and domestic relationships, it might not have fallen down so rapidly into ruin. No civilisation can maintain itself that neglects the development of the mothers that give it birth.

As we should expect we find little evidence of affection between the Athenian husband and wife. The entire separation between their work and interests would necessarily preclude ideal love. Probably Sophocles presents the ordinary Greek view accurately, when he causes one of his characters to regret the loss of a brother or sister much more than that of a wife. "If a wife dies you can get another, but if a brother or sister dies, and the mother is dead, you can never get another. The one loss is easily reparable, the other is irreparable." [2] We could have no truer indication than this as to the degradation into which woman had fallen in the sexual relationship.

That once, indeed, it had been far otherwise with the

[1] Isæus *de Pyrrhi Her.*, § 14.

[2] *Antig.* 905–13. These verses are probably interpolated, but the interpolation was as early as Aristotle. The same views are placed by Herodotus in the mouth of the wife of Intarphernes (3. 119). *See* Donaldson, *Woman*, pp. 53, 54 and note.

Athenian women the ancient legends witness. Athens was the city of Pallas Athene, the goddess of strength and power, which in itself testifies to a time when women were held in honour. The Temple of the Goddess, high on the Acropolis, stood as a relic of matriarchal worship. Year by year the secluded women of Athens wove a robe for Athene. Yet, so complete had become their subjection and their withdrawal from the duties of citizens, that when in the Theatre of Dyonysus men actors personated the great traditional women of the Greek Heroic Age, no woman was permitted to be present.[1] What wonder, then, that the Athenian women rebelled against the wastage of their womanhood. That they did rebel we may be certain on the strength of the satirical statements of Aristophanes, and even more from the pathos of the words put here and there into the mouths of women by Euripides—

> "Of all things upon earth that breathe and grow
> A herb most bruised is woman. We must pay
> Our store of gold, hoarded for that one day
> To buy us some man's love, and lo, they bring
> A Master of our flesh. There comes the sting
> Of the whole shame."[2]

The debased position of the Athenian citizen woman becomes abundantly clear when we find that ideal love and free relationship between the sexes were possible only with the *hetairæ*. Limitation of space forbids my giving any adequate details of these stranger-women, who were the beloved companions of the Athenian men. Prohibited from legal marriage by law, these women were in all other respects free; their relations with men, either

[1] "The Position of Women in History"; Essay in the volume *The Position of Woman, Actual and Ideal*, p. 37.
[2] *Medea.*

temporary or permanent, were openly entered into and treated with respect. For the Greeks the *hetaira* was in no sense a prostitute. The name meant friend and companion. The women to whom the name was applied held an honourable and independent position, one, indeed, of much truer honour than that of the wife.

These facts may well give us pause. It was not the women who were the legal wives, safeguarded to ensure their chastity, restricted to their physical function of procreation, but the *hetairæ*, says Donaldson, "who exhibited what was best and noblest in woman's nature." Xenophon's ideal wife was a good housekeeper—like her of the Proverbs. Thucydides in the famous funeral oration which he puts in the mouth of Pericles, exhorts the wives of the slain warriors, whose memory is being commemorated, "to shape their lives in accordance with their natures," and then adds with unconscious irony, "Great is the glory of that woman who is least talked of by men, either in the way of praise or blame." Such were the barren honours granted to the legal wife. The *hetairæ* were the only educated women in Athens. It was only the free-companion who was a fit helpmate for Pericles, or capable of sustaining a conversation with Socrates. We know that Socrates visited Theodota [1] and the brilliant Diotima of Mantinea, of whom he speaks "as his teacher in love." [2] Thargalia, a Milesian stranger, gained a position of high political importance.[3]

[1] Theodota, *Xen. 'Mem.,'* III. 11. Socrates conversed with Theodota on art and discussed with her how she could best find true friends.

[2] *Symposium.*

[3] *Pericles*, 24. Thargalia used her influence over the Greeks to win them over to the cause of the King of Persia.

When Alcibiades had to flee for his life, it was a "companion" who went with him, and being present at his end performed the funeral rites over him.[1] Praxiteles carved a statue of Phryne in gold, and the work stood in a place of honour in the temple of Apollo at Delphi. Apelles painted a portrait of Lais, and, for his skill as an artist, Alexander rewarded him with the gift of his favourite concubine; Pindar wrote odes to the *hetairæ;* Leontium, one of the order, sat at the feet of Epicurus to imbibe his philosophy.[2]

Among all these free women Aspasia of Miletus[3] stands forward as the most brilliant—the most remarkable. There is no doubt as to the intellectual distinction of the beloved companion of Pericles.[4] Her house became the resort of all the great men of Athens. Socrates, Phidias and Anaxagoras were all frequent visitors, and probably also Sophocles and Euripides. Plato, Xenophon and Æschines have all testified to the cultivated mind and influence of Aspasia. Æschines,

[1] Timandra, Plut., *Alcib.*, c. 39.

[2] Geoffrey Mortimer (W. M. Gallichan), *Chapters on Human Love*, p. 152.

[3] We do not know the circumstances which induced Aspasia to come to Athens. Plutarch suggests that she was led to do so by the example of Thargalia. For full accounts of the career of Aspasia see Gomperz, *Greek Thinkers*, Vol. III.; Ivo Bruns, *Frauenemancipation in Athen;* the fine monograph, *Aspasie de Milet*, by Becq Fouquières; Donaldson's *Woman*, pp. 60–67; also Ellis, *Psychology of Sex*, Vol. VI. p. 308.

[4] Pericles at the time of his meeting Aspasia was married, but there was incompatibility of temper between him and his wife. He therefore made an agreement with his wife to have a divorce and get her remarried. Aspasia then became his companion and they remained together until the death of Pericles. Their affection for one another was considered remarkable. Plutarch tells us, as an extraordinary trait in the habits of a statesman who was remarkable for his imperturbability and control, that Pericles regularly kissed Aspasia when he went out and came in. When Pericles died Aspasia is said to have formed a friendship with Lysicles, and through her influence raised him to the position of foremost politician in Athens (Donaldson, *op. cit.*, pp. 60, 61 and 63).

in his dialogue entitled "Aspasia," puts into the mouth of that distinguished woman an incisive criticism of the mode of life traditional for her sex.[1]

The high status of the *hetairæ* is proved conclusively from the fact that the men who visited Aspasia brought their wives with them to her assemblies, that they might learn from her.[2] This breaking through the accepted conventions is the more significant if we consider the circumstances. Here, indeed, is your contrast—the free companion expounding the dignity of womanhood to the imprisoned mothers! Aspasia points out to the citizen women that it is not sufficient for a wife to be merely a mother and a good housekeeper; she urges them to cultivate their minds so that they may be equal in mental dignity with the men who love them. Aspasia may thus be regarded, as Havelock Ellis suggests, as "a pioneer in the assertion of woman's rights." "She showed that spirit of revolt and aspiration" which tends to mark "the intellectual and artistic activity of those who are unclassed or dubiously classed in the social hierarchy."

It is even probable that the movement to raise the status of the Athenian women, which seems to have taken place in the fourth century B.C., was led by Aspasia, and perhaps other members of the *hetairæ*. Ivo Bruns, whom Havelock Ellis quotes, believes that "the most certain information we possess concerning Aspasia bears a strong resemblance to the picture which Euripides and Aristophanes present to us of the leaders of the woman's movement."[3]

[1] Gomperz, *Greek Thinkers*, Vol. III. p. 124.
[2] *Psychology of Sex*, Vol. VI. p. 308; Donaldson, *op. cit.*, p. 62.
[3] *Frauenemancipation in Athen*, p. 19.

It was this movement of awakening which throws light on the justice which Plato accords to women. He may well have had Aspasia in his thoughts. Contact with her cultivated mind may have brought him to see that "the gifts of nature are equally diffused in both sexes," and therefore "all the pursuits of man are the pursuits of woman also, and in all of these woman is only a weaker man." Plato did not believe that women were equally gifted with men, only that all their powers were in their nature the same, and demanded a similar expression. He insists much more on woman's duties and responsibilities than on her rights; more on what the State loses by her restriction within the home than on any loss entailed thereby to herself. Such a fine understanding of the need of the State for women as the real ground for woman's emancipation, is the fruitful seed in this often quoted passage. May it not have arisen in Plato's mind from the contrast he saw between Aspasia and the free companions of men and the restricted and ignorant wives? A vivid picture would surely come to him of the force lost by this wastage of the mothers of Athens; a force which should have been utilised for the well-being of the State.

Sexual penalties for women are always found under a strict patriarchal régime. The white flower of chastity, when enforced upon one sex by the other sex, has its roots in the degradation of marriage. Men find a way of escape; women, bound in the coils, stay and waste. There is no escaping from the truth—wherever women are in subjection it is there that the idols of purity and chastity are set up for worship.

The fact that Greek poets and philosophers speak so often of an ideal relationship between the wife and the husband proves how greatly the failure of the accepted marriage was understood and depreciated by the noblest of the Athenians. The bonds of the patriarchal system must always tend to break down as civilisation advances, and men come to think and to understand the real needs and dependence of the sexes upon each other. Aristotle says that marriage besides the propagation of the human race, has another aim, namely, "community of the entire life." He describes marriage as "a species of friendship," one, moreover, which "is most in accordance with Nature, as husband and wife mutually supply what is lacking in the other." Here is the ideal marriage, the relationship between one woman and the one man that to-day we are striving to attain. To gain it the wife must become the free companion of her husband.

It is Euripides who voices the sorrows of women. He also foreshadows their coming triumph.

"Back streams the waves of the ever running river,
Life, life is changed and the laws of it o'ertrod.

* * * * * * * * *

And woman, yea, woman shall be terrible in story;
The tales too meseemeth shall be other than of yore;
For a fear there is that cometh out of woman and a glory,
And the hard hating voices shall encompass her no more."[1]

IV.—*In Rome*

"The character of a people is only an eternal becoming . . . They are born and are modified under the influence of innumerable causes."—JEAN FINOT.

Of the position of women in Rome in the pre-historic period we know almost nothing. We can accept that

[1] *Medea*, Mr. Gilbert Murray's translation.

there was once a period of mother-rule.[1] Very little evidence, however, is forthcoming; still, what does exist points clearly to the view that woman's actions in the earliest times were entirely unfettered. Probably we may accept as near to reality the picture Virgil gives to us of Camilla fighting and dying on the field of battle.

In the ancient necropolis of Belmonte, dating from the iron age, Professor d'Àllosso has recently discovered two very rich tombs of women warriors with war chariots over their remains. "The importance of this discovery is exceptional, as it shows that the existence of the Amazon heroines, leaders of armies, sung by the ancient poets, is not a poetic fiction, but an historic reality." Professor d'Allosso states that several details given by Virgil coincide with the details of these tombs.[2]

From the earliest notices we have of the Roman women we find them possessed of a definite character of remarkable strength. We often say this or that is a sign of some particular period or people; when nine times out of ten the thing we believe to be strange is in reality common to the progress of life. In Rome the position of woman would seem to have followed in orderly

[1] Frazer thinks that the Roman kingship was transmitted in the female line; the king being a man of another town or race, who had married the daughter of his predecessor and received the crown through her. This hypothesis explains the obscure features of the traditional history of the Latin kings; their miraculous birth, and the fact that many of the kings from their names appear to have been of plebeian and not patrician families. The legends of the birth of Servius Tullius which tradition imputes to a look, or that Cœculus the founder of Proneste was conceived by a spark that leaped into his mother's bosom, as well as the rape of the Sabines, may be mentioned as traces pointing to mother-descent (*Golden Bough*, Pt. I. *The Magic Art*, Vol. II. pp. 270, 289, 312).

[2] Quoted from *Position of Woman, Actual and Ideal*; Essay on "The Position of Woman in History," p. 38.

development that cyclic movement so beautifully defined by Havelock Ellis in the quotation I have placed at the beginning of the first section of this chapter.

The patriarchal rule was already strongly established when Roman history opens; it involved the same strict subordination of woman to the one function of child-bearing that we have found in the Athenian custom. The Roman marriage law developed from exactly the same beginning as did the Greek; the woman was the property of her father first and then of her husband. The marriage ceremony might be accomplished by one or two forms, but might also be made valid without any form at all. For in regard to a woman, as in regard to other property, possession or use continued for one year gave the right of ownership to the husband. This marriage without contract or ceremony was called *usus*.[1] The form *confarreatio*, or patrician marriage, was a solemn union performed by the high Pontiff of Jupiter in the presence of ten witnesses, in which the essential act was the eating together by both the bride and bride-groom of a cake made of flour, water and salt.[2] The religious ceremony was in no way essential to the marriage. The second and most common form, was called *coemptio*, or purchase, and was really a formal sale between the father or guardian of the bride and the future

[1] Letourneau, *Evolution of Marriage*, pp. 120, 201. The *usus* was similar to the Polynesian marriage, and was the consecration of the free union after a year of cohabitation. By it the wife passed as completely under the *manum mariti* as if she had eaten of the sacred cake.

[2] Hobhouse, *Morals in Evolution*, Vol. I. p. 210. The eating of the cake would seem to the ancient mind to have been connected with magic, and was regarded as actually efficacious in establishing a unity of the man and the woman.

husband.[1] Both these forms transferred the woman from the *potestas* (power) of her father into the *manus* (hand) of her husband to whom she became as a daughter, having no rights except through him, and no duties except to him. The husband even held the right of life and death over the woman and her children. It depended on his will whether a baby girl were reared or cast out to die—and the latter alternative was no doubt often chosen. As is usual under such conditions, the right of divorce was allowed to the husband and forbidden to the wife. "If you catch your wife," was the law laid down by Cato the Censor, "in an act of infidelity, you would kill her with impunity without a trial; but if she were to catch you she would not venture to touch you with a finger, and, indeed, she has no right." It is true that divorce was not frequent.[2] Monogamy was strictly enforced. At no period of Roman history are there any traces of polygamy or concubinage.[3] But such strictness of the moral code seems to have been barren in its benefit to women. The terrible right of *manus* was vested in the husband and gave him complete power of correction over the wife. In grave cases the family tribunal had to be consulted. "Slaves and women," says Mommsen, "were

[1] *Coemption* became in time purely symbolic. The bride was delivered to the husband, who as a formality gave a few pieces of silver as payment; but the ceremony proves how completely the woman was regarded as the property of the father.

[2] Romulus, says Plutarch, gave the husband power to divorce his wife in case of her poisoning his children, or counterfeiting his keys, or committing adultery (Romulus, XXXVI.). Valerius Maximus affirms that divorce was unknown for 520 years after the foundation of Rome.

[3] Hobhouse, *op. cit.*, Vol. I. p. 211 (*note*). He states, "The concubinate we hear of in Roman Law is a form of union bereft of some of the civil rights of marriage, not the relation of a married man to a secondary wife or slave-girl."

not reckoned as being properly members of the community," and for this reason any criminal act committed by them was judged not openly by the State, but by the male members of the woman's family. The legal right of the husband to beat his wife was openly recognised. Thus Egnatius was praised when, surprising his wife in the act of tasting wine,[1] he beat her to death. And St. Monica consoles certain wives, whose faces bore the mark of marital brutality, by saying to them: "Take care to control your tongues. . . . It is the duty of servants to obey their masters . . . you have made a contract of servitude."[2] Such was the marriage law in the early days of Rome's history.

Now it followed almost necessarily that under such arbitrary regulations of the sexual relationship some way of escape should be sought. We have seen how the Athenian husbands found relief from the restrictions of legal marriage with the free *hetairæ*. But in Rome the development of the freedom of love, with the corresponding advancement of the position of woman, followed a different course. The stranger-woman never attained a prominent place in Roman society. It is the citizen-women alone who are conspicuous in history. Here, relief was gained for the Roman wives as well as for the husbands, by what we may call a clever escape from marriage under the right of the husband's *manus*. This is so important that I must ask the reader deeply to consider it. The ideal of equality and fellowship between

[1] Donaldson, *op. cit.*, p. 88. He remarks in a note, "The story may not be historical, but the Romans regarded it as such." Wives were prohibited from tasting wine at the risk of the severest penalties.

[2] St. Augustine, *Confessions*, Bk. IX. Ch. IX.

women and men in marriage can be realised only among a people who are sufficiently civilised to understand the necessity for the development and modification of legal restrictions that have become outworn and useless. Wherever the laws relating to marriage and divorce are arbitrary and unchanging there woman, as the weaker partner, will be found to remain in servitude. It can never be through the strengthening of moral prohibitions, but only by their modification to suit the growing needs of society that freedom will come to women.

The history of the development of marriage in Rome illustrates this very forcibly. Even in the days of the Twelve Tables a wholly different and free union had begun to take the place of the legally recognised marriage forms. It was developed from the early marriage by *usus*. We have seen that this marriage depended on the cohabitation of the man and the woman continued for one year, which gave the right of ownership to the husband in exactly the same way as possession for a year gave the right over others' property. But in Rome, if the enjoyment of property was broken for any period during the year, no title to it arose out of the *usufruct*. This idea was cleverly applied to marriage by *usus*. The wife by passing three nights in the year out of the conjugal domicile broke the *manus* of the husband and did not become his property.

When, or how, it became a custom to convert this breach of cohabitation into a system and establish a form of marriage, which entirely freed the wife from the *manus* of the husband, we do not know. What is certain is that this new form of free marriage by consent rapidly replaced the older forms of the *coemptio*, and even the solemn *confarreatio of the patricians.*

It will be readily seen that this expansion of marriage produced a revolution in the position of woman. The bride now remained a member of her own family, and though nominally under the control of her father or guardian, she was for all purposes practically free, having complete control over her own property, and was, in fact, her own mistress.

The law of divorce evolved rapidly, and the changes were wholly in favour of women. Marriage was now a private contract, of which the basis was consent; and, being a contract, it could be dissolved for any reason, with no shame attached to the dissolution, provided it was carried out with the due legal form, in the presence of competent witnesses. Both parties had equal liberty of divorce, only with certain pecuniary disadvantages, connected with the forfeiting of the wife's dowry, for the husband whose fault led to the divorce.[1] It was expressly stated that the husband had no right to demand fidelity from his wife unless he practised the same himself. "Such a system," says Havelock Ellis, "is obviously more in harmony with modern civilised feeling than any system that has ever been set up in Christendom."[2]

Monogamy remained imperative. The husband was bound to support the wife adequately, to consult her

[1] Letourneau, *Evolution of Marriage*, pp. 244, 245. In the ancient law, when the crime of the woman led to divorce she lost all her dowry. Later, only a sixth was kept back for adultery, and an eighth for other crimes. In the last stages of the law the guilty husband lost the whole dowry, while if the wife divorced without a cause, the husband retained a sixth of the dowry for each child, but only up to three-sixths.

[2] *Psychology of Sex*, Vol. VI. p. 396.

interests and to avenge any insult inflicted upon her, and it is expressly stated by the jurist Gaius that the wife might bring an action for damages against her husband for ill-treatment.[1] The woman retained complete control of her dowry and personal property. A Roman jurist lays it down that it is a good thing that women should be dowered, as it is desirable they should replenish the State with children. Another instance of the constant solicitude of the Roman law to protect the wife is seen in the fact that even if a wife stole from her husband, no criminal action could be brought against her. All crimes against women were punished with a heavy hand much more severely than in modern times.

Women gained increasingly greater liberty until at last they obtained complete freedom. This fact is stated by Havelock Ellis, whose remarks on this point I will quote.

> "Nothing is more certain than that the status of women in Rome rose with the rise of civilisation exactly in the same way as in Babylon and in Egypt. In the case of Rome, however, the growing refinement of civilisation and the expansion of the Empire were associated with the magnificent development of the system of Roman law, which in its final forms consecrated the position of women. In the last days of the Republic women already began to attain the same legal level as men, and later the great Antonine jurisconsults, guided by their theory of natural law, reached the conception of the equality of the sexes as the principle of the code of equity. The patriarchal subordination of women fell into complete discredit, and this continued until, in the days of Justinian, under the influence of Christianity the position of women began to suffer."[2]

[1] Hecker, *History of Women's Rights*, p. 12.
[2] Ellis, *op. cit.*, p. 395.

Hobhouse gives the same estimate as to the high status of women.

> "The Roman matron of the Empire," he says, "was more fully her own mistress than the married woman of any earlier civilisation, with the possible exception of a certain period of Egyptian history, and, it must be added, the wife of any later civilisation down to our own generation." [1]

It is necessary to note that this freedom of the Roman woman was prior to the introduction of Christianity, and that under its influence their position began to suffer.[2] I cannot follow this question, and can only say how entirely mistaken is the belief that the Jewish religion, with its barbaric view of the relationship between the sexes, was beneficial to the liberty of women.

The Roman matrons had now gained complete freedom in the domestic relationship, and were permitted a wide field for the exercise of their activities. They were the rulers of the household; they dined with their husbands, attended the public feasts, and were admitted to the aristocratic clubs, such as the *Gerousia* is supposed to have been. We find from inscriptions that women had the privilege of forming associations and of electing women presidents. One of these bore the title of *Sodalitas Pudicitiæ Servandræ*, or "Society for Promoting Purity of Life." At Lanuvium there was a society known as the "Senate of Women." There was an interesting and singular woman's society existing in Rome, with a meeting-place on the Quirinal, called *Conventus Matronarum*, or "Convention of Mothers of Families." This seems to have been a self-elected parliament of

[1] Hobhouse, *op. cit.*, Vol. I. p. 213.
[2] Maine, *Ancient Law*, Ch. V.

women for the purpose of settling questions of etiquette. It cannot be said that the accounts that we have of this assembly are at all edifying, but its existence shows the freedom permitted to women, and points to the important fact that they were accustomed to combine with one another to settle their own affairs. The Emperor Heliogabalus took this self-constituted Parliament in hand and gave it legal powers.[1]

The Roman women managed their own property; many women possessed great wealth: at times they lent money to their husbands, at more than shrewd interest. It appears to have been recognised that all women were competent in business affairs, and, therefore, the wife was in all cases permitted to assume complete charge of the children's property during their minority, and to enjoy the *usufruct*. We have instances in which this capacity for affairs is dwelt on, as when Agricola, the general in command in Britain, shows such confidence in his wife as a business woman that he makes her co-heir with his daughter and the Emperor Domitian. Women were allowed to plead for themselves in the courts of law. The satirists, like Juvenal, declare that there were hardly any cases in which a woman would not bring a suit.

There are many other examples which might be brought forward to show the public entry of women into the affairs of the State. There would seem to have been no limits set to their actions; and, moreover, they acted in their own right independently of men. On one occasion, when the women of the city rose in a body

[1] McCabe, *The Religion of Women*, p. 26 *et seq.*

against an unfair taxation, they found a successful leader in Hortensia, the daughter of the famous orator Hortensus, who is said to have argued their case before the Triumvirs with all her father's eloquence. We find the wives of generals in camp with their husbands. The *graffitti* found at Pompeii give several instances of election addresses signed by women, recommending candidates to the notice of the electors. We find, too, in the municipal inscriptions that the women in different municipalities formed themselves into small societies with semi-political objects, such as the support of some candidate, the rewards that should be made to a local magistrate, or how best funds might be collected to raise monuments or statues.

It is specially interesting to find how fine a use many of the Roman women made of their wealth and opportunities. They frequently bestowed public buildings and porticoes on the communities among which they lived; they erected public baths and gymnasia, adorned temples, and put up statues. Their generosity took other forms. In Asia Minor we find several instances of women distributing large sums of money among each citizen within her own district. Women presided over the public games and over the great religious festivals. When formally appointed to this position, they paid the expenses incurred in these displays. In the provinces they sometimes held high municipal offices. Ira Flavia, an important Roman settlement in Northern Spain, for instance, was ruled by a Roman matron, Lupa by name.[1] The power of women was especially great in

[1] *Santiago* (Mediæval Towns Series), p. 21.

Asia Minor, where they received a most marked distinction, and were elected to the most important magistracies. Several women obtained the highest Priesthood of Asia, the greatest honour that could be paid to any one.[1]

There is one final point that has to be mentioned. We have seen how the liberty and power of the Roman women arose from, and may be said to have been dependent on, the substituting of a laxer form of marriage with complete equality and freedom of divorce. In other words it was the breaking down of the patriarchal system which placed women in a position of freedom equal in all respects with men. Now, it has been held by many that, owing to this freedom, the Roman women of the later period were given up to licence. There are always many people who are afraid of freedom, especially for women. But if our survey of these ancient and great civilisations of the past has taught us anything at all, it is this: the patriarchal subjection of women can never lead to progress. We must give up a timid adherence to past traditions. It is possible that the freeing of women's bonds may lead in some cases to the foolishness of licence. I do not know; but even this is better than the wastage of the mother-force in life. The child when first it tries to walk has many tumbles, yet we do not for this reason keep him in leading strings. We know he must learn to walk; how to do this he will find out by his many mistakes.

The opinion as to the licentiousness of the Roman woman rests mainly on the statements of two satirical

[1] Donaldson, *Woman*, pp. 124–125.

writers, Juvenal and Tacitus. Great pains have been taken to refute the charges they make, and the old view is not now accepted. Dill,[1] who is quoted by Havelock Ellis, seems convinced that the movement of freedom for the Roman woman caused no deterioration of her character; "without being less virtuous or respected, she became far more accomplished and attractive; with fewer restraints, she had greater charm and influence, even in social affairs, and was more and more the equal of her husband."[2] Hobhouse and Donaldson[3] both support this opinion; the latter writer considers that "there was no degradation of morals in the Roman Empire." The licentiousness of pagan Rome was certainly not greater than the licentiousness of Christian Rome. Sir Henry Maine, in his valuable *Ancient Law* (whose chapter on this subject should be read by every woman), says, "The latest Roman law, so far as it is touched by the constitution of the Christian Emperors, bears some marks of reaction against the liberal doctrines of the great Antonine jurisconsults." This he attributes to the prevalent state of religious feeling that went to "fatal excesses" under the influence of its "passion for asceticism."

At the dissolution of the Roman Empire the enlightened Roman law remained as a precious legacy to Western civilisations. But, as Maine points out, its humane and civilising influence was injured by its fusion with the customs of the barbarians, and, in particular, by the

[1] *Roman Society*, p. 163.
[2] *Morals in Evolution*, Vol. I. p. 216.
[3] *Woman*, p. 113.

Jewish marriage system. The legislature of Europe "absorbed much more of those laws concerning the position of women which belong peculiarly to an imperfect civilisation. The law relating to married women was for the most part read by the light, not of Roman, but of Christian Canon Law, which in no one particular departs so widely from the enlightened spirit of the Roman jurisprudence than in the view it takes of the relations of the sexes in marriage." This was in part inevitable, Sir Henry Maine continues, "since no society which preserves any tincture of Christian institutions is likely to restore to married women the personal liberty conferred on them by the middle Roman law."

It is not possible for me to follow this question further. One thing is incontrovertibly certain, that woman's position and her freedom can best be judged by the equity of the moral code in its bearing on the two sexes. Wherever a different standard of moral conduct is set up for women from men there is something fundamentally wrong in the family relationship needing revolutionising. The sexual passions of men and women must be regulated, first in the interests of the social body, and next in the interests of the individual. It is the institution of marriage that secures the first end, and the remedy of divorce that secures the second. It is the great question for each civilisation to decide the position of the sexes in relation to these two necessary institutions. In Rome an unusually enlightened public feeling decided for the equality of woman with man in the whole conduct of sexual morality. The legist Ulpian expresses this view when he writes—"It seems to be very unjust that a man demands chastity from his wife while he himself shows no example of it."[1] Such deep understanding of the unity of the sexes is assuredly the finest testimony to the high status of Roman women.

I have now reached the end of the inquiry set before us at the opening of this chapter. I am fully aware of the many omissions, probable misjudgments, and the inadequacy of this brief summary. We have covered a wide field. This was inevitable. I know that to understand really the position of woman in any country it is necessary to inquire into all the customs that have built up its civilisation, and to gain knowledge upon many points outside the special question of the sexual relationships. This I have not been able even to attempt to do. I have thrown out a few hints in passing—that is all. But the practical value of what we have found seems to me not inconsiderable. I have tried to avoid any forcing of the facts to fit in with a narrow and artificial view of my own opinions. To me the truth is plain. As we have examined the often-confused mass of evidence, as it throws light on the position of woman in these four great civilisations of antiquity, we find that, in spite of the apparent differences which separate their customs and habits in the sexual relationships, the evidence, when disentangled, all points in one and the same direction. In the face of the facts before us one truth cries out its message: "Woman must be free face to face with man." Has it not, indeed, become clear that a great part of the wisdom of the Egyptians and the wisdom of the Babylonians, as also of the Romans, and,

[1] *Digest*, XLVIII. 13, 5.

in a different degree, of the Greeks, rested in this, *they thought much of the mothers of the race.* Do not the records of these old-world civilisations show us the dominant position of the mother in relation to the life of the race? In all great ages of humanity this has been accepted as a central and sacred fact. We learn thus, as we look backwards to those countries and those times when woman was free, by what laws, habits and customs the sons of mothers may live long and gladly in all regions of the earth. The use of history is not alone to sum up the varied experiences of the past, but to enlarge our vision of the present, and by reflections on that past to point a way to the future.

PART III

MODERN SECTION

PRESENT-DAY ASPECTS OF THE WOMAN PROBLEM

CONTENTS OF CHAPTER VIII

SEX DIFFERENCES

The practical application of the truths arrived at—A question to be faced—The organic differences between the sexes—Résumé of the facts already established—The error in the common opinion of the true relationship of the sexes—The male active and seeking—The female passive and receiving—Is this true ?—An examination of the passivity of the female—The delusion that man is the active partner in the sexual relationship—The economic factor in marriage—The conventional modesty of woman—Concealments and evasions—The feeling of shame in love—Woman's right of selection—How this must be regained by women—The new Ethic—The pre-natal claims of the child—The question of parenthood as a religious question—The responsibility of the mother as the child's supreme parent—The mating of the future—Another question—Woman's superior moral virtue—Its fundamental error—Woman's imperative need of love—The maternal instinct—Nature's experiments—The establishment of two sexes—The feminine and masculine characters are an inherent part of the normal man and woman—The female as the giver of life—The deep significance of this—The atrophy of the maternal instinct—Modern woman preoccupied with herself—The right position of the mother—Sex attraction and sex antagonism—Woman's relation to sexuality—The duel of the sexes—The prostitution of love—Man's fear of woman—Misogyny—The rebellion of woman against man—Coercive differentiation of the sexes in consequence of civilisation—The ideal of a one-sexed world—Woman as the enemy of her own emancipation—The attempt to establish a third sex—The danger of ignoring sex—The future progress of love.

CHAPTER VIII

SEX DIFFERENCES

"Woman is an integral constituent of the processes of civilisation, which, without her, becomes unthinkable. The present moment is a turning point in the history of the feminine world. The woman of the past is disappearing, to give place to the woman of the future, instead of the bound, there appears the free personality."—IWAN BLOCH.

AT length we are ready, clear-minded and well-prepared, to deal with the question of woman's present position in society. Our minds are clear, for we have freed them from the age-long error that the subjection of the female to the male is a universal and necessary part of Nature's scheme; we are well prepared to support an exact opposite view, with a knowledge founded on some at least of the facts that prove this, by the actual position that women have held in the great civilisations of the past and still hold among primitive peoples, as well as by a sure biological basis. We are thus far advanced from the uncertainty with which we started our inquiry; our investigation has got beyond the statement of evidence drawn from the past to a stage whence the status of woman in the social order to-day, and the meaning of her relation to herself, to man, and to the race may be estimated. The point we have reached is this: the primary value of the sexes has to some extent, at least, been reversed under the patriarchal idea, which has pushed the male destructive power into prominence at the expense of the female constructive force. This under-valuing of the one-half of life has lost to society the service of a strong unsubjugated motherhood.

I am now, in this third and last section of my book, going to deal with what seems to me the practical applications of the truth we have arrived at. And the preliminary to this is a searching question: To what extent must we accept a different natural capacity for women and men? or, in other words, How far does the predominant sexual activity of woman separate her from man in the sphere of intellectual and social work? The whole subject is a large and difficult one and is full of problems to which it is not easy to find an answer. We are brought straight up against the old controversy of the organic differences between the sexes. This must be faced before we can proceed further.

To attempt to do this we must return to the position we left at the end of the fifth chapter. We had then concluded from our examination of the sexual habits of insects, mammals, and birds that a marked differentiation between the female and the male existed already in the early stages of the development of species, and that such divergence, or sex-dimorphism, to use the biological term, becomes more and more frequent and conspicuous as we ascend to the higher types. The essential functions of females and males become more separate, their habits of life tend to diverge, and to the primary differences there are added all manner of secondary peculiarities. We found, however, especially in our study of the familial habits, that these supplementary differences could not be regarded as fixed and unalterable in either the female or the male organism; but rather that the secondary sexual characters must be considered as depending on environmental conditions, among which are included the occupational activities, the scarcity or abundance of the food supply, the relative numbers of the two sexes, and, in particular, the brain development and the strength of the parental emotions. We followed the development of the female element and the male element. The male at first an insignificant addendum to the female, but the long process of love's selection, carrying on the expansion and aggrandisement of the male, led to the reversal of the early superiority of the female, replacing it by the superiority of the male. The female led and the male followed in the evolution process. We saw that there are many curious alternations in the superiority of one sex over the other in size and also in power of function. Below the line, among backboneless animals, there is much greater constancy of superiority among the females, and this predominance persists in many higher types. Even among birds, who afford the most perfect examples of sexual development, the cases are not infrequent in which the female equals, and sometimes even exceeds, the male in size and strength and in beauty of plumage. The curious case of the Phalaropes furnished us with a remarkable example of a reversal of the rôle of the sexes. We found further that (1) an extravagant development of the secondary sexual characters was not really favourable to the reproductive process, the males thus differentiated belonging to a lower grade of sexual evolution, being bad fathers and unsocial in their conduct; (2) that the most oppressed females are as a rule very faithful wives, and (3) that the highest expression of love among the birds must be sought in the beautiful cases in which the sexes, though maintaining the essential constitutional distinctions, are, through the higher individuation of the females more alike, equal in capacity, and co-operate together in the race-work.

It were well to keep these facts clearly in sight; for, in the light of them, it becomes evident that there is an error somewhere in the common opinion of the true relationship of the sexes. Let us go first to the very start of the matter. It is always held that the sperm male-cell represents the active, and the germ female-cell the passive principle in sexuality, and on this assumption there has been based by many a fixed standard for the supposed natural relation between man and woman—he active and seeking, she passive and receiving.

But is this really a fair statement of the reproduction process? The hunger-driven male-cell certainly seeks the female—but what happens then? The female cellule, the ovule, *preserves its individuality and absorbs the masculine cellule, or is impregnated by it.* Thus, to use the term "passive" in this connection is surely curiously misleading; as well call the snake passive when, waiting motionless, it charms and draws towards it the victim it will devour. Illustrations are apt to mislead, nevertheless they do help us to see straight, and until we have come to find the truth here we shall be fumbling for the grounds of any safe conclusion as to the natural relationship of the female and the male. I think we must take a wider view of the sexual relationship, and conclude that the passivity of the female is not real, but only an apparent passivity. We may even go so far as to say that the female element has from the very first to play the more complex and difficult, the more important part. Herein, at the very start of life, is typified in a manner at once simple and convincing that differentiation which divides so sharply the sexual activity of the female from that of the male. The serious part in sex belongs to the one who gives life, while in comparison the activity of the male can almost be regarded as trifling. And I believe that this view will be found to be amply supported by facts if we turn now to consider the later and human relation of the sexes. In all cases it is the same, the serious business in sex belongs to the woman. As it was in the beginning, so, it seems to me, it continues to the end—it is woman who really leads, she who in sex absorbs and uses the male.

"The passivity of the female in love," it has been said wisely by Marro in his fine work *La Pubertà*, "is the passivity of the magnet, which in its apparent immobility is drawing the iron towards it. An intense energy lies behind such passivity, an absorbed pre-occupation in the end to be attained."[1] In the examples we have studied of the courtships of birds we saw that it is by no means a universal law that the male is eager and the female coy. I need only recall the instance noted by Darwin[2] in which a wild duck forced her love on a male pintail, and such cases, as is well known, are frequent. High-bred bitches will show sudden passions for low-bred or mongrel males. According to breeders

[1] See Havelock Ellis, "The Sexual Impulse in Woman," *Psychology of Sex*, Vol. III. p. 181, who gives this quotation from Marro.

[2] See page 111.

and observers it is the female who is always much more susceptible of sentimental selection; thus it is often necessary to deceive mares. Among many primitive peoples it is the woman who takes the initiative in courtship. In New Guinea, for instance, where women hold a very independent position, "the girl is always regarded as the seducer. 'Women steal men.' A youth who proposed to a girl would be making himself ridiculous, would be called a woman, and laughed at by the girls. The usual method by which a girl proposes is to send a present to the youth by a third party, following this up by repeated gifts of food; the young man sometimes waits a month or two, receiving presents all the time, in order to assure himself of the girl's constancy before decisively accepting her advances."[1]

In the face of this, and many similar cases, it becomes an absurdity to continue a belief in the passivity of the female as a natural law of the sexes. Such openness of conduct in courtship is, of course, impossible except where woman holds an entirely independent position. Still, it would not be difficult to bring forward similar manifestations of the initiative being taken by the woman—though often exercised unconsciously as the expression of an instinctive need—in the artificial courtships of highly civilised peoples. But enough has perhaps been said; and such examples can, I doubt not, be readily supplied by each of my readers for themselves. I will only remark that the true nature of the passivity of the woman in courtship is made abundantly clear from the

[1] Haddon, "Western Tribes of Torres Straits," *Journal of the Anthropological Society*, Vol. XIX., Feb. 1890; cited by Ellis, *op. cit.*, p. 185.

ease with which the pretence is thrown off in every case where the necessity arises.

Nothing is more astounding to me than this delusion that the man is the active partner in sex. I believe, as I have once before stated, that Bernard Shaw[1] is right here when he says that men set up the theory to save their pride. Having taken to themselves the initiative in all other matters, they claim the same privilege in love; and women have acquiesced and have helped them, so that the duplicity has become almost ineradicable. Few women are brave enough to admit this even if they have clear sight to see the truth; they know that it is not permitted to them to exercise openly their right of choice. They understand that the male pride of possession—the hunter's and the fighter's joy—must be respected. But this makes not the least difference to the result, only to the way in which that result is gained. So the whole of our society is filled with half-concealed sex-snares and pitfalls set by women for the capture of men. The woman waits *passive!* Yes, precisely, she often does. But exactly the same may be said of the female spider when she has spun her web, from which she knows full well the victim fly will not escape.

There is another point that must be noticed. Under our present sexual relationships the price the woman asks from the man for her favours is marriage as the only means of gaining permanent maintenance for herself and for her children. Now that these economic considerations have entered into love she has to act with a new and greater caution, for she has to gain her own ends as

[1] See page 66.

well as Nature's ends. In the matriarchal society the girl was allowed openly to pick her lover, and forthwith he went with her. But to the modern woman, under the patriarchal ideals, if she shows the modesty that convention requires of her, all that is permitted is the invitation of a lowered eyelid, a look, or perchance a touch, at one time given, at another withheld.

Now, I find it the opinion of most of my men friends that such half-concealed encouragements, such evasions and drawings back are a necessary part of the love-play —the woman's unconscious testing of the fussy male. There is one friend, a doctor, who tells me that the woman's dissimulation of her own inclination has come to be a secondary sexual characteristic, a manifestation of the operation of sexual selection, diluted, perhaps, and altered by civilisation, but an essential feature in every courtship, so that the woman follows a true and biologically valuable instinct when she temporises and dissembles, and tests and provokes, and entices and repels. She is proving herself and testing her lovers before she permits that awful "merging" that no afterthought can undo.

Now, on the face of it this seems true. There is a passionate uncertainty that all true lovers feel. It is, I think, a holding back from the yielding up of the individual ego—an unconscious revolt from the sacrifice claimed by the creative force before which both the woman and the man alike are helpless agents. It is very difficult to find the truth. Throughout Nature love only fulfils its purpose after much expenditure of energy. But dissimulation on the side of the woman is not, I am sure, a true or necessary incitement to love. Love, as I see it, is a breaking down of the boundaries of oneself, the casting aside of reserve and defences, with a necessary throwing off of every concealment.

In our restricted society, where the sexual instincts are at once both unnaturally repressed and unnaturally stimulated, this openness may not be possible. Concealments and evasions may be an aid at one stage of sex evolution. Just as the half-concealed body is often a more powerful sensual stimulus than nudity; the less one sees, the more does the imagination picture. But the need of such artificial excitants speaks of the poverty of love and not of its fullness. For most of us the strain of sensuality in our loves is very strong. To have lived in the bonds of slavery makes us slaves, and the price that woman has paid is the sacrifice of her purity. The feeling of shame in love, like chastity, arose in the property value of the woman to her owner; it is no more a part of the woman's character than of the man's. Woman must capture her mate because the race must perish without her travail; she is fulfilling Nature's ends, as well as her own, whatever means she uses.

So I am certain that, as woman's right of selection is given back to her to exercise without restraint, we shall see a freer and more beautiful mating. With greater liberty of action she will be far better armed with knowledge to demand a finer quality in her lovers. Her unborn children importuning her, her choice will be guided by the man's fitness alone, not, as now it is, by his capacity and power for work and protection. We are only awakening to the terrible evils of these powerful economic restraints, which now limit the woman's range of choice. It is this wastage of the Life-force that, as I believe, above all else has driven women into revolt.

The free power of Selection in Love! Yes; that is the true Female Franchise. It must be regained by woman, to be used by her to ennoble the sex relation and thereby to cleanse society of the unfit. The means by which this most important end can be attained will be brought about by giving woman such training and education and civic rights, as well as the framing of such laws and changes in the rights of property inheritance, as shall render her economically independent. Existing marriage is a pernicious survival of the patriarchal age. The "patriarch's" wife was significantly reckoned in the same category with a man's "ox" and his "ass," which any other male was forbidden "to covet." The wife was the husband's—her owner's private property—and the curse of this dependence and the old ferocious *potestas* and *manus*, from which the Roman wife freed herself, are upon women to-day. With the regaining of their economic freedom by women—by whatever means this is to be accomplished—a truer marriage will be brought within reach of every one, and the sexual relationship will be freed from the jealous chains of ownership that cause such bitter mistrusts in the wreckage of our loves.

Mating will be a much more complex affair, and yet one much more directly in harmony with the welfare of the race. A recognition of the pre-natal claims of the child is the new Ethic that is slowly but surely dawning on womankind and on man. He who destroys human life, however unfit that life may be, is remorselessly punished by society, but the woman and man who beget diseased and imbecile children—the necessarily unfit—are not only exonerated from sin, but applauded by both Church and State. Could moral inconstancy go further than this? It is only in the begetting of men that breeding from the worst stocks may be said to be the rule. As long as in our ideas on these questions superstition remains the guide there is nothing to hope for and much to fear. The new ideal is only beginning, and beginning with a tardiness that is a reproach to human foresight. But herein lies the glad hope of the future. I place my trust in the enlightened conscience of the economically emancipated mothers, and in the awakened fathers, to work out some scheme of sexual salvation as will ensure a race of sounder limb and saner intelligence than any that has yet appeared in our civilisation.

It is woman, not man, who must fix the standard in sex. The problems of love are linked on to the needs of the race. Nature has, as we have seen, made various experiments as to which of the sexes was to be the predominant partner in this relation. But the decision has been made in the favour of the mother. She it is who has to play the chief part in the racial life. There is no getting away from this, in spite of the many absurdities that man has set up, as, for instance, St. Paul's grandmotherly old Tory dogma, making "man the head of the woman."

The differences between woman and man are deep and fundamental. And, lest there be any who fear the giving back to woman of her power, let me say that in this change there will be no danger of unsexing, least of all of the unsexing of woman. Nature would not permit it, even if she in any foolishness of revolt sought such a result, for it is her body that is the sanctuary of the race. Love and courtship will not, indeed, be robbed of any charm, that would be fatal, but they will be freed from the mockeries of love that have always selfishness in them, jealous resentments and fearing distrusts—the man of the woman, not less than the woman of the man. To-day coquetry serves not only as a prelude to marriage, but very often serves as a substitute for it; an escape from the payment of the sacrifices which fulfilled love claims. There is a confusion of motives which now force women and men alike from their service to the race. Sex must be freed from all unworthy necessities. Courtship must be regarded, not as a game of chance, but as the opening act in the drama of life. And the woman who comes to know this must play her part consciously, realising in full what she is seeking for; then, indeed, no longer will her sex be to her a light or a saleable thing. At present economic and social injustices are strangling millions of beautiful unborn babes.

There is another error that I would wish to clear up now. It is a tenet of common belief that in all matters of sex-feeling and sex-morality the woman is different from, and superior to, the man. I find in the writings of almost all women on sex-subjects, not to speak of popular novels, an insistence on men's grossness, with a great deal in contrast about the soulful character of woman's love. Even so illuminated a writer as Ellen Key emphasises this supposed trait of the woman again and again.

Another woman writer, Miss May Sinclair, in a brilliant "Defence of Men" (*English Review*, July 1912), speaks of "the superior virtue of women" as being "primordially and fundamentally Nature's care." And again, woman "has monopolised virtue at man's expense," which the writer, with the most perfect humour and irony, though apparently quite unconscious, regards as "men's tragedy." The woman has received the laurel crown by "Nature's consecration of her womanhood to suffering," the man "has paid with his spiritual prospects as she has paid with her body."

Now, from this view of the sex relationship I most utterly dissent. I believe that any difference in virtue, even where it exists in woman, is not fundamental, that it is against Nature's purpose that it should be so; rather it has arisen as a pretence of necessity, because it has been expected of her, nourished in her, and imposed on her by the unnatural prohibitions of religious and social conventions. The female half of life has not been pre-ordained to suffer any more than the male half: this belief has done more to destroy the conscience of woman than any other single error. You have only to repeat any lie long enough to convince even yourself of its truth. But assuredly free woman will have to yield up her martyr's crown.

I grant willingly that men often talk brutally of sex, but I am certain that few of them think brutally. We women are so easily deceived by the outside appearance of things. The man who calls "a spade a spade" is not really inferior to him who terms it "an agricultural implement for the tilling of the soil." And women also express their sensuality in orgies of emotion, in hypocrisies of chastity, and in many other ways that are really nothing but a subtle sensuality disguised.

I confess that I doubt very much the existence of any special soulful character in woman's love. I wish that I didn't. But my experience forces me to admit that this is but another of those delusions which woman has wrapped around herself. Of course I may be wrong. I find Professor Forel and other distinguished psychologists lending their support to this idol of the woman's superior sexual virtue. Krafft Ebing goes much further, holding "that woman is naturally and organically frigid." It may be then that some difference does exist in the driving force of passion in men and women. I do not know the exact character of men's love to compare it with my own, and I hesitate to write with that assurance of the passions of the other sex with which they have written of mine. Yet I believe that the male receiving life from the female is not more mindful of the physical needs of love than the woman, though possibly she has less understanding of its joys. For the woman with a much more complex sexual nature is carried by passion further than the male; the continuance of life rests with her. Under this imperative compulsion woman, if needs be, will break every commandment in the Decalogue and suffer no remorse for having done so. I think this seeking to give life remains a necessary element in the loves of all women. At its lowest it will stoop to any unscrupulousness. Bernard Shaw tells us that "if women were as fastidious as men, morally or physically, there would be an end to the race." Perhaps this is true.

Yet I think woman's love is always different in its fundamental essence from the excitements of the male. We throw the whole burden of sex-desire on to men, because we have not yet faced the truth that they are our helpless agents in carrying on Nature's most urgent work. It has been so from the beginning, since that first primordial mating when the hungry male-cell gained renewal of life from the female, it is so still, I believe it will be thus to the end.

It is when we come to the emotions and actions connected with the maternal instinct in woman that we reach the real point of the difference between the sexes. In its essential essence this belongs to women alone. The male may be infected with the reproduction energy (we have witnessed this in its finest expression among birds, where the parental duties are shared in and, in some cases, carried out entirely by the male), but man possesses, as yet, its faint analogy only. It is the most primary of all woman's qualities, and, being fundamental, it is, I believe, unalterable, and any attempt to minimise its action is very unlikely to lead to progress. It is a two-sexed world; women and men are not alike; I hope that they never will be.

This radical truth is so plain. Yet it seems to me that in the present confusion many women are in danger of overlooking it. We saw in an earlier chapter how very early in the development of life it was found by Nature's slow but certain experiments that the establishment of two sexes in different organisms, and their differentiation, was to the immense advantage of progress. This initial difference leads to the functional distinctions between the female and the male, but it goes much further than this, finding its expression in many secondary qualities, not on the physical side alone, but on the mental and psychical, and is, indeed, a saturating influence that determines the entire development of the organism into the feminine or the masculine character. Take again the fact that this dynamic action of sex has manifested itself in a continual progress through the uncounted centuries. Developed by love's selection, the differentiation of the sexes increased in the evolution of species, and as the differentiation increased the attraction also increased, until in all the higher forms we find two markedly different sexes, strongly drawn together by the magnetism of sex, and fulfilling together their separate uses in the reproductive process. These are the natural features of sex-distinction and sex-union.

The belief, therefore, is forced upon us that the characteristic feminine and masculine characters are an inherent part of the normal woman and man, a duality that goes back to the very threshold of sexuality. So Nature created them, female and male created she them. To change the metaphor, we have the woman and the man = the unit—the race. While there is no fixing of the precise nature of this constitutional difference between the two sexes, we may yet, broadly speaking, reach the truth. The female, as the giver and keeper of life, is relatively more constructive, relatively less disruptive than the male. It is here, I believe, we touch the spring of those sex differences, which do exist, in spite of all efforts to explain them away between the woman and the man. It is a quality that crops up in many diverse directions and penetrates into every expression of the feminine character.

Now, we cannot get away from a difference so fundamental, so primordial as this. The consecration of the woman's body as the sanctuary of life—that perpetual payment in giving is not safely to be altered. And this I contest against all the Feminists: the real need of the normal woman is the full and free satisfaction of the race-instinct. Do I then accept the subjection of the woman. Assuredly not! To me it is manifest that it is just because of her sex-needs and her sex-power that woman must be free. To leave such a force to be used without understanding is like giving a weapon to a child, in whose hands a cartridge suddenly goes off, leaving the empty and smoking shell in his trembling hands.

It is well to remember, however, that for all women there is conceivably no one simple rule. It is quite possible that the maternal instincts may be overlaid and even destroyed, being replaced by others more clearly masculine. In our artificial social state this is indeed bound to be so. It may be regretted, but it cannot be blamed. And each woman must be free to make her own choice; no man may safely decide for her; she must give life gladly to be able to give it well. This is why any effort to force maternity, even as an ideal, upon women is so utterly absurd. To-day woman is coming slowly and hesitatingly to a new consciousness of herself, and this at present is perhaps preoccupying her attention. But the freed woman of to-morrow will have no need to centre her thoughts in herself, for by that time she will understand. There will come a day when women will no longer live in a prison walled up with fear of love and life. And when she has done with discovering herself and playing at conquests, she will come to the most glorious day of all, when she will know herself for what she is. And to those of us who see already the goal the way is surely clear—let us work to find how best it can be made easy for all women to love gladly and to bring forth their children in joy.

Hitherto, dating from the times of the subjection of mother-right to father-right, the woman's insecure position, with her need of protection during the period of motherhood, has forced her into a state of dependence and subordination to men, which has accentuated and made permanent that physical disadvantage which, apart from motherhood, would scarcely exist, and even with motherhood would not become a source of weakness, under a wiser social organisation, which, understanding the primary importance of the mother, so arranged its domestic and social relationships as to place its women in a position of security. We have seen how this was done in Egypt, and how happy were the results; we have seen, too, that among all primitive peoples women are practically as strong as the men, and as capable in the social duty of work. It is only under the fully established patriarchal system, with its unequal development of the sexes, that motherhood is a source of weakness to women. From the time that society comes again to recognise the position of mothers and their right as the bearers of strength to the race, not only to protection while they are fulfilling that essential function for the community, but to their freedom after they have fulfilled it—the same freedom that men claim for the work they do for the community—from that time will arise a new freedom of women which will once again unite mother-right with father-right. This change will touch and vitally affect many of the deepest problems of the sexual relationship and the race.

We hear much to-day of women, and also men, being over-sexed; to me it seems much nearer the truth to say we are wrongly sexed. It is unquestionable that the progress of civilisation has resulted in a markedly accentuated differentiation between the sexes, which, through inheritance and custom, has become continually more sharply defined. Now, up to a certain point sex differences lead to sex-attraction, but whenever such variability—whether initiated by some natural process or by some intentional guidance of the pressure of civilisation —is unduly exaggerated, the way is opened up for sex-antagonism. That this, indeed, occurs may be seen from the fact we have already established, that an exaggerated outgrowth of the secondary sexual characters is not really favourable to development; the species thus differentiated being bad parents and unsocial in their conduct. The large felines, which are often inclined to commit infanticide in their own interests, the male turkey and other members of the gallinaceæ afford examples, and so does the female phalarope, whose maternal instincts are completely atrophied. Another illustration may be drawn from the debased position of the Athenian women, where the sharp separation between the sexes led, without doubt, not only to the debasing of the marriage relationship, but to the establishment of the *hetairæ*, and also to the common practice of homo-sexual love.

Under our present civilisation, and mainly owing to the unnatural relation of the sexes, which has unduly emphasised certain qualities of excessive femininity, sex-feeling has been at once over-accentuated and under-disciplined. Thus, an extreme outward sex-attraction has come to veil but thinly a deep inward sex-antipathy, until it seems almost impossible that women and men can ever really understand one another. Herein lie the roots, as I believe, of much of the brutal treatment of women by men and the contempt in which too often they are held. For what is the truth here? In this so-called "duel of sex," while woman's moral equality has not been recognised, women have employed their sex-differences as the most effective weapon for compassing their own ends, and men in the mass—unmindful of the truth that love is an understanding of the contrasted natures, a solution of the riddle—have wished to have it so. What significance arises out of this in the so-much-lauded cry, "Woman's influence!" "By thy submission rule," really means in ninety-nine cases out of a hundred, "Rule by sex-seduction and flattery." Yes, we women cannot burk the truth—the seduction and flattery of man by woman is writ large over the face of our present society, it speaks in our literature and in our art. It is to this prostitution of love that sex-differences have carried us.

There is, of course, nothing new in these conditions; and there have always been times when men have rebelled against this sexual tyranny of woman. Misogyny is an old story. It is Euripides who betrays to us the real meaning of such revolt. In a fragment of his we read, *The most invincible of all things is a woman!*

Men are so little sure of themselves that they fear suffering from woman an annihilation of their own personality. There is nothing surprising in this; rather it is one of Nature's laws that may not be overlooked, traceable back to that first coalescence when the female cellule absorbs the male. In one way or another, for Nature's ends or for her own, the female will always absorb the male—the woman the man; she is the river of life, he but the tributary stream. Paracelsus long ago gave utterance to the profound truth, "Woman is nearer to the world than man." Hence the army of misogynists—a Schopenhauer, a Strindberg, a Weininger, even a great Tolstoi, alike moved in a rebellion of disillusion, or satiety, against the power of woman that has been turned into turbid channels of misusage. Thence, too, the hateful Christian doctrine of the fundamentally sinful, evil, devilish nature of woman.

This rebellion of men, and their efforts to free themselves from the thrall of women has been of little avail. We have reached now a new stage in the age-long conflict of the sexes—the rebellion of the woman. There has come a time when the old cry, "Woman, what have I to do with you?" is being changed. It is woman who is whispering to herself and to her sisters, and, as she gains in courage, crying it aloud, "Men, what have we to do with you? We belong to ourselves." It is to this impasse in the confusion and antagonism of the present moment of transition that sex-differences are bringing us.

In face of this we may well pause.

What to do is another matter. But I am mainly concerned just now in trying to see facts clearly. And to me it often seems that woman is in grave danger to-day of becoming intoxicated with herself. She stands out self-affirming, postulating her own—or what she thinks to be her own—nature. In her, perhaps too-sudden, awakening to an entirely new existence of a free personality, an over-consciousness of her rights has arisen, causing a confusion of her instincts, so she fails to see the revelation begotten in her inmost self.

There is no getting away from the truth that there is this vital organic distinction between woman and man; and further, that this sexual difference does, and it is well that it should, find its expression in a large number of detailed characters of femaleness and maleness, various in value, some, perhaps, trivial, and some important. These characters are natural in origin and natural also in having survived ages of eliminative selection. But the point I want to make clear is that, side by side with these fundamental differences, have arisen in women a number of what may be called coercive differentiations, inconsistent with, and absolutely hurtful to the natural distinctions, being destructive to the love and understanding of woman and man, and not less destructive to the vigour of the race. This misdifferentiation of women, it is true, is passing, but the progressive gain in this direction is counterbalanced by a new and hardly less grave danger.

I am dealing here with what seems to me to be a perilous quicksand in woman's struggle for free development. To hear many women talk it would appear that the new ideal was a one-sexed world. A great army of women have espoused the task of raising their sex out of subjection. For such a duty the strength and energy of passion is required. Can this task be performed if the woman to any extent indulges in sex—otherwise subjection to man. Sexuality debases, even reproduction and birth are regarded as "nauseating." Woman is not free, only because she has been the slave to the primitive cycle of emotions which belong to physical love. The renunciation, the conquest of sex—it is this that must be gained. As for man, he has been shown up, women have found him out; his long-worn garments of authority and his mystery and glamour have been torn into shreds—woman will have none of him.

Now obviously these are over-statements, yet they are the logical outcome of much of the talk that one hears. It is the visible sign of our incoherence and error, and in the measure of these follies we are sent back to seek the truth. Women need a robuster courage in the face of love, a greater faith in their womanhood, and in the scheme of Life. Nothing can be gained from the child's folly in breaking the toys that have momentarily ceased to please. The misogamist type of woman cannot fail to prove as futile as the misogamist man. Not "Free *from* man" is the watch-cry of women's emancipation that surely is to be, but "Free *with* man."

Let us pass to a somewhat different instance—the perversion of the natural instincts of woman which has led to the attempt to establish what has been called a "third sex,"[1] a type of woman in whom the sexual

[1] E. von Wolzogen gives this name, *The Third Sex*, to a romance in which he describes a kind of barren, stunted woman, capable, however, of holding her place in all work in competition with men. The writer compares these types of women to the workers among ants and bees. *See* p. 62. I have quoted from Iwan Bloch, *The Sexual Life of Our Times*, p. 13.

differences are obscured or even obliterated—a woman who is, in fact, a temperamental neuter. Economic conditions are compelling women to enter with men into the fierce competition of our disordered social State. Partly due to this reason, though much more, as I think, to the strong stirring in woman of her newly-discovered self, there has arisen what I should like to call an over-emphasised Intellectualism. Where sex is ignored there is bound to lurk danger. Every one recognises the significance of the advance in particular cases of women towards a higher intellectual individuation, and the social utility of those women who have been truly the pioneers of the new freedom; but this does not lessen at all the disastrous influence of an ideal which holds up the renunciation of the natural rights of love and activities of women, and thus involves an irreparable loss to the race by the barrenness of many of its finest types. The significance of such Intellectuals must be limited, because for them the possibility of transmission by inheritance of their valuable qualities is cut off, and hence the way is closed to a further progress. And, thus, we are brought back to that simple truth from which we started; there are two sexes, the female and the male, on their specific differences and resemblances blended together in union every true advance in progress depends —on the perfected woman and the perfected man.

CONTENTS OF CHAPTER IX

APPLICATION OF THE FOREGOING CHAPTER WITH SOME FURTHER REMARKS ON SEX DIFFERENCES

I.—*Women and Labour*

A further examination of the sexual differences—The knowledge we have gained does not enable us definitely to settle the problem—The necessity of considering Nurture—Woman's character to some extent the result of circumstance, to some extent organic—The difficulties of the problem—Standards of comparison—Incompleteness of our knowledge—New researches on sex-differences—The confusion of opinions—Women and men different, but neither superior to the other—The position of women in society to-day—The increasing surplus of women—How can a remedy be found?—Woman's place in the home—The changes in modern conditions—Women and labour—The damning struggle for life—Sweated work—Women's wages—The marketable value of woman's sex—This the explanation of the smallness of women's wages—The prostitute better paid than the worker—Woman's strength as compared with man's—Are women really the weaker sex?—Woman's work capacity equal to man's, but different—The Spanish women—The intolerable conditions of labour in commercial countries—Women more deeply concerned than men—The real value of women's work—This must be recognised by the State—The social service of child-bearing—The primary and most important work of women—The present revolt of women—How far is this justifiable?—A caution and some reflections.

II.—*Sexual Differences of the Mind and the Artistic Impulse in Women*

The mental and psychical sexual differences—Ineradicability of these—Can they be modified or disregarded?—The masculine and feminine intellectual qualities—Caution necessary in making any comparison—Example, a tenacious memory—Is this a feminine characteristic?—Woman's intuition—Its value—Each sex contributes to the thought power of the other—The artistic impulse—Is genius to be regarded as an endowment of the male?—An examination of the grounds for this view—Untenability of the opinion of the greater variational tendency of men—The question needs re-opening—The influence of environment and training on woman's mind—What woman can, or can not, do as yet unproved—Woman's talent for diplomacy—The separation between the mental life of the sexes—The result on woman's mind—The revolt against repression—Woman as she is represented in literature—The woman of the future—Woman the cause of emotion in men—Part played by women in early civilisations—What men learnt from them—Woman's emotional endowment—Her affectability and response to suggestion—These the qualities essential to success in the arts—A comparison between the qualities of genius and the qualities of woman—This opens up questions of startling significance—What women may achieve in the future—Some suggestions as to the effect of the entrance of women into the arts.

III.—*The Affectability of Woman—Its Connection with the Religious Impulse*

Woman's aptitude for religion—Her need for a protection—Relation between the sexual and religious emotions—Deprivation of love and satiety of love the sources of religious needs—Religious prostitution—Religio-erotic festivals—Sexual mysticism in Christianity—The lives of the saints—Religious sexual perceptions—Their influence on the emotional feminine character—A personal experience—The association between love and salvation—The same sense of the eternal in the religious and the sexual impulse—Asceticism—Its origin in the sexual emotions—Preoccupation of the ascetic with sex needs—The transformation of the sex-impulse into spiritual activities—Examples—The modern ascetic—The fear of love—This the ultimate cause of the contempt of woman—Example of Maupassant's priest—In love the way of salvation.

CHAPTER IX

APPLICATION OF THE FOREGOING CHAPTER WITH SOME FURTHER REMARKS ON SEX DIFFERENCES

I.—*Women and Labour*

"The fullest ideal of the woman-worker is she who works not merely or mainly for men as the help and instrument of their purpose, but who works with men as the instrument yet material of her purpose."—GEDDES AND THOMSON.

WHEN we come to consider the detailed differences between woman and man, a sharp separation of them into female qualities and male qualities no longer squares with the known facts. Any attempt to lessen the natural differences, as also to weaken at all the attractions arising from this divergence, must be regarded with extreme distrust. There is a real and inherent prejudice against the masculine woman and the feminine man. It is nevertheless necessary very carefully to discriminate between innate qualities of femaleness and maleness and those differences that have been acquired as the direct result of peculiarities of environmental conditions. It is certain that many differences in the physical and mental capacity of women must be referred not to Nature but to Nurture, *i.e.* the effects of conditions and training. Let me give one concrete case, for one clear illustration is more eloquent than any statement. Long ago Professor Karl Vogt pointed out that women were awkward manipulators. Thomas, in *Sex and Society*, answers this well: "The awkwardness in manual manipulation shown by these girls was surely due to lack of practice. The fastest type-writer in the world is to-day a woman; the record for roping steers (a feat depending on manual dexterity rather than physical force) is held by a woman." I may add to this an example of my own observation. In a recent International Fly and Bait Casting Tournament, held at the Crystal Palace, a woman was among the competitors, and gave an admirable exhibition of skill in salmon fly-casting. In this competition she threw one cast 34 feet and two of 33 feet, making an aggregate of 100 yards, which gained her the prize over the male competitors. It has also been recently stated that women show equal skill with men in shooting at a target.

It is plain that the more we examine the question of sex-differences the more it baffles us. The only safeguard against utter confusion and idleness of thought is to fall back on the common-sense view that *woman is what she is largely, because she has lived as she has*, and further, that in the present transition no *arbitrary rules may be laid down by men as to what she should, or should not, can, or cannot do.* Even in fear of possible danger to be incurred, woman must no longer be "grandfathered." The scope of this chapter is to make this clear.

It is no part of my purpose, even if it were possible for me within the limits at my command, to enter into an examination of all the numerous statements and theories with regard to the real or supposed secondary sexual characters of woman. For though the practical utility of such detailed knowledge is obvious, while there is no certainty of opinion even among experts to fix the distinctions between the sexes, it is wiser in one who, like myself, can claim no scientific knowledge to avoid the hazard of any conclusion. I confess that a most careful study of the many differing opinions has left me in a state of mental confusion. One is tempted to adopt those views that fit in with one's own observations and to neglect others probably equally right that do not do this. What is wanted is a much larger number of careful experiments and scientific observations. Some of these have been made already, and their value is great, but the basis is still too narrow for any safe generalisations. All kinds of error are clearly very likely to arise. I may, perhaps, be allowed to state my surprise, not to say amusement, at the conviction evidenced by some male writers in their estimate of the character of my sex. I find myself given many qualities that I am sure I have not got, and deprived of others that I am equally certain I possess. Thus, I have found myself wondering, as I sought sincerely to find truth, whether I am indeed woman or man? or, to be more exact, whether the female qualities in me do not include many others regarded as masculine? This has forced the thought—is the difference between the sexes, after all, so complete?

I am aware that what I am now saying appears to be in contradiction with my other statements. I cannot help it. The fact is, that truth is always more diverse than we suspect. This is a question that reaches so deeply that apparent contradiction is sometimes inevitable. We find we are rooted into outside things, and we melt away, as it were, into them, and no woman or man can say, "I consist absolutely of this or that"; nor define herself or himself so certainly as to be sure where the differences between the sexes end and the points of contact begin. Many qualities of the personality appear no more female than male; no more belonging to the woman than the man. And yet, underlying these common qualities there is a deep under-current in which all our nature finds expression in our sex.

Science has of late years advanced far in this matter, yet it has not much more than begun. There is, as yet, no approximation to unanimity of decision, though the way has been cleared of many errors. This is all that has really been done by the ablest observers, who seem, however, unwilling, if one may say so without presumption, to accept the conclusions to which their own experiments and observations would seem to point. Take an illustration. The early certitude on the sex-differences in the weight of the brain and in the proportion of the cerebral lobes has been completely turned upside down. The long believed opinion of the inferiority of the woman in this direction has been proved to be founded on prejudice, fallacies, and over-hasty generalisations, so that now it is allowed that the sexual differences in the brain are at most very small. An even more instructive example arises from the ancient theory that there was a natural difference in the respiratory movements of the sexes. Hutchinson even argued that this costal breathing was an adaptation to the child-bearing function in woman. Further investigations, however, with a wider basis and more accurate methods—and one may surely add more common-sense—have changed the whole aspect of the matter. This difference has been proved to be due, not to Nature at all, but wholly to the effect of corset-wearing and woman's conventional dress. There is, it would seem, no limit to the quagmire of superstition and error into which sex-difference have drawn even the most careful inquirers if once they fail to cut themselves adrift from that superficial view of Nature's scheme, by which the woman is considered as being handicapped in every direction by her maternal function.

Enough has now been said to indicate the complication of the facts, to say nothing of their practical application. I must refer my readers for further details to convenient summaries of the sexual differences, in Havelock Ellis's *Man and Woman;* Geddes and Thomson's *Sex and Evolution;* Thomas's *Sex and Society;* and H. Campbell's *Differences in the Nervous Organisation of Men and Women:* the first of these is a treasure store of facts, and may be regarded as the foundation of all later research; the last is, perhaps, the most generally interesting, certainly it is the most favourable in its estimate of women. Dr. Campbell urges with much force the fallacy of many popular views. He does not seem to believe in the fundamental origin of maleness and femaleness, holding them rather to be secondary and derived, the result, in fact, of selection.

I have already sufficiently guarded against being supposed to have any desire to establish identity between woman and man. I do, however, object to any general conclusion of an arbitrary and excessive sex-separation, without the essential preliminary inquiry being made as to the effects of conditions and training; that is, whether the opportunities of development have been at all equal. But here, to save falling into a misconception, it is necessary to point out that I do not say *the same opportunities, but equal.* This difference is so important that, risking the fear of being tedious, I must restate my belief in the unlikeness of the sexes. As Havelock Ellis says, "A man is a man to his very thumbs, and a woman is a woman down to her little toes." What I do mean, then, is this: *Have the opportunities of the woman to develop as woman been equal to the opportunities of the man to develop as man?* It is on this question, it seems to me, that our attention should be fixed.

Leaving for a little any attempt to find out in what directions this development of woman can be most fully carried out, let us now clear our way by glancing very briefly at certain plain facts of the actual position of women as they present themselves in our society to-day.

In 1901 there were 1,070,000 more women than men in this country; this surplus of women has increased slowly but steadily in every census since 1841! Thus, those who hold (as all who look straight at this matter must) that the essential need for the normal woman are conditions that make possible the fulfilment of her sex-functions, are placed in an awkward dilemma when they wish to restrict her activities to marriage and the home. By such narrowing of the sexual sphere they are not taking into consideration the facts as they exist to-day. In a society where the women outnumber the men by more than a million, it is sufficiently evident that justice can be done to these primary needs of woman only by adopting one of two courses, the placing of women in a position which secures to them the possession of property, or, if their dependence on the labours of men is maintained, the recognition of some form of polygamy. Here is no advocacy of any sexual licence or of free-love, but I do set up a claim for free motherhood, and however great the objections that may, and, as I think, must be raised against polygamy, I am unhesitating in stating my belief that any open and brave facing of the facts of the sex relationship is better than our present ignorance or hypocritical indifference, which is spread like a shroud over our national conditions of concealed polygamy for men, side by side with enforced celibacy and unconcealed prostitution for a great number of women. The most hopeful sign of the woman's movement is a new solidarity that is surely killing the fatalism of a past acquiescing in wrongs, and is slowly giving birth to a fine spiritual apprehension of the great truth that what concerns any woman concerns all women, and, I would add, also all men. This last—that there can be no woman's question that is not also a man's question—is so essentially a part of any fruitful change in our domestic and social relationship that women must not permit themselves for a moment to forget it. It is the very plain things that so often we do overlook.

So it becomes clear that the parrot cries "Woman's Place!" "Woman's Sphere!" "Her place is the home!" have lost much, even if not all, their significance. For, in the first place, it is obvious that under present conditions there are not enough homes to go round; and second, even if we neglect this essential fact, women may well answer such demands by saying "much depends on the character and conditions of the home we are to stay in." It was a many-sided home of free and full activity in which woman evolved and wherein for long ages she worked; a home, in fact, which gave free opportunities for the exercise of those qualities of constructive energy that women, broadly speaking, may be said to possess. The woman's so-called natural position in the home is not now natural at all. The conditions of life have changed. Everything is drifting towards separation from worn-out conditions. We are increasingly conscious of a growing discontent at waste. The home with its old full activities has passed from women's hands. But woman's work is not less needed. To-day the State claims her; the Nation's housekeeping needs the vitalising mother-force more than anything else.

The old way of looking at the patriarchal family was, from one point of thought, perfectly right and reasonable as long as every woman was ensured the protection of, and maintenance by, some man. Nor do I think there was any unhappiness or degradation involved to women in this co-operation of the old days, where the man went out to work and the woman stayed to do work at least equally valuable in the home. It was, as a rule, a co-operation of love, and, in any case, it was an equal partnership in work. But what was true once is not true now. We are living in a continually changing development and modification of the old tradition of the relationship of woman and man. It is very needful to impress this factor of constant change on our attention, and to fix it there. To ignore it, and it is too commonly ignored, is to falsify every issue. "The Hithertos," as Mr. Zangwill has aptly termed them, are helpless. Things are so, and we are carried on; and as yet we know not whither, and we are floundering not a little as we seek for a way. The women of one class have been forced into labour by the sharp driving of hunger. Among the women of the other class have arisen a great number who have turned to seek occupation from an entirely different cause; the no less bitter driving of an unstimulating and ineffective existence, a kind of boiling-over of women's energy wasted, causing a revolt of the woman-soul against a life of confused purposes, achieving by accident what is achieved at all. Between the women who have the finest opportunities and the women who have none there is this common kinship—the wastage not so much of woman as of womanhood.

Let us consider for a moment the women who have been forced into the cheating, damning struggle for life. There are, according to the estimate of labour experts, 5,000,000 women industrially employed in England. The important point to consider is that during the last sixty years the women who work are gaining numerically at a greater rate than men are. The average weekly wage paid is seven shillings. Nine-tenths of the sweated work of this country is done by women. I have no wish to give statistics of the wages in particular trades; these are readily accessible to all. Unfortunately the facts do not allow any exaggeration; they are saddening and horrible enough in themselves. The life-blood of women, that should be given to the race, is being stitched into our ready-made clothes; is washed and ironed into our linen; wrought into the laces and embroideries, the feathers and flowers, the sham furs with which we other women bedeck ourselves; it is poured into our adulterated foods; it is pasted on our matches and pin-boxes; stuffed into our furniture and mattresses; and spent on the toys we buy for our children. The china that we use for our foods and the tins in which we cook them are damned with the lead-poison that we offer to women as the reward of labour.

It is these wrongs that the mothers with the fathers of the race have to think out the way to alter. There is no one among us who is guiltless in this matter. Things that are continuously wrong need revolutionising, and not patching up.

What, then, is the real cause of the lowness of remuneration offered to women for work when compared with men? Thousands of women and girls receive wages that are insufficient to support life. They do not die, they live; but how? The answer is plain. Woman possesses a marketable value attached to her personality which man has not got. This enables her to live, if she has children, to feed them, and also not infrequently to support the man, forced out of work by the lowness of the wages she can accept. The woman's sex is a saleable thing. Prostitution is the door of escape freely opened to all women. It is because of the reserve fund thus established that their honest wages suffer. Not all sweated women are prostitutes. Many are legally married, they exist somehow; but the wages of all women are conditioned by this sexual resource. It can be readily seen that this is a survival of the patriarchal idea of the property value of woman. To-day it affords a striking example of the conflict between the old rights of men with the rising power of women. The value of woman is her sexual value; her value as a worker is as yet unrecognised, except as a secondary matter. You may refuse to be convinced of this. Yet the fact remains that our society is so organised that women are more highly paid and better treated as prostitutes than they are as honest workers.

I shall say no more on this question here, as I propose to deal with prostitution more fully in a later chapter. I would, however, point out that what I have said in no way implies an opinion that women should be driven out of the labour market. This is as unfair as that they should be driven into it. It is the conditions of labour that must be changed. I am not even able to accept the opinion that the strength of woman is necessarily less than that of man, only that it is different. It is, in fact, just this difference that is so important. If woman's capacity in work was the same as men's no great advantage could arise from women's entrance into the work of the State. It might well lead to even worse confusion. It is the special qualities that belong to woman that humanity is waiting for. Just as at the dawn of civilisation society was moulded and in great measure built up by women, then probably unconscious of their power and the end it made towards, so, in the future, our society will be carried on and humanised by women, deliberately working for the race, their creative energy having become self-conscious and organised in a final and fruitful period of civilisation.

I want to look a little further into this question of the strength of woman as compared with the strength of man. On the whole it seems right to say that the man is the more muscular type, and stronger in relation to isolated feats and spasmodic efforts. But against this may be placed the relative greater tenacity of life in women. They are longer lived, alike in infancy and in old age; they also show a greater power of resisting death. The difference in the incidence of disease, again, in the two sexes is far from furnishing conclusive evidence as to the greater feebleness of women. Their constitution seems to have staying powers greater than the man's. The theory that women are "natural invalids" cannot be accepted. Every care must be taken to guard against any mis-differentiation of function in the kind of work women are to do, but there is no evidence to prove that healthy work is less beneficial to women than to men. Indeed, all the evidence points in the opposite direction. Even in the matter of muscular power it is difficult to make any absolute statement. The muscular development of women among primitive peoples is well known. Japanese women will coal a vessel with a rapidity unsurpassable by men. The pit-brow women of the Lancashire collieries are said to be of finer physical development than any other class of women workers. I have seen the women of Northern Spain perform feats of strength that seem extraordinary.

It is worth while to wait to consider these Spanish women, who are well known to me. The industrial side of primitive culture has always belonged to women, and in Galicia, the north-west province of Spain, the old custom is still in active practice, owing to the widespread emigration of the men. The farms are worked by women, the ox-carts are driven by women, the seed is sown and reaped by women—indeed, all work is done by women. What is important is that these women have benefited by this enforced engaging in activities which in most countries have been absorbed by men. The fine physical qualities of these workers can scarcely be questioned. I have taken pains to gain all possible information on this subject. Statistics are not available, because in Galicia they have not been kept from this point of view. I find, however, that it is the opinion of many eminent doctors and the most thoughtful men of the province, that this labour does not damage the health or beauty of the women, but the contrary, nor does it prejudice the life and health of their children. As workers they are most conscientious and intelligent, apt to learn, and ready to adopt improvements. From my personal observations I can bear witness that their children are universally well cared for. What impressed me was that these women looked happy. They are full of energy and vigour, even to an advanced age. They are evidently happy, and the standard of beauty among them will compare favourably with the women of any other nation. I once witnessed an interesting episode during a motor-ride in the country. A robust and comely Gallegan woman was riding *a ancas* (pillion fashion) with a young *caballero*, probably her son. The passing of our motor-car frightened the steed, with the result that both riders were unhorsed. Neither was hurt, but it was the woman who pursued the runaway horse. She caught it without assistance and with surprising skill. What happened to the man I cannot say. When I saw him he was standing in the road brushing the dust from his clothes. I presume the woman returned with the horse to fetch him.

Women were the world's primitive carriers. In Galicia I have seen women bearing immense burdens, unloading boats, acting as porters and firemen, and removing household furniture. I saw one woman with a chest of drawers easily poised upon her head, another woman bore a coffin, while another, who was old, carried a small bedstead. A beautiful woman porter in one village carried our heavy luggage, running with it on bare feet, without sign of effort. She was the mother of four children, and her husband was at the late Cuban war. She was upright as a young pine, with the shapeliness that comes from perfect bodily equipoise. I do not wish to judge from trivial incidents, but I saw in the Gallegan women a strength and a beauty that has become rare among women to-day. I recall a conversation with an Englishman I met at La Coruña, of the not uncommon strongly patriotic and censorious type. We were walking together on the quay; he pointed to a group of the Gallegan burden-bearers, who were unloading a vessel, remarking in his indiscriminate British gallantry, "I can't bear to see women doing work that ought to be done by men." "Look at the women!" was the answer I made him.

It is, of course, impossible to compare the industrial conditions of such a country as Spain with England. We may associate the position of women in Galicia with some of the old matriarchal conditions. Women are held in honour. There is a proverb common over all Northern Spain to the effect that he who is unfortunate and needs assistance should "seek his Gallegan mother." Many primitive customs survive, and one of the most interesting is that by which the eldest daughter in some districts takes precedence over the sons in inheritance. In no country does less stigma fall upon a child born out of wedlock. As far back as the fourth century Spanish women insisted on retaining their own names after marriage. We find the Synod of Elvira trying to limit this freedom. The practice is still common for the children to use the name of the mother coupled with that of the father, and in some cases, alone, showing the absence of preference for the paternal descent.[1] The introduction of modern institutions, and especially the empty forms of chivalry, has lowered the position of women. Yet there can be no question that some feature of the ancient mother-right customs have left the imprint on the domestic life of the people. Spanish women have, in certain directions, preserved a freedom and privilege which in England has never been established and is only now being claimed.[2]

How completely all difficulties vanish from the relationship of the sexes where society is more sanely organised—with a wiser understanding of the things that really matter. The question is not: are our women fit for labour? but this: are the conditions of labour in

[1] Velazquez is known to us only by the name of his mother; his father's name was de Silva.

[2] I have taken these passages from the chapter on "The Women of Galicia," in my *Spain Revisited*.

England fit either for women or men? The supply of cheap labour on which the whole fabric of our society is built up is giving way—and it has to go. We have to plan out new and more tolerable conditions for the workers in every sort of employment. But first we have to organise the difficult period of transition from the present disorder.

I will not dwell on this. I would, however, point out that women must be trained and ready to take their part with men in this work of industrial re-organisation. They are even more deeply concerned than men. The conditions of under-payment for woman's work are not restricted to sweated workers; it is the same in skilled work, and in all trades and professions that are open to women. For exactly the same work a lower rate of payment is offered. Female labour is cheap, just as slave labour is cheap, the woman is not considered as belonging to herself.

There is no question here of the real value of woman's labour. The cry of man to woman under the patriarchal system has always been, and still for the most part is, "Your value in our eyes is your sexuality, for your work we care not." But mark this! The penalty of this false adjustment has fallen upon men. For women, in their turn, have come to value men first in their capacity as providers for them, caring as little for the man's sex-value as men care for woman's work-value. From the moment when woman had to place the economic considerations in love first, her faculties of discrimination were no more of service for the selection of the fittest man. Here we may find the explanation of the kind of men girls have been willing to marry—old men, the unfit fathers, the diseased. Yes, any man who was able to do for them what they have not been allowed to do for themselves. And it is the race that suffers and rots; the sins of the mother must be visited on the child.

It is clear, then, there is one remedy and one alone. This separation of values must cease. All women's work must be paid at a rate based on the quality and quantity of the work done; not upon her sexuality. I do not mean by this that there should be any ignoring of woman's special sex-function; to do this, in my opinion, would be fatal. The bearing of fit children is woman's most important work for the State. The economic stress which forces women into unlimited competition with men is, I am certain, harmful. *Women do not do this because they like it, but because they are driven to it.*

The true effort of women, I conceive, should be centred on the freeing of the sexual relationship from the domination of a viciously directed compulsion, and from the hardly less disastrous work-struggle of sex against sex. The emancipated woman must work to gain economic recognition, not necessarily the same as the man's, but her own. It is to the direct interest of men to stop under-cutting by women; but the way to do this is not to force women out of labour, compelling their return to the home—that is impossible—rather it rests in an equal value of service being recognised in both sexes. The fully developed woman of the future is still to be, and first there must be a time of what may well prove to be dangerous experiments. This may be regretted, it cannot be avoided. The finding out of new paths entails some losing of the way.

Women have to find out what work they can best do; what work they want to do, and *what work men want them to do.* I must insist, against all the Feminists, on this factor of men's wishes being equally considered with woman's own. It may not safely be neglected. Woman without man at her side, after obtaining her freedom, will advance even less far than man has advanced with his freedom, without her help. To deny this is to show an absurd misunderstanding of the problem. Neither the male-force alone, nor the female-power is sufficient; no theory of sex-superiority shall prevail. The setting up of women against men, or men against women, to the disadvantage of one or the other, belongs to a day that is over. We must recognise that both the work of women and the work of men are in equal measure essential to satisfy the needs of the State; the force of both sexes must be united to plan and carry out those measures of reform now called for by the new ideals of a civilised humanity. It is only by loosening all the chains of all women and all men alike that the inherent energies of the world's workers can be set free for the eventual ennobling of the race.

There is a fundamental difference in respect to the modes of energy in woman and man. Is it, then, too much to hope for, that in the enlightened civilisation, whose dawn is even now breaking the darkness, we shall recognise and use this difference in work-power and claim from women the kinds of labour they can give best to the State; and reward them for doing this in such a way that their primary social service of child-bearing is in no way impaired? But as yet the day is not. There is an outlook that causes foreboding. The female sex is in a dangerous state of disturbance. New and strange urgencies are at work amongst us, forces for which the word "revolution" is only too faithfully appropriate. Little is being done to allay these forces, much conspires to exasperate them. Whither are they taking us? To this we women have to find an answer.

Other questions force themselves as wisely we wait to think. What will women do when they have gained the voice to control the attitude the State shall assume in the regulation of their work? Will their decisions be founded on wide knowledge, that recognises all the facts and accepts the responsibilities and restrictions that any true freedom for their sex entails, or will it be merely continued revolt, tending to embitter and intensify the struggle of sex against sex? Will their action reveal the wise patience, the sympathy and understanding of the mother, or will it prove to be the illogical, short-sighted, and bewildered behaviour of the spoilt child? No one can answer these questions. Hitherto, it has seemed that women stand in danger of losing sight of great issues in grasping at immediate gains. Goaded by the wrongs they see so plainly waiting to be righted, they are in such a desperate hurry. But "hurry" should not belong to the woman's nature. There is a "grasp" quality of this age that can bring nothing but harm to women. It is a great thing to be a woman, greater, as I believe, than to be a man. For the first time for long ages women are beginning again to understand this and all that it signifies. Women and not men are the responsible sex in the great things of life that really matter. They are that "Stubborn Power of Permanency" of which Goethe speaks. The female not only typifies the race, she is the race. It is man who constitutes the changing, the experimenting, sex. Thus, woman has to be steadier than man, yes, and more self-sacrificing. She may not safely escape from her work as "the giver," and if she does not give in life, she must give in something. We have got to do more than bear men, we have to carry them with us through life—our sons, our lovers, our husbands. We must free them now as well as ourselves, if our freedom is to count for anything. Let us not, then, in any impatience, neglect to pause, to prepare, to be ready, that the pregnancy of the present may bring fair birth when the days are fulfilled. For, after all, what shall it profit women if, in gaining the world, they lose themselves?

II.—*Sexual Differences in Mind and the Artistic Impulse in Women*

"The most secret elements of woman's nature, in association with the magic mystery of her organisation, indicate the existence in her of peculiar and deep-lying creative ideas."—Theodor Mundt.

What is true of the physical differences between women and men is true also of the mental differences. We may readily accept the saturating influence of sex on woman's mind. I mean a deep-lying distinction, not superficial and to be explained away as due to outside things, but based on the essential fact of her womanhood—her capacity for maternity. But the impracticability of making any definite statement as to the exact nature or extent of such mental sexual differentiation is evident. First must be cleared up the difficulty of distinguishing between those differences that are fundamental and constitutional as being directly dependent on the woman character and those that have, or seem to have, arisen through distinction of training or environment, which may be termed evolutionary differences, and are likely to be changed by altered conditions. Even the trained biologist is unable to draw an undisputed line of demarcation between the two kinds of differences, and, even if it were drawn, the conclusion would not help us very much. For with regard to these evolutionary differences that are liable to change many questions have to be considered. Can they safely be modified or disregarded? Do we want them changed? Will the alteration really be of benefit to women? Only such qualities as can be proved clearly to be mis-differentiations—*i. e.* directly harmful—can be contemptuously dismissed. Thus the problem is an extraordinarily difficult one. I can only touch its outer fringe.

It is held that men have greater mental variability and more originality, while women have greater stability and more common sense. In this connection may be noticed the characteristic male restlessness; man is probably more inclined to experiment with his body and his mind and with other people, while woman's constitution and temper is relatively more conservative. It is held that women have the greater integrating intelligence, while men are stronger in differentiation. The thinking power of woman is deductive, that of man inductive; woman's influence on knowledge is thus held to be indirect rather than direct. But women have greater receptive powers, retain impressions better and have more vivid and surer memories; for which reason women are generally more receptive for facts than for laws, more for concrete than for general ideas. The feminine mind shows greater patience, more open-mindedness and tact, and keener insight into character, greater appreciation of subtle details and, consequently, what we call intuition. The masculine mind, on the other hand, tends to a greater height of sudden efforts, of scientific insight and experiment, greater frequency of genius, and this is associated with an unobservant or impatient disregard of details, but a stronger grasp of general ideas.

Now it is easy to make comparisons of this kind, but to accept them as at all final calls for great caution. Let me take, as an instance, the opinion so continuously affirmed, that women are distinguished by good memories, in particular, for details. Now to regard this as necessarily a mental sexual character is entirely to mistake the facts. A tenacious memory for details that are often quite unimportant, belongs to all people of limited impressions and unskilled in thought; it may be noticed in all children. Without a wide experience of life and practice in constructive thinking the mind inevitably falls back on fact-memory. I knew an agricultural labourer who could only tell his age by reckoning the years he had been dung-spreading. Thus a good memory for details may be a sign of an untrained mind. It is an entirely different thing from that acuteness of true memory, which ensures the retention of all experiences that have made an impression on the mind, with a corresponding rejection of what has failed to interest. Thus before anything can be said with regard to this memory power of woman, we have to decide on what it depends—*i. e.* is it really a mental quality of woman, or is it simply dependent on, and brought about by, the circumstances of her life and a limited experience? But to answer this question I shall wait till later in this chapter.

It would be easy to follow a similar train of argument with regard to each of these mental differences of the sexes. Few women have yet entered even the threshold of the mental world of men, and those who have done this stand in the position of strangers or visitors. To be in it, in any true sense, would be to be born into it and to live in it by right; to absorb the same experiences, not consciously and by special effort, but unconsciously as a child absorbs words and learns to speak. Whenever this happens, and not till then, shall we be in a position to compare positively the mental efficiency of woman with men. At present no more can be affirmed than that the differences in woman's mental expression are no greater than they must be in view of the existing differences in their experience. And I am not sure, even if such similarity of mental life were possible, that it would be of benefit to women. Indeed, I am almost sure that it would not. What is needed is an ungrudging recognition of the value of the special feminine qualities. This would do much to lessen the regrettable competition that undoubtedly prevails at present, which is due, it seems to me, to the foolish denial of the value of any save masculine characteristics in our art, as also in our public and professional life.

But leaving this point for the present, there is another question arising from this first that also brings me doubt. Few will deny that women are more instinctive than logical; more intuitive than cerebral. Men find their conclusions by searching for and observing facts, while women, to a great extent, arrive at the same end by instinct. *They know, rather than know how, or why, they know.* Now, too often we hear these qualities of woman treated with contempt. Is this wise? What I doubt is this: when women by education and evolution have been able to learn and to practise the inductive process of reasoning—if, indeed, they do come to do this—will they lose their present faculty of gaining conclusions by instinct? I believe that they must do so to a large extent, and I am not convinced that the gain would at all fully make up for the loss. Looking at human conduct, it is regulated quite as much by instinct as by reason. I think it will be impossible to prevent this being so, and if this is true, woman's instinct may remain of greater service to her than the gaining of a higher reasoning faculty. The true distinction between the psychology of woman and man is as the difference between feeling and thought. Woman thinks through her emotions, man feels through his brain. This is obviously an exaggeration, but it will show what I mean by the different process of thought that, broadly speaking, is usual to the two sexes. Mistakes are, of course, made by both processes, but more often, as I believe, by reasoning than by instinct—this is probably because I am a woman. But it is certain that each sex contributes to the thought-power of the other, each is indispensable to the other, on the mental plane no less than on the physical.

The importance of the above will become obvious when we consider, as we will now do, the artistic impulse in woman. Strange difficulties have been raised on all sides concerning the occurrence of genius among women. It seems to be accepted that in respect of artistic endowment the male sex is unquestionably superior to the female. Havelock Ellis, for instance, in dealing with this question says, " The assertion of Möbius [1] that the art impulse is of the nature of a male secondary sexual character, in the same sense as the beard, cannot be accepted without some qualification, but it may well represent an approximation of the truth." By some it is held that genius is linked with maleness: that it represents an ideal masculinity in the highest form; and from genius the feminine mind must, therefore, be excluded. But in truth it is not easy to credit such assumptions, or to see the strangeness of the difficulties in an exact opposite view, if we understand the significance of those qualities of femaleness which are allowed to women by those who most deny to her the possibility of genius. Such a denial serves only to show the absurd presumption of present knowledge of this kind in its hope to solve a problem so difficult.

Let me try to sift out the facts. And first we must inquire on what grounds this opinion is based. I have already alluded to the general belief in the greater degree of variability in men, which, if established, would on the psychical side involve an accentuated individualism and

[1] *Man and Woman*, p. 377; Möbius, *Stachylogie*, 1901.

hence a greater possibility of genius. This view has been supported by John Hunter, Burdach, Darwin, Havelock Ellis, and others. Ellis, in the chapter on "The Artistic Impulse" in *Man and Woman*, says, "The rarity of women artists of the first rank is largely due to the greater variational tendency of men." Now, this biological fact is certainly of great importance, *if it can be proved*. But can it? It has recently been contested by anthropologists at least as distinguished as those who have given it their support. Manouvrier, Karl Pearson, Frossetto, and especially Guiffrida-Ruggieri have brought forward evidence to prove the fallacy of this belief in the slighter variability and infantile character of woman. Now, it is clearly impossible for me in the space at my command to go into the conclusions brought forward on both sides of this difficult question. What I want to make clear is that this greater variability of man has not been established, and therefore cannot be accepted as a condition of male genius. I am glad to be able to give a statement on this question by Professor Arthur Thomson, which will sufficiently show that my opinion is not put forward wantonly and without due consideration, but that it coincides with the conclusion of one who is an acknowledged leader in the advanced biological study of the sexes.

Professor Thomson writes thus [1]—

"We would guard against the temptation to sum up the contrast of the sexes in epigrams. We regard the woman as relatively

[1] The passage occurs in a lecture by Prof. Thomson and Mrs. Thomson on "The Position of Woman Biologically Considered," and was one of a series delivered in Edinburgh to consider and estimate the recent changes in the position of woman. The addresses have been published in a book entitled *The Position of Woman, Actual and Ideal.*

more anabolic, man as relatively more katabolic, and whether this biological hypothesis is a good one or not, it certainly does no social harm. But when investigators begin to say that woman is more infantile and man more senile, that woman is "undeveloped man" and man is "evolved woman," we get among generalisations not only unscientific but practically dangerous. Not the least dangerous of these generalisations is one of the most familiar, that man is more variable than woman, that the raw materials of evolution make their appearance in greatest abundance in man. There seems to be no secure basis for this generalisation; it seems doubtful whether any generalisation of the kind is feasible. Prof. Karl Pearson has made seventeen groups of measurements of different parts of the body, in eleven groups the female is more variable than the male, and in six the male is more variable than the female. *Moreover the differences of variability are slight, less than those between members of the same race living in different conditions.* Furthermore, an elementary remark may be pardoned. Since inheritance is bi-parental, and since variation means some peculiarity in the inheritance, a greater variability in men, if true, would not mean that men had any credit for varying. The stimulus to variation may have come from the mother as well as the father. *If proved it would only mean that the male constitution gives free play to the expression of variations, which are kept latent in the female constitution.* But what is probably true is that some variations find expression more readily in man and others more readily in woman."

The italics in the passage are mine, for they make abundantly clear the falseness of the old view, and show how much the question needs reopening from the common-sense standpoint of opportunity. I shall, therefore, only restate my opinion that it is impossible to assume a fundamental difference in individuality as existing between woman and man until it can be proved that the same free-play to the expression has been common alike to both sexes.

To me it seems probable that what Samuel Butler insists upon is true, and that the origin of variations must be looked for in the needs and experiences of the creature varying. But let this pass, as it opens up too large and difficult a question to enter upon here. The effects of environment and function must act as a kind of arbiter directing conduct and, in particular, mental expression. It is the very A B C of the question that appropriate training and opportunities of use are essential if any mind is to develop. Supply such mental stimuli to the boy and man, deny them to the girl and woman, and then call "the art impulse of the nature of a male secondary sexual character," because woman has as yet played but a small and secondary part in any of the arts! The source of error is so plain that one can only wonder at the fallacies that have been accepted as truth. Thus, when one finds so just and careful an investigator as Havelock Ellis saying, "It is unthinkable that a woman should have discovered the Copernician system!" it can but be regarded as an example of that sex-bias which marks so strikingly men's statements on this subject of mental sex-differences. We may well ask, Why unthinkable? As answer I will give the finely just acknowledgment of Iwan Bloch on this very question. He refers to this statement of Havelock Ellis, and then says, "I need merely call to mind the widely known physical discoveries of Madame Curie, whose thoroughly independent work qualified her to succeed her husband as professor at the Sorbonne. We cannot, therefore, exclude the possibility that in the sphere of the natural sciences notable discoveries and inventions may be made in the future in consequence of the independent work of women."[1] To take another instance. We find the fact

[1] *Sexual Life of Our Times*, p. 74.

that so far women have gained very small distinction in music, contrasted with the great number of girls who are trained to play on musical instruments. But this is surely to show a complete misunderstanding of the question. It is like saying that the best preparation for a painter to know the colours reflected on water by a cloudy or sunny sky would be a course of optics. Music is at once the most imaginative and the most severely abstract of the arts, and the absence of women from music must be referred to deeper causes, which yet, it seems to me, are not far to seek.

Mind, I make no claim for women. I acknowledge fully that in all the arts, except in acting and in dancing, woman's achievement has been infinitely less than man's. There have been a few great women poets—notably a Sappho, many good writers of fiction, and some capable painters. But to bring forward these particular women and to try either to exaggerate or belittle their importance can serve nothing. This search for ability among women is absurd. It already exists widely, though unused or directed into channels of waste. Of this I am convinced. The thing that has been rare is opportunity. The fact that some few women have struggled up out of obscurity does not so much show that they possessed a special masculine superiority as that they have been less inextricably bound down than others by the conventional bonds of a man-ruled society. I believe that this could be proved in the case of every woman who has attained to fame. And there is another point. The women who have succeeded in bursting these bonds have, in most cases, done so at such great cost of energy and fighting, that their work is rendered crude and often valueless.

Self-assertion can never be the best preparation for achievement. All this narrows the mental horizon and tends to make the results gained superficial and unenduring. We have here the explanation of much that has been, and still is, futile in women's efforts.

The face of the world, however, is changing for women. It may be that the future will reveal creative ability in them as yet unsuspected. It is not safe to prophesy, and no one can say, as yet, just in what direction women will develop. It may prove that their special qualities will not find expression in the realm of imagination, but will be turned to diplomacy and to administration and financial work. I simply affirm that what women can or cannot do is as yet unproved. Throughout the ages of patriarchal faith one ideal of womanhood has been impressed upon the world, which is only now being shaken —the ideal of self-repression and submission to the will of man, of society, and of God. Women's minds have reflected only the minds of men. I think that much of the failure of women's work arises from the arrogance of men, who have always preferred the flattering image of woman in their own minds to woman herself. Woman has had to accept this. She could only realise herself through man, not with man, while he has been able to realise himself, either with her help or without her.

There is a wide difference between the mental and social attitudes of men and women. Men have been responsible to society at large for their work and conduct, woman's outlook has been much narrower; she has been responsible to men, and has only touched outside life through them. In this way women have developed on wrong lines. It is significant, for instance, how many women have written books under men's names. Women's work and conduct has been largely restricted by this adjustment to men, with the result that not only their mental capacity and work-power has suffered, but their attention has been fixed, for the most part, to the enhancing of the attractiveness of their persons as an aid to hold men to their service. The feminine mind and interests have been set so strongly towards personal display that they will not easily be diverted. The clothes-peg woman is familiar to all: she gratifies any whim, well knowing that it is her male protector who will have to pay, not she. She will, on occasions, use her children for such base ends. She knows the game is in her hand. Even if the man resists her for a time, she understands how easily she can break down his objections by a seductive display of silk stockings! The character of woman as the inherent coquette is very deeply rooted. It is only a little more baneful to the freedom of the sexes than that opposite pernicious side of woman as a sort of angel-child, which we all know to be such a preposterous pretence.

Nor do I think that the change from these conditions can, or will, be easy. Women may, and do, protest against the triviality of their lives, but emotional interests are more immediate than intellectual ones. Human nature does not drift into intellectual pursuits voluntarily, rather it is forced into them in connection with urgency and practical activities. It is much easier to be kept, dressed, and petted, than to work. Women have not participated in the mental activities of men because it has not been necessary for them; to do this has been, indeed, a hindrance to their success. The contrast between the sexes in this respect has been well compared by Thomas [1] to the relation of the amateur and the professional in games. "Women may be desperately interested and work to the limit of endurance at times; but, like the amateur, they enter into the work late, and have not had a lifetime of practice. . . . No one will contend that the amateur has a nervous organisation less fitted to the game than the professional; it is admitted that the difference lies in the constant practice." It is only in the case of woman that the obvious conclusion is passed over for assumptions that cannot be proved.

The revolt against repression has taken amongst many women another form of abandonment to lives of sexual preoccupation and intrigue. Scan the history of woman as she is presented in our literature and drama, and you will find one expression of her character, one idea alone of her sphere. It is a point of such interest that I would like to linger upon it. Wherever woman enters she is a disturbing influence; she is the centre of emotional action, it is true, but with no recognised position in life outside of her sex; around her rage seas of stormy passions, which sometimes she calms, sometimes lashes into angrier foam. In a sense it may be said that she has scarcely an individual existence; it is solely in her relation to man that her nature is considered. If she works, or practises one of the arts, she does this only until marriage.

[1] *Sex and Society*, pp. 306, 307.

It does not seem to be conceived as possible that she can follow work, as the artist must, for herself. It is curious how far we have been misled by that giving-power of woman, which, in part, is right and natural to her, but also, in much greater part, has been harmfully forced upon her. The creator's need to find expression is, I am certain, at least as strongly rooted in woman as in man, but no plant can attain to growth unless fitting nourishment is given to it. To ignore this leads very directly to deception. Thus we find Mr. Wells, usually so true in his insight, keeps up an old pretence and affirms in his latest novel, *Marriage*—

> "They don't care for art or philosophy, or literature or anything except the things that touch them directly. And the work——? It's nothing to them. No woman ever painted for the love of painting, sang for the sounds she made, or philosophised for the sake of wisdom as men do."

So it is always. Without question it has been taken for granted by those who have depicted woman that her sole occupation is an emotional one; here alone is she justified in literature, as in life.

The fully complete woman of the future is still to be created; assuredly she is not to be found among the women who have been portrayed so widely for us by recent writers. These are portraits arising out of the present confusion; as such they are interesting, but they are quite unreal in their relation to life. They show us women, and men too, in revolt. Often these women are really nothing more than feminist stump-orators preaching the doctrine of an unconsidered individualism · "Free Motherhood," "Free Love"—free anything, in fact. These portraits are far removed, indeed, from the perfected woman that is to be. We want something much more than this—woman with all sides of her nature adequately worked upon and fully developed.

Now, to look for a moment at the other side of the question. Woman has been the cause of emotion in men, the fine instrument by which the poet has sung and the musician played his exquisite music; the sculptor, the painter, the writer, all have drawn their inspiration from her. Have men, then, any right to pride themselves to such a degree on their achievement in the arts? Could they without woman have advanced anything like so far? And this becomes abundantly evident if we look a little deeper and back to the beginning of the arts. "Not," writes Karl Bücher,[1] "upon the steep summits of society did poetry originate, it sprang rather from the depths of the pure, strong soul of the people. Women have striven to produce it, and as civilised man owes to woman's work much the best of his possessions, so also are her thoughts interwoven in the spiritual treasure handed down from generation to generation."

A glance back at the beginnings of human civilisation show that women were equal, if not superior, to men in productive poetic activity. To a large extent men first learned from women the elements of the various handicrafts. I have already referred to this fact in the historical section, where we see the reasons whereby women lost their early control over the industrial arts. I wish to refer to a point of special importance now, which I find is brought forward, in this connection, by Iwan

[1] Quoted by Bloch, *Sexual Life of Our Times*, p. 80.

Bloch.[1] In the start of the industrial occupations, in sowing and thrashing and grinding the grain, in baking bread, in the preparation of food and drinks, of wine and beer, in the making of pots and baskets, and in spinning, the women worked together; and, as is common still among primitive peoples, these occupations were largely carried on in a rhythmical manner. From this co-operation of the women it resulted that they were the first creators of poetry and music. The men, on the other hand, hunted singly in the forests. The birth of their poetic activity followed only after they had monopolised the labours of material production. Even to-day among many races the influence of woman's poetry can be followed for a long way into the literary period. I have myself witnessed something similar to this among the peasants in the rural districts of Spain. I have heard women in the evenings relate to one another and to their children the rich legends of their land, carrying on the old traditions that have come down from generation to generation, and thus creating among themselves a communion of heroes. Then, again, these Spanish women seem never to cease from singing as they carry on their many and heavy labours. The women sing far more frequently than the men. Music is to them an instinctive means of expression; they do not learn it, it belongs to them, like dancing belongs to the natural child. And these folk songs, where the words are often improvised by the singer, seem to give utterance to natural out-door things—a symbol of the people's life, of its action, its work, very strong in its appeal, which blends so strangely

[1] *Sexual Life of Our Times*, pp. 80, 81.

joy with sadness. A special quality that often surprised me in these songs was the way in which the people translate and use the music of other countries. I have heard popular English tunes sung by the women as they work, which have ceased to be common in their sentiment and become full of a tenderness into which passion has fallen; even slangy music-hall tunes take a new character, a lively brilliance that no longer is vulgar. This music is the true singing of the people, and if you would feel all the beauty of its appeal you must be in touch with the spirit that cries in it, with work, and passion, and life.

It may seem that all this has taken us rather far away from our inquiry into the strength of the artistic impulse in women. The way, however, is largely cleared. We have proved that there is, at least, a possible mistake in the opinion that those experiments in creative expression, which we call variations, are necessarily inherent in the male, rather than in the female. Speaking biologically, we may regard woman, in common with man, as a potentially creative agent with a striving will, and thus able to change under the stimulus of appropriate opportunity.

Now, to look at the question for a moment in a different light—in relation to the special qualities that are facts of actual experience in woman's character as it is to-day. It is proved—if scientific determination of such qualities were necessary—that women are more sensitive to suggestion and receptive of outward influences; that they have keener affectability, and thus tend to be more emotional and, within certain limits, more imaginative than men. They react to both physical and psychical stimuli more readily, and it would seem that their brain action is more rapid. Experimental tests have shown that in respect of quickness of comprehension and intellectual mobility women are distinctly superior to men.

It is, of course, an open question how far all this is due to Nature and how far merely to education. Must we regard this emotional endowment of woman as permanent or alterable? Havelock Ellis has detected a decline in the emotivity of modern women under the influence of new conditions, especially as the result of the more healthy life and out-door games among girls. But he does not believe that any present or future change in activities can lead to a complete abolition of the emotional differences between the sexes. These qualities are correlated with the essential physical function of women, and are probably in part of similar deep origin, and are therefore not likely to change. Nietzsche, as is well known, denies this emotional capacity of women, and considers them much more remarkable for their intelligence than for their sensitiveness and feeling. I believe, however, the view of Havelock Ellis to be the right one. Throughout Nature it would seem to be indispensable that the mother should have finer and quicker sensibility than the father. The female selects the male that she may use him for the race. Women, for the reasons we have seen, have, as I believe, lost much of the fineness of their selective sensitiveness. But whether this greater emotional power in women has been weakened or not, it is—as all nature proves to us—an actual quality of the female, and in it we have, therefore, a positive ground to start from in estimating the potential artistic endowment of women.

Let us accept, then, this sensitiveness both physical and psychical, as at least the natural character of femaleness. How does it place women in her relation to the arts?

Consider what are the qualities essential to success in any one of the arts. Are not the most essential of these a quick reception of impressions, added to an acute memory for all that has been experienced? The poet and the writer can reach deeper into the nature of others, the architect, the sculptor, the painter can see more clearly, the musician hear more finely; and so it is with all the arts. Does not the genius, or even the man of talent, take his place as one who understands incomparably more than others; or, to express it a little differently, the genius is he who is conscious of most and of that most acutely. And what is it that enables him to do this, if it is not a greater sensitiveness and a finer response to every outward suggestion? It would seem, then, that genius must possess the emotional qualities that are the natural endowment of woman; while woman herself is to be excluded from genius. A conclusion that is plainly absurd.

The further we follow this the more striking the likeness between the qualities of genius and the high, nervous affectability of woman becomes. The intuition of woman is really direct vision and may mean only a quicker power of reasoning. Exactly the same quality must be acknowledged as distinguishing the genius. He, too, *knows, rather than reasons how he knows.*

Take, again, the alleged superiority of the feminine mind in matter of memory. There is the same difference between the memory of the ordinary man and the man of genius. Mental recognition is proportional to the intensity of consciousness. Because the life of the genius is more continuously emotional—nearer, in fact, in its nature to the woman's—he is more ready to receive impressions and to keep them. And here we may note the incitement towards autobiography common to gifted men, which would seem to arise from the same psychological condition which forces women so strongly to self-revelations. So also with all the mental qualities we shall find, I believe, the same connection between the special characters of woman and those of genius. Woman's mental mobility, her tendency towards nervous outbursts, with a corresponding irritability and greater susceptibility to fatigue, except under the support of excitement, as also in the resulting qualities of her power of ready adaptation to changes of habits and response to new influences, her tact, her keener insight into character, her quickness in pity, her impulsiveness, her finer discrimination, her innate sense of symmetry or fitness—each of these qualities may be said to accord also with the character of genius, but no one among them is common to the ordinary man.

Even in so obvious a point as facial expression the same relation may be traced. It is a matter of constant observation that women's faces are more expressive than men's, showing greater mobility, through the instinctive response to suggestions from without and within. A similar mobility will be readily noted in the appearance of almost all men of special giftedness. The faces of such men rarely exhibit the stereotyped expressions that characterise most male countenances. No one mood leaves a permanent imprint on the features, for through the amplitude of feeling a new side of the mind is continuously revealed. Faces with an unchanging expression belong really to people low in artistic endowment.

Of some significance, again, is the variability in the mental power of genius, leading to what may be called "a periodicity in production." Goethe has spoken somewhere of "the recurrence of puberty" in the artist. This idea may perhaps, without too much straining, be compared with the functional periodicity of woman. The periods in the life of a creative artist often assume the character of a crisis—a kind of climax of vital energy. Sterile years precede productive periods, to be followed by more barren years. The circle of activity is not broken, it is but interrupted; the years of apparent sterility really leading up to, and preparing for, the creative periods. I may point out here a thought in passing in connection with the child-bearing functions of women. This is brought forward by many as the most serious objection to women being able to attain success in any of the arts. The objection is not really sound. No creative work can be carried on without interruptions. The important part in all such work is not to be uninterrupted, but to be able to begin again. The new experiences gained give new power; a fresh and wider view. And woman has in her supreme function of motherhood—an experience denied to men; this should give her greater, and not less, creative capacity. What is really needed is the freedom, the training and the desire that shall direct expression, so that woman may enrich the arts with her own special experience.

It is useless to argue that woman's past record in the arts holds out no such promise. We know really very little about woman's genius. One thing is, however, certain: the only possible test of it is trial, for without this there is no basis of judgment, no means of deciding whether there be genius or no. If, as I believe, woman's creative capacity arises out of, and is essentially connected with, her sexual functions, how can it have been possible to employ such power in the arts in a society where the natural use of her sex has been restricted and not allowed a free expression?—a society, moreover, in which the pregnant woman has been regarded as an object of shame or ridicule.

To look at this question of woman's achievement in the arts in the old way is no longer possible. We have proved that the natural emotional endowment of woman is rich and varied. But there are two things necessary for achievement: inherent aptitude and opportunity—that is, a favourable environment for expression, in which power may be directed into useful channels and saved from wastefully expending itself. To deny genius to women when the opportunity for its development has been absent is obviously unjust. The influence of education, and the stronger driving of habit and social opinion, must be taken into the account. Women have up till now been without two essential qualities necessary for creating—subjectivity and initiative. In practice they have not been able, or only very rarely, to get beyond imitation. Through the circumstances of their lives they have lacked the courage and conviction, even if opportunity had arisen, necessary for creative work. For the highest achievement in the arts they have missed the concentration, the severe devotion to work, the control of thought and complete self-restraint, which can come only from discipline, from long training, and freedom. Yet I make the claim that woman, from her constitutional femininity, is a compound of all those qualities that genius demands. The channels of woman's energy have been everywhere choked. No great creative art has ever been produced by a subjugated class. Art comes with freedom, with the strong incentive of the communal spirit, and with the sense of power. For centuries woman has been artificially individualised. Her special function of motherhood has remained unacknowledged as a communal work. Her emotional and mental capacities have been turned back upon herself and her immediate belongings, with the result that her social usefulness has been suppressed or thwarted. The emotional feelings of woman are ever pressing, and only need to be brought into stricter command in order to achieve. What women will accomplish no man can say.

One word more. Let us look in this new direction, the direction of the future, because it is there that this possible future entrance of women into the arts becomes important. We stand in the first rush of a new movement. It is the day of experiments. The extraordinary enthusiasm now sweeping through womanhood reveals behind its immediate fevered expression a great power of emotional and spiritual initiative. Wide and radically sweeping are the changes in woman's social outlook.

So much stronger is the promise of a vital force, when they are free to enter and to work in the various departments of the arts. It is the commonest error to think of art as if it stood outside the other activities of life. Under the cloak of art much self-amusement and vulgar self-display tries to justify itself, and many mercenary interests are concerned in stinting its vitality. All living and valuable art is really communal. It must fit into its right place with all phases of human activities, and to do this it must have somewhere in it the social citizen spirit.

You see how women stand in this matter. The social ideal is becoming a very near ideal to women. And this quickening in her of the citizen spirit may well come to revive our art to a more true and social service. This is no idle fancy. Throughout the ages of patriarchal faith women have been confined in the home, so that an understanding of the needs of the home is in their blood. May not the old ideals remain for service and find expression in the new work? Much that has passed with us as art has to be swept away. Let women bring this sense of home into our civic life, and surely it will be reflected in the arts. It is the sense of fitness to the common use and needs of the larger family of the State that has been almost wholly eliminated from our architecture, our statues, our paintings, our music, and much of our literature. The arts have withered and lost their vitality in our narrow and blighting commercial society.

I do not want to weary the reader with what can only be suggestions. I am certain, however, that this vital factor of the home cannot safely be excluded from the

State. Consider any one of the old mediæval towns, with its buildings, its cathedral, its churches, its halls, its homes—all that it contains a splendid witness to the civic life of its people. Contrast this with what we have been willing to accept as art in our industrial towns. In the old days the city was in a very literal sense the home of its citizens, now it is merely a centre of trade. Is it unfair to connect this with the subjection of women and the rush of male activities, that has destroyed the need of beauty and fitness which once was the possession of all? For art you must have human qualities, and you must have emotion. The time has come when we are yielding to the new forces, that yet are old. This age will leave its own track behind it, and those, who are beating out the way now, must start on the right path—freeing for the service of the future all the intellectual and emotional forces of women as well as men.

To think boldly, untrammelled by conventions from the past, to search sedulously for the truth within themselves and follow it fearlessly, this should be the faith of all those women who love art. Let them have the courage of their own deep emotions. Let them look forward into the future, instead of clinging timorously to the stone wall of their past imitation of men. Then, indeed, woman may be freed—able to give expression to those creative ideas which are wrapped up with the elements of her nature. But women must beware of sham emotion and lachrymose sentimentality. It is her own feelings she must voice, not the feelings that have been supposed to belong to her. Then, indeed, the work of women will begin to count. The two things most peculiar to woman—her pursuing-love of man and her need of a child, will find their expression in women's art.

It is an appalling commentary on the condition of our thoughts on this subject that the pregnant woman was but recently considered unfit to be represented in the statues placed on one of our public buildings. How convincingly this speaks to women, "Be not ashamed of anything, but to be ashamed."

III.—*The Affectability of Woman—Its Connection with the Religious Impulse*

"Religion shares with the sexual impulse the unceasing yearning, the sentiment of everlastingness, the mystic absorption into the depths of life, the longing for the coalescence of individualities in an eternally blessed union, free from earthly fetters."—IWAN BLOCH.

Now, this affectability, that we have found to be a characteristic feminine feature, leads us directly to an inquiry into the part religion has played in the lives of women, and to the wider consideration of the religious impulse in general, and its close connection with the sexual instinct. I had intended to treat this subject in some detail, especially in relation to religious hypnotic phenomena, a matter of very deep significance in estimating woman's character. I should have liked, too, to have traced the influence of the early and late Christian teaching upon woman's mind, to have examined her position in the social and domestic relationship, and then to have contrasted this with the almost complete liberty and distinction enjoyed by women in Pagan culture. But the field opened up by these inquiries is too wide. The previous sections of this chapter have grown to such length that all that is possible to me now, if I am to have space for the matters I want still to investigate, are a few scattered remarks and suggestions which seem to me to throw some light on this important side of woman's life.

No one will question woman's aptitude for religion, whatever the opinion held as to what the organic basis of that aptitude may be. If we accept that woman is more sensitive to suggestion, more emotional, and more imaginative in her nature, it is plain why religion affects her more deeply than men. The extraordinary way in which woman can be influenced by religious suggestion is similar in its nature to that saturation of her innermost thoughts with love, which is due in part, as I believe, to the special qualities of her sex-functions, but also, in part, to the over-emphasised sexuality produced in her by an artificial existence. Women have accepted religious beliefs as they have accepted man's valuation of temporal things, even although these may be utterly at variance with their nature and their desires.

It has been said that the disposition of woman makes her peculiarly conservative and uncritical of religious beliefs. Others suggest that there is a "specific religious sense" in women related with a higher standard of character. This I do not believe: it is part of the fiction of woman's superior morality. I think in most women is hidden an immense appetite for life, an immense capacity for expenditure of force. She does not often dare to listen to these deeps within her soul; yet the insurgent voices fill her. There is in the life of most women something wanting, some general idea, some aim to hold life together. The effort of woman—often unconscious, but always present—to realise herself in love has forced her to practise duplicity and to accept dependence. And this sense of dependence in her on a protector, not always forthcoming, and, even when present, not always able to protect, has sent her in search of something outside and beyond the known and fallible, and has prepared her to accept with eagerness any professed revelation of the infallible unknown.

We have seen again and again in the course of our inquiry how deep and natural the sex impulse is in woman, and this, combined with the much greater complexity of her sexual life, renders her position peculiarly liable to be affected disastrously by any failure of love. It must be recognised that unbounded piety is often no more than a sex symptom, proceeding from deprivation or from satiety of love, as also from love's failure in loveless marriage. It seems to me that this connection of the religious impulse with sexuality is a very important thing for women to understand. In our achievement of facing the truth in the place of evasions about fundamental things, lies the path, I believe along which woman can escape, if ever she is to escape, from the confusion of purposes that distract her at present.

The intimate association between religious ideas and feelings and the sexual life is abundantly proved by the history of all peoples. We first meet it in the widespread early practice of religious prostitution, which has aptly been called "lust sacrifice." It is even more manifest in the ancient religious erotic festivals. Of these we have examples in the festivals of Isis in Egypt, in the Dionysian and Eleusinian festivals of the Hellenes, in the Roman Bacchanalia and festival of Flora, and among the Jews in the feast of Baal-peor. In these festivals the frenzy of religious mysticism merges with the wildest sexual licence. Sexual mysticism found its way also into Christianity, a fact to which the lives of the saints furnish an illuminating witness. And down to the present day we may notice its manifestations in the most diverse sects during any period of religious revival. We still meet with sexual excesses under the shadow of faith, as, for instance, occurred in the late revival in Wales.

Havelock Ellis has laid stress on the leading significance of religious sexual perceptions, and their special importance on the emotional feminine character. This subject is so deeply connected with women that I shall, I hope, be pardoned if I pause for a moment to relate a personal experience which may help to make this truth more clear.

In my girlhood I was strongly drawn to religion, partly through training and example, but more, as I now know, by the affectability of my strongly feminine temperament. My religious enthusiasm was so intense that often I was in a condition which must have been closely connected with erotic religious ecstasy. Salvation was the essential fact of my life; seeking for it brought me the excitement I unconsciously craved of conflicts and fulfilled desires. I sought for God as the passionate woman seeks her lover. I recall a period—I was approaching womanhood—during which I prayed continuously and earnestly that it might be granted to me, as to the saints of old, to see God and the Risen Christ. For long I received no answer. This did not weaken my faith, but the great trouble of my mind became for long a consciousness of my own unworthiness. I began an absurd and childish system of self-punishments, and what I thought would lead to purification. Then there came a night—it was summer and I was looking from my window out at the beautiful evening sky—when my prayer was answered. I seemed, in very truth, to see God. From that time, and for long, I lived in extraordinary happiness. I am sure that I must have become hysterical. I felt that I was set apart by God; I conceived the idea of founding a new religious sect. That I made no attempt to do this was due to circumstances, which forced me into active work to gain my own living. Religion continued very largely in my life, but I was too healthily occupied to be favoured with any more visions. But the essential point in all this is its close connection with my sexual development. So far I had never been in love. I believe that the natural sex desires awakened consciously in me much later than is common. My need for religion lasted until my sex needs were fully satisfied, then, little by little, it faded. I want to state the truth. I did not then trace, nor should I have understood, this connection. The knowledge came to me long years afterwards; how it does not matter, but I am certain that in me the religious impulse and the sex impulse are one.

Love has in it much of the same supernatural element as religion. Both the sex-act and the act of finding salvation come into intimate association with woman's need of dependence; hence arises the remarkable relation between the two, and that easy transition of sexual emotion into religious emotion which is manifest in so many women. In both cases the surrender, the renunciation of personal will, is an experience fraught with passionate pleasure. "Love," as H. G. Wells has said, "is the individualised correlation of salvation, like that it is a synthetic consequence of conflict and confusions." It is true that few women render love the compliment of taking it seriously. To many it is merely this: a little amusement, clothes, a home, money to buy new toys; some mild pleasure, a little chagrin, a little weariness, and then the end. They do not realise or ever desire love in its full joy of personal surrender. So, too, many women never, save in some time of personal bewilderment, desire or seek salvation. But such aimlessness brings its own emptiness, and women strain and seek towards the god-head. For the truth remains, woman's need of love is greater than man's need, and for this reason, where love fails her, her desire for salvation is deeper than man's desire. And here again, and once again, we see the difference between the sexes. The woman pays the higher price for her implicit, unquestioning, and unconscious obedience to Nature. And society has made the payment still heavier. Let us for this last pity women! The dice they have had to throw in the game of life is their sex, and they have only been allowed one throw, and when they have thrown wastefully—yes, it is here that religion has entered into the game. It may almost be said to measure the failures and false boundaries in women's loves. The songs of love and the songs of faith are alike; and women act worship as also they are often driven to act love. The woman who knows her own heart must know that this is true. And one cannot wish to see the opium of religion taken from women until the game is made a fairer one for them to play.

There is another point to consider.

Many great thinkers have striven against this profound and primitive connection between the bodily and spiritual impulses, which has seemed to them an intrusion of evil, impairing their pure spirituality by the sexual life. They have thus recommended and followed asceticism in order to arrive at a heightened spirituality. The error here is obvious. The spiritual activities cannot be divided from the physical; as well cut the flower off from its roots, and then expect to gather the fruit. This is why sex-denial and sex-excesses so often go together. Hence the undeniable unchastity of the mediæval cloisters. Nor need the manifestations of sex be physical. Erotic imagination and voluptuous revelations are expressions of sex-passion. The monstrous sexual visions of the saints reflect in a typical manner the incredible violence of the sexual perception of ascetics.

We observe it, then, as a fact of wide experience that the ascetic life is rooted really in the functional impulses; and further, that it is only through sexual perception that the spiritual and imaginative can be grasped and reached. What the ascetic has done is to fear overmuch. It must not be overlooked that this continual battle with the primary force of life is necessarily futile in accomplishing its own aim. For the woman or man who, for the religious or any other ideal, wishes to overcome the sex-needs must keep the subject always before her, or his, consciousness. Thus it comes about that the ascetic is always more occupied with sex than the normal individual. It seems to me that this is a truth few women have learnt to face.

I am not for a moment denying that the potential energy of the sexual impulse may be transformed with benefit into productive spiritual activities, finding its vent in religion, as also in poetry, in art, and in all creative work. Plato must have had this in his mind when he speaks of "thought as a sublimated sexual impulse." Schopenhauer, and many other thinkers, lay stress on the connection between the work of productive genius and the modification of the sexual impulse. This may be illustrated—if examples are needed in proof—by the power that has been exercised so conspicuously by women throughout the world in religious movements. Two of the greater festivals of the Catholic Church, for instance, owe their origin to the illumination of women; the mystic writings of Santa Teresa of Avila give classic expression to the highest powers of the spirit. Take again the part played by women as religious leaders of the convents in the early Middle Ages. In them women of spirit and capacity found a wide and satisfying career, many of them showing great administrative ability and a quite remarkable power for government. In recent times mention may be made of the Theosophists, the most important modern religious movement established in this country and led by women; and of Christian

Science, which, under the able guidance of Mrs. Eddy, has sprung up and flourished. It is instructive to note that both these religions are connected with, and largely established on, magical faith and esoteric doctrines and practices. In almost all the religions founded by women we may trace a similar relation with hypnotic phenomena which must be regarded as closely dependent on sexual sources. The proof is wider even than these particular instances. It is without doubt the transformation of suppressed sexual instincts that has made women the chief supporters of all religions.

It may be said that the religious impulse has to a large extent lost its hold upon women. This is true. A new age must expect to see a new departure. As women take active participation in the work of the world their sense of dependence and need for protection will diminish, and we may look for a corresponding decrease in that display of excessive religious emotion that dependence has fostered. But the needs of woman can never be satisfied alone with work. The natural desires remain imperative; deny these, and there will be left only the barren tree robbed of its fruits. Sexuality first breathes into woman's spiritual being warm and blooming life.

The religious ascetic is not common among us to-day. Yet the old seeking for something is there. The impulse towards asceticism has, I think, rather changed its form than passed from women. The place of the female saint is being taken by the social ascetic. Desire is not now set to gain salvation, but is turned towards a heightened intellectual individuation, showing itself in nervous mental activity. No one can have failed to note the immense egoism of the modern woman. Women are still in fear of life and love. They have been made ascetics through the long exercise of restraint upon their explosively emotional temperament. They have restrained their natures to remain *pure*. This false ideal of chastity was in the first place forced upon them, but by long habit it has been accentuated and has been backed up by woman's own blindness and fear. Thus to-day, in their new-found freedom, women are seeking to bind men up in the same bonds of denial which have restrained them. In the past they have over-readily imbibed the doctrine of a different standard of purity for the sexes, now they are in revolt—indeed, they are only just emerging from a period of bitterness in relation to this matter. Men made women into puritans, and women are arising in the strength of their faith to enforce puritanism on men. Is this malice or is it revenge? In any case it is foolishness. Bound up as the sexual impulse is with the entire psychic emotional being, there would be left behind without it only the wilderness of a cold abstraction. The Christian belief in souls and bodies separate, and souls imprisoned in vile clay, has wrought terrible havoc to women. I believe the two—soul and body—are one and indivisible. Women have yet this lesson to learn: the capacity for sense-experience is the sap of life. The power to feel passion is in direct ratio to the strength of the individual's hold upon life; and may be said to mark the height of his, or her, attainment in the scale of being. It is only another out of many indications of the strength of sexual emotion in women that so many of them are afraid of the beauty and the natural joys of love.

There is one thing more I would wish to point out in closing this very insufficient survey of an exceedingly complicated and difficult subject. To me it seems that here, in this finer understanding of love, we open the door to the only remedy that will wipe out the hateful fear of women, which has wrought such havoc in the relationship between the sexes. Woman, restrained to purity, has of necessity fallen often into impurity. And men, knowing this better than woman herself, have feared her, though they have failed in any true understanding of the cause. Let me give you the estimate of woman which Maupassant, in *Moonlight*, has placed in the mouth of a priest. It is the most illuminating passage in one of the most exquisite of his stories—

> "He hated woman, hated her unconsciously and instinctively despised her. He often repeated to himself the words of Christ: 'Woman, what have I to do with thee?' And he would add, 'It seems as if God Himself felt discontented with that particular creation.' For him was that child of whom the poet speaks, impure, through and through impure. She was the temptress who had led away the first man, and still continued her work of perdition; a frail creature but dangerous, mysteriously disturbing. And even more than their sinful bodies he hated their loving souls. . . . God, in his opinion, had created woman solely to tempt man, to put him to the proof."

One lesson women and men have to learn: so easy to be put into words, so difficult to carry out by deeds. To get good from each other the sexes must give love the one to the other. The human heart in loneliness eats out itself, causes its own emptiness, creates its own terrors. Nature gives lavishly, wantonly, and woman is nearer to Nature than man is, therefore she must give the more freely, the more generously. There can be no such thing as the goodness of one-half of life without the goodness of the other half. Love between woman and man is mutual; is continual giving. Not by storing up for the good of one sex or in waste for the pleasure of the other, but by free bestowing is salvation. Wherefore, not in the enforced chastity of woman, but in her love, will man gain his new redemption.

CONTENTS OF CHAPTER X

THE SOCIAL FORMS OF THE SEXUAL RELATIONSHIP

I.—*Marriage*

The difficulty of the problem of marriage—Facts to be considered—Marriage and the family among the animals—Among primitive peoples—Progress from lower to higher forms of the sexual association—An examination of the purpose of marriage—The fear of hasty reforms—Practical morality—Marriage an institution older than mankind—The practical moral ends of marriage—The racial and individual factors—No real antagonism between the two—What is good for the individual must react also for the benefit of the race—Various systems of marriage—Monogamy the form that has prevailed—The higher law of the true marriage—Conventional monogamic marriage—Its failure in practical morality—Co-existence with polygamy and prostitution—Chief grounds for the reform of marriage—An indictment by Mr. Wells—Our marriage system based upon the rights of property—This not necessarily evil—The Egyptian marriage contracts—The Roman marriage—The influence of Christianity—Asceticism and the glorification of virginity—Confusions and absurdities—The failure of our sexual morality—Mammon marriages—Sins against the race—Two examples from my own experience—The iniquity of our bastardy laws—The waste of love—Free-love—Its failure as a practical solution—The reform of marriage—The tendency to place the form of the sexual relationship above the facts of love—The dependence of the consciousness of duty upon freedom—The sexual responsibility of women.

II.—*Divorce*

Traditional morality—Practical conditions of divorce—The moral code—This must be modified to meet new conditions—The enforced continuance of an unreal marriage—This the grossest form of immorality—The barbarism of our divorce laws—The action of the Church and State—Confusion and absurdities—Divorce relief from misfortune, not a crime—Personal responsibility in marriage—A recognition of the equality of the mother with the father—Sanction by the State of free divorce—The example of Egypt and Babylon—The Roman divorce by consent—The condemnation of free divorce not the outcome of true morality—The immorality of indissoluble marriage—Loyalty and duty in love—The claims of the child—One advantage of free divorce—Adoption of children under the State—Growing disinclination against coercive marriage—The waste to the race—Our responsibility to the future.

III.—*Prostitution*

The dependence of prostitution upon marriage—The extent and difficulties of the problem involved—Prostitution essentially a woman's question—Women's past attitude towards it—The diffusion of disease by means of prostitution—Apathy and ignorance of women—This changing—What action will women take in the future?—Grounds for fear—The White Slave Bill—Its absurd futility—The opinion of Bernard Shaw—Poverty as a cause of prostitution—This not the only factor—The real evil lies deeper—The economic reformer — The moral crusade — Men's passions — Seduction — These causes need careful examination—Lippert's view—Idleness, frivolity, and love of finery as causes—The desire for excitement—The need for personal knowledge of the prostitute—What I have learnt from different members of this profession—The prostitute's attitude towards her trade—The sale of sex very profitable to the expert trader—The sexual frigidity of the prostitute—Importance and significance of this—A further examination into the causes of the evil—Poverty seldom the chief motive for prostitution—The influence of inheritance upon the sexual life—The degradation of our legitimate loves the ultimate cause of prostitution—The demand for the prostitute by men—Causes of this demand—Repression of the primitive sexual instincts by civilisation—The foolishness of casting blame upon men—The duplex morality of the sexes—Its influence on the degradation of passion—Woman's unprofitable service to chastity—The connection with prostitution—My belief in passion as the only source of help.

CHAPTER X

THE SOCIAL FORMS OF THE SEXUAL RELATIONSHIP

I.—Marriage

"The race flows through us, the race is the drama and we are the incidents. This is not any sort of poetical statement; it is a statement of fact. In so far as we are individuals, in so far as we seek to follow merely individual ends, we are accidental, disconnected, without significance, the sport of chance. In so far as we realise ourselves as experiments of the species for the species, just in so far do we escape from the accidental and the chaotic. We are episodes in an experience greater than ourselves."—H. G. WELLS.

"THERE is no subject," says Bernard Shaw in his delightful preface to *Getting Married*, "on which more dangerous nonsense is talked and thought than marriage." And, in truth, it is not easy to avoid such foolishness if we understand at all the complexity of the relationship of the sexes. Sentiment rules our actions in this connection, whereas our talk on the subject is directed by intellect. And the demands of the emotions are at once more imperious and tyrannical, and more fastidious and more critical, than are the demands of the mind. Thus the more firmly reason checks the riot of imagination the greater the danger of error. Of all of which what is the moral? This: It is useless to talk or to think unless it is also possible and expedient to act.

Be it noted, then, first that our marriage customs and laws are founded and have been framed not for, or by, the personal needs—that is, the likes and dislikes of men and women, but by the exigencies of social and economic necessities. Now, from this it will be readily seen that individual inclinations are very likely, even if not bound, to clash with, as they seek to conform to, the usages of society. Always there will tend to be prevalent everywhere a hostility—at times latent, at others active—between these two forces; against the special desires of women and men on the one hand, and the laws enforced by a social and economic community on the other. Always there will tend to arise some who will desire to change the accepted marriage form, those who, considering first the personal needs, will advocate the loosening or the breaking of the marriage-bond; while others, looking only to the stability which they believe to be founded in law and custom, will seek to keep and to make the tie indissoluble.

This perpetual conflict is, it seems to me, the greatest difficulty that has to be faced in any effort to readjust the conditions of marriage. In our contemporary society there is a deep-lying dissatisfaction with the existing relations of the sexes, a yearning and restless need for change. In no other direction are the confusions and uncertainty of the contemporary mind more manifest. The change that has taken place so rapidly in the attitudes of women and men has brought with it a very strong and, what seems to be a new, revolt against the ignominious conditions of our amatory life as bound by coercive monogamy. We are questioning where before we have accepted, and are seeking out new ways in which mankind will go—will go because it must.

Yet just because of this imperative urging the greater

caution is called for in introducing any changes in the laws or customs affecting marriage. Present social and economic conditions are to a great extent chaotic. It would be a sorry thing if in haste we were to establish practices that must come to an end, when we have freed ourselves from the present transition; changes that would not be for the welfare of generations still unborn. It will, however, hardly be denied by any one that reform is needed. All will admit that a change must be made in some direction, and an attempt to say where it should be tried must therefore be faced.

Does Nature give us any help in solving the problem? None whatever. It would seem, indeed, that Nature has in some ways arranged the love relation in regard to the needs of the two sexes very badly. But putting this aside for the present, it is clear that in regard to the form of marriage Nature has no preference; all ways are equal to her, provided that the race profits by them, or at least does not suffer too much from them. We found abundant proof of this in our examination of marriage and the family as established already in the animal kingdom; the modes of sexual association offer great variety, no species being of necessity restricted to any one form of union. Polygamy, polyandry, and monogamy all are practised. The family is sometimes patriarchal, though more often it is matriarchal, with the female the centre of it, and her love for the young infinitely stronger and more devoted than the male, though even in this direction there are many and notable exceptions. When we came to study the history of mankind we found similar conditions persisting. Separate groups living as they best could without caring about theories; their sexual conduct ordered by a compromise between the procreative needs on the one hand, and the necessities of the social conditions on the other. Marriage forms, as we understand them, were for long unknown, the relations of the sexes slowly evolving from a more or less restricted promiscuity to a family union at first merely temporary, and only later becoming fixed and permanent. Thus very gradually the primitive instinctive sex impulses underwent expansion, and always in the direction of the control of the individual desires in the interest of the family.

The unit of the group or state is the family, therefore sex-customs arise and laws are made not to suit the convenience of the woman or the man, but for the preservation and good of the family. In a word, the children—they are the pivot about which all regulations of marriage should turn.

It is certain, however, that such control and such laws have never in the past, and never in the future can be fixed to one unchanging form. In proof of this I must refer the reader back to the historical section of this book, where nothing stands out clearer than that the most diverse morality and customs prevail in matters of sex. Wherever for any reason there arises a tendency towards any form of sexual association, such form is likely to be established as a habit, and, persisting, it comes to be regarded as right, and is enforced by custom and later by law, and also sometimes sanctified by religion. It comes to be regarded as moral, and other forms become immoral.

Now, all this may seem to be rather far away from the matter we are discussing—the present dissatisfaction with our marriage system. But the point I want to make clear is this: there is no rigid and unchangeable code of right or wrong in the sexual relationship. Our opinions here are based for the most part on traditional morality, which accepts what is as right because it is established. A small but growing minority, looking in an exact opposite direction, turn to an ideal morality, considering the facts of sex not as they are, but as they think they ought to be. Both these attitudes are alike harmful. The one refuses to go forward, the other rushes on blindly, goaded by sentiment or by personal desires. And to-day the greater danger seems to me to rest with the hasty reformers. It is an essentially feminine crusade. By this I do not mean that it is advocated alone by women, but that in itself it must be regarded as *feminine;* a view which elevates a subjective ideal relationship of sex above all objective facts. The desires and feelings and sentiments are set up in opposition to historical experience and communal tradition. We hear much, and especially in the writings and talk of women, of such vapid phrases as "Self-realisation in love," "The enhancement of the individual life," and "The spiritualising of sex." Such personal views, which exalt the passing needs of the individual above the enduring interests of the race, are in direct opposition to progress. What is rather needed is an examination of marriage and other forms of our sexual relationships by practical morality, by which I mean the estimating of their merits and defects in relation to the vital needs of the community under the circumstances of the present.

To do this we must first clear our minds from the belief that regards our present form of monogamic marriage as ordained by Nature and sanctified by God. He who accepts the development of the love of one man for one woman from other and earlier forms of association may well look forward in faith to a future progress from our existing marriage: yet, though eager for reform, he will, remembering the slowness of this steady upward progress in love's refinement in the past, refrain from acting in haste, understanding the impossibility of forcing any Utopia of the sexes. No change can be made in a matter so intimate as marriage by a mere altering of the law. Only such reforms as are the natural outgrowth of an enlightened public feeling can be of benefit, and thus permanent in their result. I must go further than this and say that what may very possibly be right for the few cannot be regarded as practically moral and good until it can be accepted and acted upon by the people at large. In sex more than in any other department of life we are all linked together; we are our brother's keeper, and the blood of the race will be required at our hands. Many women, and some men, do not realise at all the immense complications of sex and the claims passion makes on many natures. I am sure that this is the explanation of much of the foolish talk that one hears. I tried to make clear in the first chapters of this book the irresistible elemental power of the uncurbed sexual instincts. And this force is at least as strong now as it was in the beginning of life. For in sex we have, as yet, learnt very little. We who are living among the sophistication of aeroplanes, the inheritors of the knowledge of all the ages, have still to pass in wonder along the paths of love, entering into it blindly and making all the old mistakes.

Am I, then, afraid that I plead thus for caution? No, I am not. I rest my faith in the development of the racial element in love side by side with its personal ends of physical and spiritual joy. For the sex impulses, which have ruled women and men, will assuredly come to be ruled by them. Just as in the past life has been moulded and carried on by love's selection, acting unconsciously and ignorant of the ends it followed, so in the future the race will be developed and carried onwards by deliberate selection, and the creative energy of love will become the servant of women and men. The mighty dynamic force will then be capable of further and, as yet, unrealised development. This is no vain hope. It has its proof in the past history of the selective power of love. The problems of our individual loves are linked on to the racial life. The hope for improvement rests thus in a growing understanding of the individual's relation to the race, and in an expansion of our knowledge and practice of the high duties love enforces.

Let us look now at the practical direction of the present. We have reached these conclusions as a starting-point—

(1) We have inherited marriage as a social, nay more, a racial institution.

(2) The practical moral end of marriage, whether we

regard it from the wider biological standpoint or from the narrower standpoint of society, is a selection of the sexes by means of love, having as its social object the carrying on of the race, and as its personal object a mutual life of complete physical, mental, and psychical union.

(3) The first of these, the racial object, is the concern of the State; the second, the personal need of love, is the concern of the individual woman and man.

(4) It is the business of the State to make such laws that the interests of the race, *i.e.* the children, are protected.

From this it would seem to follow that beyond such care the State has nothing to do with the sexual relationship. Here I am placed in a difficulty. I cannot accept this view. I do not believe that the loves of women and men, even apart from children being born from such union, can ever be merely a personal matter between the two individuals concerned. For this reason any woman and man is a potential mother or father, and may become so in a later union. We cannot break the links which bind the individual to the race. I am very clear in my mind, however, of the need of recognising this perpetual duality in the objects of love. It is not necessary to bring forward any proof of the profound significance of the individual side of the sexual passion in the progress of civilisation. We may accept what is really proved by all of us in our acts, that love and love's embrace are not exercised only, or indeed chiefly, for the purpose of procreation, but are of quite equal importance to the parents, necessary for the complete life—the physical and mental development and the joy of the woman and the man.

It may seem, then, that we are thus faced by two opposing forces. That is not the case. There is real harmony underlying the apparent opposition of these two interests, and each is, indeed, the indispensable complement of the other. Both the personal and the further-reaching racial objects of love alike belong to the great synthesis of life. I do not, of course, deny, what every one knows, that there is at present an opposition and even conflict in certain individual cases. This is but one sign of chaos and the wastage of love. But this does not change the truth; there can be no gain for the individual in the personal ends of love unless there is also a corresponding gain to the wider racial end. The element of self-assertion in our loves must be brought into correlation with the universal and immortal development of life. This is so evident that I will not wait to elaborate it further. I will only point out that all the good, as also all the evil, that the individual is able to gain from love must ultimately react also for the benefit, or the wastage, of the race. Thus we have to get every good that we can out of our sexual experiences for ourselves for this very reason that we do not stand alone. It is because the race flows through us that we have to make the utmost of our individual opportunities and powers, so that, understanding our position as guardians to the generations yet unborn, we may use to the very full, but refrain from any misuse of love's possibilities of joy. We know that all we gain for ourselves we gain in trust for the race, and what we lose for ourselves we waste for the life to come. This has, of course, been said before by numberless people, but it seems to me it has been realised by very few, and until it is realised to the fullest extent it will never begin to be practised. We shall continue at a crossed purpose between our own interests and desires and the interests of the race, and shall go on wasting the forces of love needlessly and riotously.

Armed with these conclusions I shall now attempt to examine our existing marriage in its relation (1) to the needs of the children, (2) to the individual needs apart from parentage. The extent of the problems involved is almost illimitable, thus all that I can do is to touch very briefly and insufficiently on a few facts.

As we question in turn the various systems of marriage it becomes clear that monogamy is the form which has most widely prevailed, and will be likely to be maintained, because of its superior survival value. In other words, because it best serves the interests of the race by assuring to the woman and her children the individual interest and providence of the father. I believe further that monogamy of all the sexual associations serves best the personal needs of the parents; and, moreover, that it represents the form of union which is in harmony with the instincts and desires of the majority of people. The ideal of permanent marriage between one woman and one man to last for the life of both must persist as an ideal never to be lost. I wish to state this as my belief quite clearly. The higher love in true marriage is the veritable law of the life to be; and beside it all experiments in sensation will rot in their emptiness and their self-love.

But this faith of mine in an ideal and lasting union does not lessen at all my scepticism in the moral inefficacy of our present marriage system. It is not the particular form of marriage practised that, after all, is the main thing, but the kind of lives people live under that form. The mere acceptance of a legally enforced monogamy does not carry us very far in practical morality; we must claim something much deeper than this.

And this brings us to the base counterfeit of monogamy that is accepted and practised by many among us to-day; base because it is a monogamy largely mitigated by clandestine transitory loves—tipplings with sensation and snackings at lust which betray passion. Facts of daily observation may not be shuffled out of consideration by any hypocrisy. They must be faced and dealt with. Our marriage system is buttressed with prostitution, which thus makes our moral attitude one of intolerable deception, and our efforts at reform not only ineffective, but absurd. Without the assistance of the prostitution of one class of women and the enforced celibacy of another class our marriage in its present form could not stand. It is no use shirking it; if marriage cannot be made more moral—and by this I mean more able to meet the sex needs of all men and all women—then we must accept prostitution. No sentimentalism can save us; we must give our consent to this sacrifice of women as necessary to the welfare and stability of society. But with this question I shall deal in a later section of this chapter. There is, however, more than this to be said. Marriage is itself in many cases a legalised form of prostitution. From the standpoint of morals, the woman who sells herself in marriage is on the same level as the one who sells herself for a night, the only difference is in the price paid and the duration of the contract. Nay, it is probably fair to say that at the lowest such sale-marriage results in the greater evil, for the prostitute does not bear children. If she has a child it has, as a rule, been born first; such is our morality that motherhood often drives her on to the streets!

Any woman who marries for money or position is departing from the biological and moral ends of marriage. A child can be born gladly only as the fruit of love. It is in this direction, rather than in maintaining a barren virginity, that woman's chastity should be guarded. We may excuse women on the grounds of possible ignorance, but, none the less, have the conditions of marriage been unfavourable to the development of a fine moral feeling in women or in men. No one can have failed to feel surprised at the men many girls are content to marry; it is one thing that must be set against the claim women make as the morally superior sex. Mr. Wells, whom I have already quoted in this matter, places in the mouth of one of his characters, in his recent book, *Marriage*, a true and terrible indictment of women.

"If there was one thing in which you might think woman would show a sense of some divine purpose in life it is in the matter of children, and they show about as much care in the matter—oh, as rabbits! Yes, rabbits. I stick to it. Look at the things a nice girl will marry; look at the men's children she'll submit to bring into the world. Cheerfully! Proudly! For the sake of the home and the clothes!"

The fact is our marriage in its present legal form is primarily an arrangement for securing the rights of property. This in itself is not necessarily evil. Economic necessities cannot be ignored in any form of the sexual relationship; it is rather a readjustment that is called for here. We have seen how admirably a marriage system based upon property in the form of free contracts worked in Egypt, and how happy were the family relationships under this system of equal partnership between the wife and husband. I would again recommend the careful study of these marriage contracts to all those interested in marriage reform. The contracts were never fixed in one form; all that was required being that the interests of the woman and the children were in all cases protected. Take again the Roman marriage which, in its latest fine developments, has special interest, as the history of modern marriage systems may be traced back to it. The Romans came, like the Egyptians, to regard marriage as a contract rather than a legal form. In the custom of *usus*, which supplanted the earlier and sacred *confarreatio*, there was no ceremony at all. I would recall to the memory of my readers the significant fact that in both these great countries this freedom in marriage was associated with the freedom of woman. It must be recognised that these two forces tac together.

Traditional customs in marriage, as in all other departments of life, tend to become worn out, and whenever any form presses too heavily on a sufficient number of individuals acting against, instead of for, the interests of those concerned, there arises a movement towards reform. This happened in Rome, and led to the establishment of marriage by *usus*, which was further modified by the practice known as *conventio in manus*, whereby the wife by passing three nights in the year from her husband was able to break through the terrible right of the husband's *manus*. It is possible that by some such simple way of escape we may come to change the pressure of our coercive marriage.

The briefest glance at our marriage system proves it to be founded on the patriarchal idea of woman as the property of man, which is sufficiently illustrated by the fact that a husband can claim sums of money as compensation from any man who sexually approaches his wife, while a woman, on her side, is granted compensation in the case of a breach of promise of marriage. If we seek to find how this condition has arisen we must look backwards into the past. To the fine legacy left by the Roman law (which, regarding marriage as a contract, placed the two sexes in a position of equal freedom) was added the customs of the barbarians and the base Jewish system, giving to the husband rights in marriage and divorce denied to the wife. Later, in the twelfth century, came the capture of marriage by the Church and the establishment of Canon law, whereby the property-value of marriage became inextricably mingled with the sanctification of marriage as a sacrament, which, strengthened by Christian asceticism and the glorification of virginity, involved a corresponding contempt cast on all love outside of legal marriage.[1] The action of this double standard of sexual morality has led on the one side to the setting-up of a theoretical ideal, which, as few are able to follow it, tends to become an empty form, and this, on the other side, leads to a hidden laxity that rushes to waste love out to a swift finish. The puritan view has left us an inheritance of denials. It is small wonder, under such circumstances, that marriage is often immoral, so often ending in repulsion and weariness. "Our sexual morality," it has been said with fine truth by Havelock Ellis, "is in reality a bastard born of the union of property-morality with primitive ascetic morality, neither in true relationship to the vital facts of life."

It may, indeed, be doubted if apart from property considerations we have left any sexual morality at all. How else were it possible for marriage (which, if it is to fulfil its moral biological ends, must be based on physical and mental affinity and fitness) to be contracted, as it often is, without knowledge or any true care of these essential factors, and, moreover, to guarantee a permanence of a relationship thus entered into blindly. At least it should be considered necessary that a certificate of the health of the partners be obtained before marriage. What is required to ensure our individual life ought to be demanded before we create new life. Here, as I believe, is one direction in which the State should take action. Parentage on the part of degenerate human

[1] I would refer my readers to the Chapters on "Sexual Morality" and "Marriage" in Havelock Ellis's *Psychology of Sex*, Vol. VI. The only way to estimate aright the value of our present marriage system is to examine the history of that system in the past. I had hoped to have space in which to do this, and it is with real regret I am compelled to omit the section I had written on this subject.

beings is a crime, and as such it ought to be prevented. It may be, and is, argued that any action of the State in this direction entails an interference with the rights of the individual. Just the same may be said of all laws. The man who wishes to steal or to kill either another or himself may, with equal reason, hold that it is an interference of the law that he is not permitted to follow his inclinations in these matters. The sins that he may wish to commit are assuredly less evil in their results than the sin of irresponsible parentage. You see what I mean. For if this unceasing crime against the unborn could somehow be stopped there would be so great a reduction of all other sins that we might well be freed from many laws. As an example I would refer the reader back to the wise Spartans, to consider how great was the gain to them as individuals by their strict and unceasing care for the welfare of the race.

There are many who attribute to mammon-marriages all the terrible evils of our disordered love-life of to-day. It is, therefore, well to remember that such conditions are not really a new thing, and cannot be regarded as the result of our commercialised civilisation. The intrusion of economics into marriage is of very ancient origin, and may be found among peoples who are almost primitive. But there is this important difference. In earlier and more vigorous societies such property-based marriages occur side by side with other forms of sexual associations, on a more natural basis, which are openly accepted and honoured. Our marriage system by its rigorous exclusions closes this way of escape. Morality may be outraged to any extent provided that law and religion have been invoked in legal marriage.

Let me give my readers two cases from my own experience; facts speak more forcibly than any mere statements of opinion. In a village that I know well a woman, legally married, bore five idiot children one after the other; her husband was a confirmed drinker and a mental degenerate. One of the children fortunately died. The text that was chosen as fitting for his funeral card was, "Of such is the kingdom of heaven." About the same time in the same village a girl gave birth to an illegitimate child. She was a beautiful girl; the father, who did not live in the village, was strong and young; probably the child would have been healthy. But the girl was sent from her situation and, later, was driven from her home by her father. At the last she sought refuge in a disused quarry, and she was there for two days without food. When we found her her child had been born and was dead. Afterwards the girl went mad. I will add no comment, except to record my belief that under a saner social organisation such crimes against love would be impossible.

As was said years ago by the wise Senancour, "The human race would gain much if virtue were made less laborious." Let us view these large questions in the light of their results to the individual and the race. This practical morality will serve us better than any traditional code. So only shall we learn to see if we cannot rid love of stress and pain that is unendurable. We force women and men into rebellion, into fearing concealments, and the dark and furtive ways of vice. For this reason we must, I believe, make the regulations of law as wide as possible, taking care only that mothers and all children must be safeguarded, whether in legal marriage or outside. All of which forces the conclusion: the same act of love cannot be good or bad just because it is performed in or out of marriage. To hold such an opinion is really as absurd as saying that food is more or less digestible according to whether grace is, or is not, said before the meal. All marriage forms are only matters of custom and expediency.

In face of the iniquity of our bastardy laws we may well pause to doubt the traditional ideas of our sexual code and conventional morality. It seems to me that in these questions of sex we have receded further and further from the reality of things, and become blinded and baffled by the very idols to love that men have set up. One thing renders love altogether and incurably wrong, and that is waste. The terribly high death-rate among illegitimate children alone suffices to illustrate the actual conditions, to say nothing of the greater waste often carried on in those children who live. The question of the maintenance of such unfathered children is a scandal of our time. We may surely claim that the birth of any child, without exception, must be preceded by some form of contract which, though not necessarily binding the mother and the father to each other, will place on both alike the obligation of adequate fulfilment of the duties to their child. This, I believe, the State must enforce. If inability on the part of the parents to make such provision is proved, the State must step in with some wide and fitting scheme of insurance of childhood. The carrying out of even these simple demands will lead us a great step forward in practical morality. It will open up the way to a saner and more beautiful future.

But here, in case I am mistaken and thought to be desiring the loosening of the bonds between the sexes, I must repeat again how firmly I accept marriage as the best, the happiest, and the most practical form of the sexual association. The ideal union is, I am certain, an indestructible bond, trebly woven of inclination, duty, and convenience. Marriage is an institution older than any existing society, older than mankind, and reaches back, as Fabre's study of insects has so beautifully shown us, to an infinitely remote past. Its forms are, therefore, too fundamentally blended with human and, further back, with animal society for them to be shaken with theories, or even the practices of individuals or groups of individuals. Thus I accept marriage: I believe that its form must be regulated and cannot be left to the development of individual desires against the needs of the race.

There are some who, in seeking liberation from the ignominious conditions of our present amatory life, are wishing to rid marriage from all legal bonds, and are pointing to Free-love as the way of escape. To me this seems a very great mistake. I admit the splendid imaginative appeal in the idea of Love's freedom as it is put forward, for instance, by the great Swedish feminist, Ellen Key; I am unable to accept it as practical morality. This, I believe, should be the only sound basis for reform. The real question is not what people *ought to do*, but what they *actually do* and are likely *to go on doing*. It is these facts that the idealist fails to face. Love is a very mixed game indeed. And all that the wisest reformer has ever been able to do is to make bad guesses at the solution of its problems.

The fundamental principle of the new ideal morality is that love and marriage must always coincide, and, therefore, when love ceases the bond should be broken. This in theory is, of course, right. I doubt if it is, or ever will be, possible in practice. Experience has forced the knowledge that the most passionate love is often the most likely to end in disaster. Nor do I think that the evil is much lessened when no legal bond is entered into. Those few people who have made a success of Free-love would probably have made an equal success of marriage. I know personally several cases in which the same woman, and many in which the same man, has tried in succession legal marriage and free unions and has been equally unhappy in both.

All the facts seem to me to point in another direction for reform. I do not think that life's great central purpose of carrying on the race (not alone giving birth to fit children, but the equally necessary work of both parents uniting in caring for and bringing them up) can be left safely to be confused and wasted by its dependence on the gratification of personal desires. I wish that I thought otherwise. It would make it all so much easier. It is useless to point back here to the action of love's selection in the past history of life. As civilisation progresses, and as individual needs become elaborated and wealth increases, we tend to get further and further away from the realities of love. We choose our partners without understanding, and think very little of the needs of the future. What I want is to free marriage from those bonds that can be proved to act against practical morality. I do not wish at all to lessen its binding, only to defend it against the conventions of a false and narrow traditional morality. In love, as in every human relationship, it is character that avails and prevails—nothing else. Marriage is, or ought to be, the most practically moral institution that any civilisation is able to produce. Women and men are likely to get out of any form of the sexual association results in proportion to that which they put into it. A great many people put nothing into marriage, and they are disappointed when they get out of it—nothing. We shall put more into marriage, and not less, in proportion as we come to understand it and to value its enduring importance.

After all it is the people of any race who make marriage, not marriage the people. The form of union is but a symbol of the people's character, their desires, and capacities. If we have evolved the wrong women and men, then any reform of marriage is vain. Have we in our weakened civilisation drifted so far from life that the inherent attributes of loyalty and discipline to the future are no longer with us in sufficient measure adequately to respond to the enduring realities of love? The answer is with women. We must demand from the fathers of our children, as we demand from ourselves, loyalty to the well-being of the race; the discipline of our personal desires and loves that we may maintain ourselves fit as the bearers and protectors of those wider interests, which belong not to ourselves, not to this generation alone, but to the life and the future history of our race. Woman must again assert, as she did in the past, that she is the maker of men. She must reclaim her right, held by the female from the beginning of life, as the director of love's selective power. And more even than this. Woman with man must be the framer of the law, and the guide and director of all the relations of the sexes. But it is not sufficient to do this by mere proclamation. Virile nations are not made by theories or by the blast of the trumpet. They are reared in the bonds of marriage, and what we incorporate in that bond will be manifest in our children.

II.—*Divorce*

"The result of dissolving the formal stringency of the marriage relationship, it is sometimes said, would be a tendency to an immoral laxity. Those who make this statement overlook the fact that laxity tends to reach a maximum as the result of stringency, and that where the merely external authority of a rigid marriage law prevails then the extreme excesses of licence must flourish. It is also undoubtedly true, and for the same reason, that any sudden removal of restraints necessarily involves a reaction to the opposite extreme of licence. A slave is not changed in a stroke into an autonomous free man."—HAVELOCK ELLIS.

In putting forward a practical morality for marriage we have to remember that we are not really uprooting traditional morality. There is no necessity. Of its own decay the old morality has fallen in a confusion of ruin. The ideal marriage is the union of one woman with one man for life. This we have established. We have now to look at the question from another side and ask, How far is this ideal monogamy possible in practice? I think the answer must be that, as we stand at present, it is possible to very few. For marriage is essentially a state of bondage—there is no getting away from this—a state which calls upon the individual to surrender his personal freedom in the interests of the race and the stability of social structure. I have proved that this bondage acts really for the benefit and happiness of the individual, but this deep truth I must now leave. Marriage is, thus, a concession of the individual to the general welfare of the future and of the State. Now, with human nature as it is in its present development, it is clearly claiming the impossible to demand indissoluble marriage. Divorce is really implicit in the conditions of marriage itself, and the firmest believers in monogamy must be the supporters of practical and moral conditions of divorce.

The moral code of any society represents the experience of its members. But experience is continually changing and enlarging, and moral codes must also change and enlarge, or they become worn-out and useless. Those people who are unable to modify their moral code to fit new conditions and growth are doomed to extinction, while the people who adjust their customs and laws to meet new requirements open up the way to move on, and still onwards, in continual progress.

It were well to remember this as we come to question the conditions of our law of divorce. There can be no possible doubt that if marriage is to remain and become moral there must be an easier dissolution of its bonds. The enforced continuance of an unreal marriage is really the grossest form of immorality, harmful not only to the individuals concerned, but to the children. The prejudices handed down to us by past tradition have twisted morals into an assertion that a husband or wife who have ceased to love must continue to share the rites of marriage in mutual repugnance, or live in an unnatural celibacy.

The question as to how this condition arose may be answered very briefly. The Church ordained that marriage is indissoluble, but, this being found impossible to maintain in practice, the State stepped in with a way of escape—a kind of emergency exit. But what a makeshift it is! how flagrantly indecent! how inconsistent! Adultery must be committed. To escape the degradation of an unworthy partner another partner must first be sought, and love degraded in an act of infidelity. Adultery is, in fact, a State-endowed offence against morality, just as the indissolubility of marriage is a theological perversion of the plainest moral law, that the true relationship between the sexes is founded on love. This bastard-born morality of Church and State is as immoral in theory as it is evil in practice.

For if we look deeper it becomes clear that the test to be applied here is the same as in every relation between the sexes: the conditions of divorce, like the conditions of marriage, must be such as best serve the interests of the race. This means, in the first place, that both partners in a marriage must have the assurance that when the moral conditions of the contract are broken, or through any reason become inefficient, they can be liberated, without any shame or idea of delinquency being attached to the dissolution. "Divorce is relief from misfortune and not a crime," to quote from the admirable statute-book of Norway, a saying which should be one of universal application in divorce. This must be done not merely as an act of justice to the individual; it is called for equally in the interests of the race. The woman or man from whom a divorce ought to be obtained is in almost all cases the woman or man who ought not to be a parent. We may go further than this. Divorce cannot be considered on the physical side alone, there is a psychological divorce which is far deeper, and also far more frequent. The woman or man who for any reason is unhappy in marriage is unfitted to be a parent in that marriage, and the way should be opened to them, if they desire, to have other children born in love in a new marriage with a more fitting mate. Our eyes are shut to the damning facts which confront us on every side. Take, for instance, the case of the drunkard, the insane, the syphilitic, the consumptive, parent bound in marriage. On biological and economic grounds it is folly to leave in such hands the protection of the race. It is the business of the State, as I believe, to regulate the law to prevent, as far as possible, the birth of unfit children; at least we may demand that Church and State cease to grant their sanction to this flagrant sin.

It is of the utmost importance to realise that Divorce Law Reform is needed to bring our jurisprudence up to the level of the modern civilised State. Our law in this respect lags far behind that of other countries, and is only one example out of many of our hide-bound attachment to ancient abuses. The opposition shown against the splendid and fearless recommendations for the extension of the grounds of divorce, voiced by the Majority Report in the recent Divorce Law Commission, prove how far we are still from understanding the higher morality of marriage. The recent Commission and the strong movement in favour of reform will, without doubt, lead to a change in the glaring injustice and inconsistencies of our law. It is, however, certain that an enlightened divorce law must go much further than providing ways of escape from marriage. Such exits tend to destroy the true sanctity of marriage; also they are unable to meet the needs of all classes, no matter how wide and numerous they are. They can never form the ultimate solution. They tend to make marriage ridiculous, and there are real grounds in the objections raised against them. There must be no special exits; the door of marriage itself must be left open to go out of as it is open to enter. This will come. When personal responsibility in marriage is developed, when all the relationships of sexes are founded on the recognition of the equality of the mother with the father—the woman with the man, then will come divorce by mutual consent.

Whenever divorce is difficult, there woman's lot is hard and her position low. It is a part of the patriarchal custom which regards women as property. It would be easy to prove this by the history of marriage in the civilisations of the past, as also by an examination of the present divorce laws in civilised countries. I cannot do this, but I make the assertion without the least shadow of doubt. I would point back in proof to the Egyptian and Babylonian divorce law, and to the splendid development of Roman Law in this direction. Consent is accepted as necessary to marriage; it should be the condition of divorce. This, I believe, is the only solution which women will be content to accept, when once they are awakened to their responsibilities in marriage. And here I would quote the wise dictum of Mr. Cunninghame Graham: "Divorce is the charter of Woman's Freedom."

The condemnation of divorce and the pillorying of divorced persons are not really the outcome of any concern for true morality, though most people deceive themselves that they are. They are predominantly the outcome of ignorance, of prejudices and false values, based, on the one hand, on the primitive patriarchal view of the wife (hence the insistence on woman's chastity and the inequality of the law), and, on the other, on the ecclesiastical doctrine of the indissolubility of marriage and the sin of all relationships outside its bonds. It is only when we realise how deeply and terribly these worn-out views have saturated and falsified our judgments that we come to understand the barbarism of our present laws of divorce.

It is significant that those who talk most of the sanctity of marriage are the very people who fear most the extension of divorce, seeming to believe that any loosening of its chains would lead to a dissolution of the institution of marriage. One marvels at the weakness of faith shown in such a view. It is not possible to hold the argument both ways. If the partners in marriage are happy, why lock them in? if not, why pretend that they are? The best argument I ever heard for divorce was a remark made to me in a conversation with a working man. He said, "When two people are fighting it is not very safe to lock the door." After all, what you do is this: you give occasion for the locks to be broken.

I have already spoken of loyalty and duty in relation

to marriage, and nothing that I say now must be thought to lessen at all my deep belief in the personal responsibility of the individual in every relationship of the sexes. Living together even after the death of love may, indeed, be right if this is done in the interests of the children. But it can never be right to compel such action by law. For then in ninety-nine cases out of every hundred what is regarded as duty is really a question of expediency. It is very easy to deceive ourselves. And it requires more courage than most people possess to face the fact that what has perhaps been a happy and fruitful marriage has died a slow and bitter death. But the higher morality claims that a child must be born in love and reared in love, or, at the lowest, in an atmosphere from which all enmity is absent. Only the parent who is strong enough to subordinate the individual right to the rights of the child can safely remain in a marriage without love.

One great advantage of free divorce is that the wife and husband would not part, as is almost inevitable under present conditions, in hatred, but in friendship. This would enable them to meet one another from time to time and unite together in care of any children of the marriage. If such reasonable conduct was for any reason impossible on the part of either or both parents, then the State must appoint a guardian to fill the place of one parent or both. No child should be brought up without a mother and a father. The adoption of children under the State might in this way open up fruitful opportunities whereby childless women and men might gain the joys of parenthood.

This condition of safety by free-divorce once established, would do much to mitigate the hostility against marriage which is so unfortunately prevalent among us to-day. Practical morality is teaching us the immorality of indissoluble marriage. In Spain, a country that I know well, where marriage is indissoluble, an increasing number of men—and these the best and most thoughtful—are refraining from marriage for this very reason. It follows, as a result, that in Spain the illegitimate birth-rate is very high. The difficulty of divorce is also a strong factor that upholds prostitution.

Many women and men of exceptional gifts and character, conscious of an increasing intolerance against the makeshift morality imposed upon our sexual life, are standing outside of marriage and evading parentage. For this waste we are responsible to the future. Thus, finally, we find this truth: the principle of divorce reform forms the most practical foundation—and one waiting ready to our hands—for the reformation of marriage and the re-establishment of its sanctity. It also has direct and urgent bearing on many of the problems of womanhood.

III.—*Prostitution*

"Nought so vile that on the earth doth live
But to the earth some special good doth give;
Nor nought so good but strained from that fair use,
Revolts from true birth, stumbling on abuse:
Virtue itself turns vice being misapplied,
And vice sometimes by action dignified."—*Romeo and Juliet.*

"In nature there's no blemish but the mind,
None can be called deformed but the unkind."—*Twelfth Night.*

A brief and final section of this chapter on the sexual relationships must be devoted to the question of the conditions of prostitution, which are really part of the conditions of marriage, being correlated with that institution in its present coercive form, in fact, part of it and growing out of it.

The extent of the problems involved here are so immense, the difficulties so great and the issues so involved that I hesitate at making any attempt to treat so wide a subject briefly and necessarily inadequately in the short space at my disposal. Yet it seems to me impossible to take the easy way and pass it over in silence, and I may be able to contribute a word or two of worth to this very complex social phenomenon. I shall limit myself to the aspects of the question that seem to me important, choosing in preference the facts about which I have some little personal knowledge.

Essentially this is a woman's question. What do women know about it? Almost nothing. We are really as ignorant of the character, moral, mental and physical of "the fallen woman," as if she belonged to an extinct species. We know her only to pity her or to despise her, which is, in result, to know nothing that is true about her. To deal with the problem needs women and men of the finest character and the widest sympathy. There are some of them at work now, but these, for the most part, are engaged in the almost impossible task of rescue work, which does not bring, I think, a real understanding of the facts in their wider social aspect.

Women are, however, realising that they cannot continue to shirk this part of their civic duties. These "painted tragedies" of our streets have got to be recognised and dealt with; and this not so much for the sake of the prostitute, but for all women's safety and the health of the race. The time is not far distant when the mothers of the community, the sheltered wives of respectable homes, must come to understand that their own position of moral safety is maintained at the expense of a traffic whose very name they will not mention. For the prostitute, though unable to avenge herself, has had a mighty ally in Nature, who has taken her case in hand and has avenged it on the women and their children, who have received the benefits of our legal marriage system. M. Brieux deals with this question in *Les Avariés:* it is a tragedy that should be read by all women.

For this reason, if for no other, the existence of prostitution has to be faced by women. Apathy and ignorance will no longer be accepted as excuse, in the light of the sins against the race slowly piled up through the centuries by vice and disease. But what will be the result of women's action in this matter? What will they do? What changes in the law will they demand? The importance of these questions forces itself upon all those who realise at all the difficulties of the problem. What we see and hear does not, I think, give great hopes. Every woman who dares to speak on this great burked subject seems to have "a remedy" ready to her hand. What one hears most frequently are unconsidered denunciations of "the men who are responsible." For example, I heard one woman of education state publicly that *there was no problem of prostitution!* I mention this because it seems to me a very grave danger, an instance of the feminine over-haste in reform, which, while casting out one devil, but prepares the way for seven other devils worse than the first. Women seem to expect to solve problems that have vexed civilisation since the beginnings of society. This attitude is a little irritating. Every attempt hitherto to grapple with prostitution has been a failure. Women have to remember that it has existed as an institution in nearly all historic times and among nearly all races of men. It is as old as monogamic marriage, and maybe the result of that form of the sexual relationship, and not, as some have held, a survival of primitive sexual licence. The action of women in this question must be based on an educated opinion, which is cognisant with the past history of prostitution, recognises the facts of its action to-day in all civilised countries, and understands the complexity of the problem from the man's side as well as the woman's. Nothing less than this is necessary if any fruitful change is to be effected, when women shall come to have a voice to direct the action the State should assume towards this matter. The one measure which has recently been brought forward and passed, largely aided by women, especially the militant Suffragists—I refer to the White Slave Traffic Bill—is just the most useless, ill-devised and really preposterous law with which this tremendous problem could be mocked. As Bernard Shaw has recently said—

"The act is the final triumph of the vice it pretends to repress. There is one remedy and one alone, for the White Slave Traffic. Make it impossible, by the enactment of a Minimum Wage law and by the proper provision of the unemployed, for any woman to be forced to choose between prostitution and penury, and the White Slaver will have no more power over the daughters of labourers, artisans and clerks than he (or under the New Act she) will have over the wives of Bishops."

Now all this is true, but is not all the truth. Remove the economic pressure and no woman will be driven, or be likely to be trapped, into entering the oldest profession in the world; but this does not say that she *will not enter it.* The establishment of a minimum wage will assuredly lighten the evil, but it will not end prostitution. The economic factor is by no means the only factor. It is quite true that poverty drives many women into the profession—that this should be so is one of the social crimes that must, and will, be remedied.

The real problem lies deeper than this. Want is not the incentive to the traffic of sex in the case of the dancer or chorus girl in regular employment, of the forewoman in a factory or shop who earns steady wages, or among numerous women belonging to much higher social positions. These women choose prostitution, they are not driven into it. It is necessary to insist upon this. The belief in the efficacy of economic reform amounts almost to a disease—a kind of unquestioning fanatical faith. Again and again I have been met by the assurance, made by men who should know better, as well as by women, that no woman would sell herself if economic causes were removed. Such opinion proves a very plain ignorance of the history and facts of prostitution. It is only a little more scientific than the view of the woman moral crusader, who believes that the "social evil" can easily be remedied by self-control on the part of men. One of the worst vices common to women at present is spiritual pride. One wonders if these short-cut reformers have ever been acquainted with a single member of this class they hope to repress by legal enactments or other measures, such as early marriage, better wages for women, moral education, the censorship of amusements, and so forth. It is not so simple. You see, what is needed is an understanding of the conditions, not from the reformer's standard of thought, but from that of the prostitute, which is a very different matter. How can any one hope to reform a class whose real lives, thoughts, and desires are unknown to them?

My effort to reach bed-rock facts had led me to seek first-hand information from these women, many of whom I have come to know intimately, and to like. I have learnt a great deal, much more than from all my close study of the problem as it is presented in books. Problems are never so simple in the working out as they appear in theories. Moral doctrines fall to pieces; even statistics and the estimates of expert investigators are apt to become curiously unreal in the light of a very little practical knowledge. I have learnt that there is no one type of prostitute, no one cause of the evil, no one remedy that will cure it.

And here, before I go further, I must in fairness state that I have been compelled to give up the view held by me, in common with most women, that men and their uncontrolled passions are chiefly responsible for this hideous traffic. It is so comfortable to place the sins of society on men's passions. But as an unbiassed inquirer I have learnt that seduction as a cause of prostitution requires very careful examination. We women have got to remember that if many of our fallen sisters have been seduced by men, at least an equal number of men have received their sexual initiation at the hands of our sex. This seduction of men by women is often the starting-point of a young man's association with courtesans. It is time to assert that, if women suffer through men's passion, men suffer no less from women's greed. I am inclined to accept the estimate of Lippert (*Prostitution in Hamburg*) that the principal motives to prostitution are "idleness, frivolity, and, above all, the love of finery." This last is, as I believe, a far more frequent and stronger factor in determining towards prostitution than actual want, and one, moreover, that is very deeply rooted in the feminine character. I do not wish to be cynical, but facts have forced on me the belief that the majority of prostitutes are simply doing for money what they originally did *of their own will* for excitement and the gain of some small personal gift.

There are, of course, many types among these unclassed women, as many as there are in any other class, probably even more. Yet, in one respect, I have found them curiously alike. Just as the members of any other trade have a special attitude towards their work, so prostitutes have, I think, a particular way of viewing their trade in sex. It is a mistake of sentiment to believe they have any real dislike to this traffic. Such distaste is felt by the unsuccessful and by others in periods of unprofitable business, but not, I think, otherwise. To me it has seemed in talking with them—as I have done very freely—that they regard the sexual embraces of their partners exactly in the light that I regard the process of the actual writing down of my books—as something, in itself unimportant and tiresome, but necessary to the end to be gained. This was first made clear to me in a conversation with a member of the higher *demi-monde*, a woman of education and considerable character. "After all," she said, "it is really a very small thing to do, and gives one very little trouble, and men are almost always generous."

This remarkable statement seems to me representative of the attitude of most prostitutes. They are much better paid, if at all successful, than they ever could be as workers. The sale of their sex opens up to them the same opportunities of gain that gambling on the stock-exchange or betting on the racecourse, for instance, opens up to men. It also offers the same joy of excitement, undoubtedly a very important factor. There are a considerable number of women who are drawn to and kept in the profession, not through necessity, but through neurosis.

There is no doubt that prostitution is very profitable to the clever trader. I was informed by one woman, for instance, that a certain country, whose name I had perhaps better withhold, "Is a Paradise for women." Quite a considerable fortune, either in money or jewels, may be reaped in a few months and sometimes in a few weeks. But the woman must keep her head; cleverness is more important even than beauty. I learnt that it was considered foolish to remain with the same partner for more than two nights, the oftener a change was made the greater the chance of gain. The richest presents are given as a rule by young boys or old men: some of these boys are as young as fifteen years.

Now the really extraordinary thing to me was that my

informant had plainly no idea of my moral sensibility being shocked at these statements. Of course, if I had shown the least surprise or condemnation, she would at once have agreed with me—but I didn't. I was trying to see things as she saw them, and my interest caused her really to speak to me as she felt. I am certain of this, as was proved to me in a subsequent conversation, in which I was told the history of a girl friend, who had got into difficulties and been helped by my informant. (These women are almost always kind and generous to one another. I know of one case in which a woman who had been trapped into a bogus marriage and then deserted, afterwards helped with money the girl and bastard child, also left by the man who had deceived her.) The story was ended with this extraordinary remark, "*It was all my friend's own fault, she was not particular who she went with; she would go with any man just because she took a fancy to him. I often told her how foolish she was, but she always said she could not help it.*"

It was then that I realised the immensity of the gulf which separated my outlook from that of this successful courtesan. To her *to be not particular* was to give oneself without a due return in money: to me——! Well, I needed all my control at that moment not to let her see what I felt. I have never been conscious of so deep a pity for any woman before, or felt so fierce an anger against social conditions that made this degradation of love possible. For, mark you, I know this woman well, have known her for years, and I can, and do, testify that in many directions apart from her trade, her virtue, her refinement and her character are equal, even if not superior, to my own. This is the greatest lesson I have learnt. The degradation of prostitution rests not with these women, but on us, the sheltered, happy women who have been content to ignore or despise them. Do you come to know these women (and this is very difficult) you are just as able to like them and in many ways to respect them, as you are to like and to respect any "straight" woman. You may hate their trade, you cannot justly hate them.

I would like here to bring forward as a chief cause of prostitution a factor which, though mentioned by many investigators,[1] has not, I think, been sufficiently recognised. To me it has been brought very forcibly home by my personal investigations. I mean sexual frigidity. This is surely the clearest explanation of the moral insensibility of the prostitute. I have not enough knowledge to say whether this is a natural condition, or whether it is acquired. I am certain, however, that it is present in those courtesans whom I have known. These women have never experienced passion. I believe that the traffic of love's supreme rite means less to them than it would do to me to shake hands with a man I disliked.

Now, if I am right, this fact will explain a great deal. I believe, moreover, that here a way opens out whereby in the future prostitution may be remedied. This is no fanciful statement, but a practical belief in passion as a

[1] Lombroso mentions the prevalence of sexual frigidity among prostitutes (*La Donna Delinquente*, p. 401). See also Havelock Ellis, *Psychology of Sex*, Vol. VI. pp. 268–272. This writer does not support the view of the sexual frigidity of prostitutes, but in this, I believe, he is influenced by statistics and outward facts, rather than personal knowledge gained from the women themselves.

power containing all forces. To any one who shares the faith I have been developing in this book, what I mean will be evident. If we consider how large a factor physical sex is in the life of woman, it becomes clear that any atrophy of these instincts must be in the highest degree hurtful. Moral insensibility is almost always combined with economic dependence. If all mating was founded, as it ought to be, on love, and all children born from lovers, there would follow as an inevitable result a truer insistence on reality in the relationships of the sexes. With a strengthening of passion in the mothers of the race, sex will return to its right and powerful purpose; love of all types, from the merest physical to the highest soul attraction, will be brought back to its true biological end—the service of the future.

I know, of course, as I have said already, that, just as there are many different forms of prostitution, there are many and varied types of prostitutes, and that, therefore, it is foolishness to hold fast in a one-sided manner to a single theory. There are undoubtedly voluptuous women among prostitutes. These I have not considered. For one thing I have not met them. I have preferred to speak of the women I have known personally. In the light of what I have learnt from them, I have come to believe that only in comparatively few cases does sexual desire lead any woman to adopt a career of prostitution, and in still fewer cases does passion persist. The insistence so often made on this factor as a cause of prostitution is due, in part, to ignorance as to the real feelings of these women, and also, in part, to its moral plausibility. We are so afraid of normal passion that we readily assume abnormal passion to be the cause of the evil. But far truer causes on the women's side are love of luxury and dislike of work. I think the estimates given by men on this subject have to be accepted with great caution. It must be remembered that it is the business of these women to excite passion, and, to do this, they must have learnt to simulate passion; and men, as every woman who is not ignorant or a fool knows, are easy to deceive. It may also be added that to the woman of strong sexuality the career of prostitution is suited. It is possible that in the future and under wiser conditions such women only will choose this profession.

For the same reason I have passed very lightly over the economic factor as a cause of prostitution. I believe that this will be changed. I do not under-estimate the undoubted importance of the driving pressure of want. But, as I have tried to make clear, it does not take us to the root of the problem. Poverty can only be regarded as probably the strongest out of many accessory causes. The socialists and economic apostles have to face this: no possible raising of women's wages can abolish prostitution.[1]

We must hold firmly to the fact that characterlessness, which is incapable of overcoming opposition and takes the path that is easiest, is the result of the individual's inherited disposition, with the addition of his, or her, own experience; and of these it is the former that, as a rule, determines to prostitution. Every kind of moral and intellectual looseness and dullness can, for the most

[1] Women in marriage have been for so long protected by men from the necessity of doing work, that why should we expect the prostitute to prefer uncongenial work?

part, be traced to this cause. At all events it is the strongest among many. Not alone for the prostitute's sake must this subject be seriously approached, but for society's sake as well. As things stand with us at present, moral sensitiveness has a poor chance of being cultivated, and those who realise that this is the case are still very few. Women have yet to learn the responsibilities of love, not only in regard to their duties of child-bearing and child-rearing, but in its personal bearing on their own sexual needs and the needs of men. I believe that the degradation of our legitimate love-relationships is the ultimate cause of prostitution, to which all other causes are subsidiary.

If we look now at the position for a moment from the other side—the man's side—a very difficult question awaits us. It is a question that women must answer. What is the real need of the prostitute on the part of men? This demand is present everywhere under civilisation; what are its causes? and how far are these likely to be changed? Now it is easy to bring forward answers, such as the lateness of marriage, difficulty of divorce, and all those social and economic causes which may be grouped together and classed as "lack of opportunity of legitimate love." Without question these causes are important, but, like the economic factor which drives women into prostitution, they are not fundamental; they are also remediable. They do not, however, explain the fact, which all know, that the prostitute is sought out by numberless men who have ample opportunity of unpriced love with other women. Here we have a preference for the prostitute, not the acceptance of her as a substitute taken of necessity. It is, of course, easy to say that such preference is due to the lustful nature of the male. There was a time when I accepted this view —it is, without doubt, a pleasant and a flattering one for women. I have learnt the folly of such shallow condemnations of needs I had not troubled to understand. Possibly no woman can quite get to the truth here; but at least I have tried to see facts straight and without feminine prejudice.

This is what seems to me to be the explanation.

We have got to recognise that there are primitive instincts of tremendous power, which, held in check by our dull and laborious, yet sexually-exciting, civilisation, break out at times in many individuals like a veritable monomania. In earlier civilisations this fact was frankly recognised, and such instincts were prevented from working mischief by the provision of means wherein they might expend themselves. Hence the widespread custom of festivals with the accompanying orgy; but these channels have been closed to us with a result that is often disastrous. No woman can have failed to feel astonishment at the attractive force the prostitute may, and often does, exercise on cultured men of really fine character. There is some deeper cause here than mere sexual necessity. But if we accept, as we must, the existence of these imperatively driving, though usually restrained impulses, it will be readily seen that prostitution provides a channel in which this surplus of wild energy may be expended. It lightens the burden of the customary restraints. There are many men, I believe, who find it a relief just to talk with a prostitute—a woman with whom they have no need to be on guard. The prostitute fulfils that need that may arise in even the most civilised man for something primitive and strong: a need, as has been said by a male writer, better than I can express it, "for woman in herself, not woman with the thousand and one tricks and whimsies of wives, mothers and daughters."

This is a truth that it seems to me it is very necessary for all women to realise. It is in our foolishness and want of knowledge that we cast our contempt upon men. Women flinch from the facts of life. These women who, regarded by us as "the supreme types of vice," are yet, from this point of view, "the most efficient guardians of our virtue." Must we not then rather see if there is no cause in ourselves for blame?

It has been held for generations that woman must practise principles of virtue to counteract man's example. This has led to an entirely false standard. A solving compromise has been found in the ideal of purity in one set of women and passion in another. And this state of things has continued indefinitely until it has become to some extent true. Numberless women have withered in this unprofitable service to chastity. The sexual coldness of the modern woman, which sociologists continually refer to, exists mainly in consequence of this constant system of repression. Female virtue has been overcultivated, the flower has grown to an enormous size, but it has lost its scent. A hypocritical and a lying system has been set up professing disbelief in that which it knows is necessary to the needs of the individual woman and to the larger needs of the race. Physical love is only inglorious when it is regarded ingloriously. Why this horror of passion? The tragedy of woman it seems is this, that with such power of love as she has in her there should be so little opportunity for its use—so much for its waste. Those of us who believe in passion as the supreme factor in race-building, must know that this view of its shamefulness is weakening the race.

I, therefore, hold firmly as my belief that the hateful traffic in love will flourish just as long, and in proportion, as we regard passion outside of prostitution with shame. Each one of us women is responsible. Do we not know that there is not this difference between our sexual needs and those of men? Let us tear down the old pretence. Do not instincts arise in us, too, that demand expression, free from all coercion of convention? And if we stifle them are we really the better—the more moral sex? I doubt this, as I have come to doubt so many of the lies that have been accepted as the truth about women.

The true hope of the future lies in the undivided recognition of responsibility in love, which alone can make freedom possible. Freedom for all women—the women of the home and the women of the streets. The prostitute woman must be freed from all oppression. We, her sisters, can demand no less than this. If we are to remain sheltered, she must be sheltered too. She must be freed from the oppression of absurd laws, from the terrible oppression of the police and from all economic and social oppression. But to make this possible, these women, who for centuries have been blasted for our sins against love, must be re-admitted by women and men into the social life of our homes and the State. Then, and then alone, can we have any hope that the prostitute will cease to be and the natural woman will take her place.

CONTENTS OF CHAPTER XI

THE END OF THE INQUIRY

The future of Woman—Indications of progress—The re-birth of woman—Woman learning to believe in herself—The sin of sterility—The waste of womanhood—The change in woman's outlook—The quickening of the social conscience—A criticism of militancy—It does not correspond with the ideal for women—The new free relationship of the sexes—The conditions which make this possible—The recognition of love as the spiritual force in life—The importance of woman's freedom to the vital advance of humanity—The end brings us back to the beginning—The supreme importance of Motherhood—Woman the guardian of the Race-life and the Race-soul—This the ground of her claim for freedom.

CHAPTER XI

THE END OF THE INQUIRY

"Among the higher activities and movements of our time, the struggle of our sisters to attain an equality of position with the strong, the dominant, the oppressive sex, appears to me, from the purely human point of view, most beautiful and most interesting: indeed, I regard it as possible that the coming century will obtain its historical characterisations, not from any of the social and economical controversies of the world of men, but that this century will be known to subsequent history distinctively as that in which the solution of the 'woman's question' was obtained."—GEORGE HIRTH.

LOOKING back over the long inquiry which lies behind us, we have come by many and various paths to seek that standpoint from which we started—the Truth about Woman. We must now try to give a brief answer to a difficult question. What is the future of woman? Are we able to recognise in the present upward development of the sex signs of real progress towards better conditions? Is it within the capacity of the female half of human-kind to acquire and keep that position of essential usefulness held by the females of all other species? Will women learn to develop their own nature and to express their own genius? Can their present characteristic weakness, vices, and failings be really overcome under different and freer conditions of domestic and social life? Are we of to-day justified in looking forward to the new woman of the future, with saner aspirations and wider aims, who lives the whole of her life;

who will restore to humanity harmony between the sexes, and transform the miseries of love back to its rightful joys? Can these things, indeed, be?

The answer is a confident and joyful "Yes!"

The re-birth of woman is no dream.

We have become accustomed to listen to the opinion voiced by men. We have heard that belief in women is a symptom of youth or of inexperience of the sex, which a riper mind and wider knowledge will invariably tend to dissipate. So woman has come to regard herself as almost an indiscretion on the part of the Creator, necessary indeed to man, but something which he must try to hide and hush up. We have, in fact, put into practice Milton's ideal: "He, for God only, she, for God in him." Some such arguments from the lips of disillusioned men have been possible, perhaps, with some measure of reason. But the time has come for men to hold their peace.

Woman is learning to believe in herself.

Now, so far, the great result of the long years of repression has been the sterility of women's lives. Sterility is a deadly sin. To-day so many of our activities are sterile. The women of our richer classes have been impotent by reason of their soft living; the women of our workers have had their vitality sweated out of them by their filthy labours; they could bear only dead things. Life ought to be a struggle of desire towards adventures of expression, whose nobility will fertilise the mind and lead to the conception of new and glorious births. Women have been forced to use life wastefully. They have been spiritually sterile;

consuming, not giving: getting little from life, giving back little to life.

But woman is awakening to find her place in the eternal purpose. She is adding understanding to her feeling and passion.

Never before throughout the history of modern womankind has her own character evoked so earnest and profound an interest as to-day: never has she considered herself from so truly a social standpoint as now. It is true that the change has not yet, except in very few women, reached deep enough to the realities of the things that most matter. Women have to learn to utilise every advantage of their nature, not one side only. They will do this; because they will come to have truer and stronger motives. They are beginning even now to be sifted clean through the sieve of work. The waste of womanhood cannot for long continue.

One great and hopeful sign is a new consciousness among all women of personal responsibility to their own sex. The most fruitful outgrowth from the present agitation for the rights of citizens—the Vote! the symbol of this awakening—is a solidarity unknown among women before, which now binds them in one common purpose. Yet there is a possible danger lurking in this enthusiasm. Women will gain nothing by snatching at reform. Many have no eyes to see the beyond; they are hurried forward by a cry of wrongs, while others are held back by fear of change. Woman is by her temperament inclined to do too much or to do nothing. Looked at from this standpoint of the immediate present, when only the semi-hysterical and illogical aspects of the struggle are manifest, the future may appear dark. The revolution is accompanied by much noise and violence. Perhaps this is inevitable. I do not know. There is, what must seem to many of us who stand outside the fight, a terrible wastage, a straining and a shattering of the forces of life and love. To earn salvation quickly and riotously may not, indeed, be the surest way. It may be only a further development of the sin of woman, the wastage of her womanhood.

Women say that the fault rests with men. Again I do not know. Certainly it is much easier and pleasanter to see the mote in our brother's eye than it is to recognise a possible beam as clouding our own sight. One of the worst results of the protection of woman by man is that he has had to bear her sins. Women have grown accustomed to this; they do not even know how greatly their sex shields them. They will not readily yield up their scapegoat or sacrifice their privileges. But the personal responsibility that is making itself felt among women must teach them to be ready to answer for their own actions, and, if need be, to pay for them. Freedom carries with it the acceptance of responsibility. Women must accept this: they are working towards it.

In a new and free relationship of the sexes women have at least as much to learn as men. The possession of the vote is not going to transform women. Changes that matter are never so simple as that. Women estimating their future powers tend to become presumptuous. One is reminded sometimes of the people Nietzsche describes as "those who 'briefly deal' with all the real problems of life." It frequently appears as if the modern woman expects to hold tight to her old privileges as the protected child, as well as to gain her new rights as the human woman. In a word, to stay on her pedestal when it is convenient, and to climb down whenever she wants to. This cannot be. And the grasping of both sides of the situation leads to what is worse than all else—strife between women and men. Just in measure as the sexes fall away from love and understanding of each other, do they fall away from life into the mere futility of personal ends. It is to *go on with man*, and not to *get from man*, that is the goal of Woman's Freedom. There are other conditions of change that women have to be ready to meet. This must be. For however much some may sigh for the ease and the ignorant repose of the passing generation, we cannot go back. It is as impossible to live behind one's generation as before it. We have to live our lives in the pulse of the new knowledge, the new fears, the new increasing responsibilities. Women must train themselves to keep pace with men. There is a price to be paid for free womanhood. Are women ready and willing to pay it? If so, they must cease to profit and live by their sex. *They must come out and be common women among common men.* This, as I believe, is a better solution than to bring men up to women's level. For, as I have said before, I doubt, and still doubt. if women are really better than men.

If the constructive synthetic purpose of life, which I have tried to make the ruling idea of my book, is that all growth is a succession of upward development through the action of love between the two sexes, then not only must woman in her individual capacity—

physically as wife and mother, and mentally as home-builder and teacher—contribute to the further progress of life by a nobler use of her sex; but the collective work of women in their social and political activities must all be set towards the same purpose. It is in this light, the welfare of the lives of the future and the building up of a finer race—that the individual and collective conduct of women must be judged. Women have talked and thought too much about their sex, and all the time they have totally under-estimated the real strength of the strongest thing in life. I think the force, the power, the driving intensity of love will come as a surprise and a wonder to awakened women. I think they will come to realise, as they have never realised before, the tremendous force sex is.

The Woman's movement is inextricably bound up with all the problems of our disorganised love-relationships; and although politicians with their customary blindness have chosen to treat it as a side issue, it is, for this reason, the most serious social question that has come to the front during the century. Woman's position and her efforts to regain her equality with man can never be a thing apart—a side issue—to a responsible State. Love and the relationship of the sexes is the foundation of the social structure itself; it forms the real centre of all the social and economic problems—of the population problem, of the marriage problem, of the problems of education and eugenics, of the future of labour, of the sweating question, and the problem of prostitution. As the Woman's Movement presses forward each and all of these questions will press forward too. All women and men have got to be concerned with sex and its problems until some at least of these wrongs are righted. That any woman can ever regard love as merely a personal matter, "an incident in life," that can be set aside in the rush of new activities, makes one wonder if the delusions of women about themselves can ever end. This misunderstanding of love ought never to be possible to any woman or any man: it is going to be increasingly difficult for it to be possible for the new woman and her mate that is to be. In love all things rest. In love has gathered the strength to be, growing into conscious need of fuller life, growing into completer vision of the larger day.

My faith in womanhood is strong and deep. The manifestations of the present, many of which seem to give cause for fear, are, after all, only the superficial evidence of a deep undercurrent of awakening. The ultimate driving force behind is shaping a social understanding in the woman's spirit. So surely from out of the wreckage and passion a new woman will arise.

For this Nature will see to. Woman, both by physiological and biological causes is the constructive force of life. Nothing that is fine in woman will be lost, nothing that is profitable will be sacrificed. No, the essential feminine in her will be gathered in a more complete, a more enduring synthesis. Woman is the predominant partner in the sexual relationship. We cannot get away from this. It is here, in this wide field, where so many wrongs wait to be righted, that the thrill of her new passion must bring well-being and joy. The female was the start of life, and woman is the main stream of its force. Man is her agent, her helper: hers is the supreme responsibility in creating and moulding life. It is thus certain that woman's present assertion of her age-long rights and claim for truer responsibilities has its cause rooted deep in the needs of the race. She is treading, blindly, perhaps, and stumblingly, in the steps laid down for her by Nature; following in a path not made by man, one that goes back to the beginning of life and is surer and beyond herself; thus she has time as well as right upon her side, and can therefore afford to be patient as well as fearless.

"I have caused thee to see it with thine eyes, but thou shalt not go over hither."

From the height of Pisgah there is revealed to women to-day a glimpse of the promised land. But shall we enter therein to take possession? I believe not. It will be given to those who follow us and carry on the work which our passion has begun. For our children's children the joys of reaping, the feast, and the songs of harvest home.

What matter? We shall be there in them.

Shall we, then, complain if for us is the hard toil, the doubts, and the mistakes, the long enduring patience, and the bitter fruits of disappointment? We have opened up the way.

And is not this one with the very purpose of life? We are obeying Nature's law in dedicating ourselves and our work to those who follow us. We have made our record, we can do nothing more. The race flows through us. All our effort lies in this—the giving of all that we have been able to gain. And it is sufficient. This is the end and the beginning.

Thus we are brought back to the truth from which we started. Women are the guardians of the Race-life and the Race-soul. There is no more to be said. It is because we are the mothers of men that we claim to be free. We claim this as our right. We claim it for the sake of men, for our lovers, our husbands, and our sons; we claim it even more for the sake of the life of the race that is to come.

> "Then comes the statelier Eden back to men;
> Then ring the world's great bridals, chaste and calm;
> Then springs the crowning race of human-kind.
> May these things be."

BIBLIOGRAPHY

N.B.—This bibliography is intended as a guide to the student; it is merely representative, not in any way exhaustive.

The books to which direct reference is made are marked with an asterisk.

BIOLOGICAL PART

*AUDUBON: Scènes de la nature dans les États Unis (*French trans.*).

Ornithological Biography: an Account of the Habits of the Birds of the United States of America.

BATESON, W.: Materials for the Study of Variation.

Mendel's Principles of Heredity.

*BONHOTE, J. LEWIS: Birds of Britain.

BREHM: Tierleben.

Ornithology, or the Science of Birds. (*From the text of Brehm.*)

BROOKS, W. K.: The Law of Heredity.

The Foundations of Zoology.

*BÜCHNER: Mind in Animals (*Eng. trans.*).

Liebe und Liebesleben in der Tierwelt.

*BUTLER, SAMUEL: Life and Habit.

Evolution Old and New.

*DARWIN, CHARLES: The Descent of Man.

The Origin of Species.

The Variation of Animals and Plants under Domestication.

The Expression of the Emotions in Men and Animals.

*DARWIN, FRANCIS: Life and Letters of Charles Darwin.

*ELLIS, HAVELOCK: Psychology of Sex. Vol. III.

*ESPINAS: Sociétés animales.

CC 2

FABRE, J. HENRI : Mœurs des insectes.
Life and Love of Insects (*trans.*).
Insect Life (*trans.*).
Social Life in the Insect World (*trans.*).

*FORBES, H. O. : A Naturalist's Wanderings.

*GALTON, FRANCIS : Natural Inheritance.
Average Contribution of Each Several Ancestor to the Total Heritage of the Offspring. *Pro. Roy. Soc., London, LXI.*

*GEDDES, PATRICK : *Articles:* "Reproduction," "Sex," "Variation" and "Selection" : *Encycl. Brit.*

*GEDDES AND THOMSON, J. A. : The Evolution of Sex. (*Cont. Sci. Series.*) *Rev. ed.*
Problems of Sex.

*HÄCKER : Der Gesang der Vögel.

*HAECKEL : Generelle Morphologie der Organismen.
Evolution of Man (*trans.* by J. McCabe).

HERTWIG : The Biological Problem of To-day (*trans.* by P. Chalmers Mitchell).

HOUZEAU : Études sur les facultés mentales des animaux comparés à celles de l'homme.

*HUDSON, W. H. : Argentine Ornithology.
The Naturalist in La Plata.
Birds and Man.

*HUXLEY, T. H. : A Manual of Invertebrate Animals.

KELLOGG : Studies of Variation in Insects.
Evidence as to Man's Place in Nature.

LETOURNEAU : Evolution of Marriage. (*Cont. Sci. Series.*)

*MILNE-EDWARDS, HERNI : Leçons sur la physiologie et l'anatomie comparée de l'homme et des animaux.
A Manual of Zoology (*trans.*).
Histoire naturelle des insectes.

MIVART, ST. GEORGE : Lessons from Nature as manifested in Mind and Matter.
The Common Frog. (*Nat. Series.*)
Man and Apes : an Exposition of Structural Resemblance upon the Questions of Affinity and Origin.
On the Genesis of Species.

*MORGAN, C. LLOYD : Animal Life and Intelligence.
Habit and Instinct.
Animal Behaviour.

POULTON, E. B. : The Colours of Animals.

PUNNETT, R. C. : On Nutrition and Sex-determination in Man. (*Proc. Cambridge Phil. Soc.*, XII.)

RIBOT, TH. : Heredity (*Eng. trans.*).

ROMANES, G. J. : Darwin and after Darwin.
Animal Intelligence. (*Int. Sci. Series.*)
Mental Evolution in Animals.

*THOMSON, J. A. : Synthetic Summary of the Influence of the Environment upon the Organism. (*Proc. Roy. Phys. Soc., Edinburgh, IX.*)
Heredity. (*Pro. Sci. Series.*)
The Science of Life.

VARIGNY, DE : Experimental Evolution. (*Nat. Series.*)

VERNON, H. M. : Variation in Animals and Plants. (*Int. Sci. Series.*)

VREIS, HUGO DE : Species and Varieties (*trans.*).

*WALLACE, A. R. : Darwinism.

*WARD, LESTER : Pure Sociology.

*WEISSMANN : Essays upon Heredity (*trans.*).
The Germ-plasma Theory of Heredity (*trans.*).
The Effect of External Influences on Development. *Romanes Lecture, Oxford.*
The Evolution Theory (*trans.* by A. J. Tompson).

WILSON, E. B. : The Cell in Development and Inheritance.

HISTORICAL PART

*AMÉLINEAU : La Morale égyptienne.

*ARNOT, F. S. : Garenganzas.

*BACHOFEN : Das Mutterrecht. (*French trans. of Intro. by Giraud-Teulon.*)

BACKER, LOUIS DE : Le Droit de la femme dans l'antiquité.

BADER, MLLE. C. : La femme grecque : étude de la vie antique.
La femme romaine : étude de la vie antique.

BANCROFT, H. H. : The Native Races of the Pacific States of North America.

*BECQ DE FOUQUIÈRES : Aspasie de Milet.

*BONWICK, J. : Daily Life and Origin of the Tasmanians.

Brandt, P. : Sappho.

Brugsch, E. : Histoire d'Égypte.

*Bruns, Ivo : Frauenemancipation in Athen.

*Budge, E. A. Wallis : Book of the Dead (*trans.*).

*Burton, Sir R. F. : First Footsteps in East Africa.

*Buttles, J. R. : The Queens of Egypt : *with a preface by Maspero.*

*Charlevoix, Le P. de : Histoire et description générale de la Nouvelle France.

Crawley : The Mystic Rose.

*Crooke, W. : The Tribes and Castes of the North-west Provinces and Oudh.

*Cushing, F. H. : Zünie Folk Tales.

*Dalton, E. J. : Descriptive Ethnology of Bengal.

Dargun, L. von : Mutterrecht und Vaterrecht.

*Davy, J. : An Account of the Interior of Ceylon and its Inhabitants.

Dawson, J. : Australian Aborigines.

*Dennett, R. S. : "At the Back of the Black Man's Mind." Journal of the African. Vol. I.

*Dill : Roman Society. *Three volumes.*

*Donaldson, J. : Woman; Her Position and Influence in Greece and Rome and among the Early Christians.

*Ellis, Havelock : Man and Woman.
Psychology of Sex. Vol. VI.

*Ellis, W. : History of Madagascar.

Featherman, A. : A Social History of the Races of Mankind.

Fink : Primitive Love and Love Stories.

*Fison and Howitt : Kamilaroi and Kurnia; Group Marriage and Relationship, etc.

*Frazer, J. G. : The Golden Bough : *The Magic Art*, 3rd ed.

*Giraud-Teulon, A. : Les Origines de mariage et de la famille.

*Gladstone, W. E. : Homeric Studies. Vol. II.

*Gomperz : Greek Thinkers.

*Gray, J. H. : China, a History of the Laws, Manners and Customs of the People.

*Griffith : The World's Literature.

*Hartland, E. S. : Primitive Paternity.

*Hecker, E. A. : History of Woman's Rights.

*HOMMEL, F.: Geschichte Babyloniens.
The Civilisation of the East (*trans.*).
*HOBHOUSE, L. T.: Morals in Evolution.
HOWARD, G. E.: History of Matrimonial Institutions.
HOWITT, A. W.: The Native Tribes of South-east Australia.
The Organisation of the Australian Tribes.
JACOB, P. L.: Les Courtisanes de l'ancienne Rome.
*JOHNS, C. H. W.: Hammurabi, King of Babylon. The Oldest Code of Laws in the World.
Babylonian and Assyrian Laws, Contracts and Letters.
*KINGSLEY, MARY H.: Travels in West Africa.
*KOHLER AND PEISER: Aus dem babylonischen Rechtsleben.
LABOULAYE, ED.: Recherches sur la condition civile et politique des femmes, depuis les Romains jusqu'à nos jours.
LACOMBE, PAUL: La Famille dans la société romaine: étude de moralité comparée.
*LAFITEAU, J. F.: Mœurs des sauvages américains.
LATHAM: Descriptive Ethnology.
*LECKY, W. E. H.: History of European Morals, from Augustus to Charlemagne.
LEFEVRE, M.: La Femme à travers l'histoire.
LEGOUVÉ, E.: Histoire morale des femmes.
*LENZ, C. S.: Geschichte der Weiber im heroischen Zeitalter.
*LETOURNEAU: Evolution of Marriage. (*Cont. Sci. Series.*)
La Condition de la femme dans les diverses races et civilisations.
*LIPPERT, J.: Kulturgeschichte, etc.
Geschichte der Familie.
*LUBBOCK, LORD AVEBURY: Origin of Civilisation.
Marriage, Totemism and Religion.
*MACDONALD, D.: Africana.
MAHAFFY, J. P.: Social Life in Greece.
*MAINE: Ancient Law.
*MARSDEN, W.: History of Sumatra.
MARTIN, L. A.: Histoire de la femme; sa condition politique, civile, morale et religieuse.
MARX, V.: Die Stellung der Frauen in Babylonien.
*MASON, OTIS: The Origin of Inventions, a Study of Industry among Primitive Peoples. *Cont. Sci. Series.*
Woman's Share in Primitive Culture. *Anthro. Series.*

*Maspero, Sir G.: The Dawn of Civilisation (*trans.*).
Les Contes populaires de l'Égypte ancienne.
Ancient Egypt and Assyria (*trans.*).
New Light on Ancient Egypt (*trans.*).

*McCabe, J.: The Religion of Woman.

*McGee, W. J.: The Beginning of Marriage. (*Am. Anthro. Soc. Printed for private circulation.*)
The Aborigines of the District of Columbia and the Lower Potomac.
The Indians of North America.

*Mommsen: History of Rome.

*Morgan, L. H.: Ancient Society; or Researches in the Lines of Human Progress.
House and House-life of the American Aborigines. *Cont. to N. Am. Ethn. Vol. IV.*
Systems of Consanguinity and Affinity of the Human Family. *Smithsonian Contributions.*

Morillot, L.: De la condition des enfants nés hors mariage dans l'antiquité et au moyen âge en Europe.

*Müller, W. Max: Liebespoesie der alten Aegypter.

*Munzinger, W.: Ostafrikanische Studien.

*Nietzold, J.: Die Ehe in Aegypten, etc.

*Owen, M. A.: Folk-lore of the Musquakie Indians of North America.

*Paturet, G.: La condition juridique de la femme dans l'ancienne Égypte.

*Pearson, Karl: The Chances of Death.

*Peiser: Skizze der babylonischen Gesellschaft.

Perry, W. C.: The Women of Homer.

*Petherick, J.: Egypt, the Soudan and Central Africa.

*Petrie, Flinders: Religion and Conscience in Ancient Egypt.
Egyptian Tales translated from the Papyri.

*Ploss, H.: Das Weib in der Natur- und Völkerkunde.

*Powell, J. W.: Wyandot Government. *Report of the Bureau of Am. Ethn.*

Rainneville, J. de: La Femme dans l'antiquité et d'après la morale naturelle.

*Ratzel, T.: History of Mankind.

*Reclus, Élie: Les Primitifs (*Eng. trans.*, Primitive Folk. *Cont. Sci. Series*).

*REVILLOUT, E. : Cours de droit égyptien.
Les obligations en droit égyptien, comparées aux autres droits de l'antiquité.
Etudes égyptologiques.

*RHYS AND BRYNMOR JONES : The Welsh People.

ROBY, H. J. : Roman Private Law in the Times of Cicero and of the Antonines.

*SACHOT : L'Île de Ceylon.

SAYCE : Records of the Past.

*SCHOOLCRAFT, H. R. : History, Condition, and Prospects of the Indian Tribes of the United States.

*SIBREE, J. : The Great African Island.

*SIMCOX, E. J. : Primitive Civilisations.

*SPENCER AND GILLEN : The Native Tribes of Central Australia.

*SPENCER, H. : Descriptive Sociology.

STARCKE, C. N. : The Primitive Family.

*THOMAS, W. J. : Sex and Society.

*TURNER : Thibet.

*TYLOR, ED. B. : Researches into the Early History of Mankind.
Primitive Culture.
The Matriarchal Family System. *Nineteenth Century, July*, 1896.

*WAITZ-GERLAND, F. : Anthropologie der Naturvölker (*Eng. trans.*).
Introduction to Anthropology.

WAKE : Evolution of Morality.

*WESTERMARK : The History of Human Marriage.
Origin and Development of Moral Ideas.

WHITE, R. E. : Women in Ptolemaic Egypt.

WIESE, L. : Zur Geschichte und Bildung der Frauen.

*VOTH, H. R. : Traditions of the Hopi.

MODERN PART

ALBERT, C. : Free Love.

BEBEL, H. : Woman in the Past, Present, and Future (*trans.*).

BLACKWELL, ELIZ. : The Human Element in Sex.

BLASCHKO, A. : Prostitution in the Nineteenth Century.

*BLEASE, W. L.: The Emancipation of English Women.

BOUCHACOURT: La Grossesse.

BRAUN, LILY: Die Frauenfrage.

"BRITISH MEDICAL JOURNAL": "The Unborn Child: Its Care and its Rights," *Aug.* 1907; "The Influences of Antenatal Conditions on Infantile Mortality," *Aug.* 1904; "Physical Deterioration," *Oct.* 1905; "Infant Mortality. Huddersfield Scheme," *Dec.* 1907.

FÉRÉ, C. S.: La Pathologie des émotions. (*Eng. trans.*, The Pathology of the Emotions.)
L'Instinct sexuel.

FREUD, S.: Contributions to the Sexual Theory (*trans.*).
Article on Sex abstinence, *Sexual Problem,* March 1908.

*GALTON, F.: Restrictions in Marriage and Eugenics as a Factor in Religion.

GODFREY, J. A.: The Science of Sex.

GROSS-HOFFINGER, A. J.: The Fate of Woman and Prostitution, etc.

HALL, STANLEY: Adolescence.

HAYNES, E. S. P.: Our Divorce Law.

HINTON, JAMES: MS., written 1870, and left unpublished. Quoted by H. Ellis, *Psychology of Sex,* Vol. VI.

HIRSCHFELD, M.: Sexual Stages of Transition.

*HIRTH, GEORGE, Wege zur Liebe.
Wege zur Heimat.

HOWARD: History of Matrimonial Institutions.

JEANNEL, J.: Prostitution in Large Towns in the Nineteenth Century.

KEY, ELLEN: On Love and Marriage.
The Century of the Child.
The Woman Movement.

KISCH: Sexual Life of Women.

KRAFFT-EBING: Psychopathia Sexualis.

LAPIE, PAUL: La Femme dans la famille.

*LEA: History of Sacerdotal Celibacy.

*LIPPERT, H.: Prostitution in Hamburg.

LOMBROSO E FERRERO: La donna delinquente, la prostituta, e la donna normale.
(*Incom. Eng. trans.*) The Female Offender. (*Eng. Criminology Series.*)

LÖWENFELD: Sexuelleben und Nervenleiden.

*MANTEGAZZA, P. L'Amore. (*French trans.*, L'amour dans l'humanité.)
The Art of Choosing a Wife (*trans.*).
The Art of Choosing a Husband (*trans.*).

MARCUSE, MAX: Unmarried Mothers. (*Vol. XVII. of Documents of Great Towns.*)

*MARRO, A.: La Puberté chez l'homme et chez la femme.

MAYREDER, ROSA: Zur Kritik der Weiblichkeit.

MILL, J. S.: Subjection of Women.

*MÖIBUS, P. J.: Stachyologie.

MOLL, A.: Hypnotism. (*Trans., Cont. Sci. Series.*)

MORRISON, W. D.: Crime and its Causes.

*MORTIMER, GEOFFREY (W. M. GALLICHAN): Chapters on Human Love.

NEWMAN, G.: Infant Mortality.

NORTHCOTE, H.: Christianity and Sex Problems.

PARENT-DUCHATELET, A. J. B.: De la prostitution dans la ville de Paris.

PARSONS, C. E.: The Family.

*PEARSON, KARL: The Chances of Death.
Ethics of Free Thought.
The Groundwork of Eugenics.

PÉCHIN: La Puériculture avant la naissance.

RYAN, M.: Prostitution in London, with a Comparative View of that of Paris and New York (in 1839).

SANGER, W. M.: The History of Prostitution.

SCHMID, MARIE VON: Mutterdienst.

*SCHREINER, OLIVE: Woman and Labour.
The Woman Movement of our Day. (*Harper's Bazaar, Jan.* 1902.)

SÉNANCOUR: De l'amour.

*SHAW, G. B.: Man and Superman.
Getting Married.

*STETSON (Mrs. Perkins Gilman): Woman and Economics.
The Man-made World.

STOCKER, HELEN: Die Liebe und die Frauen.

TARDE: La Morale sexuelle. (*Archives d'anthropologie criminelle.*)

*THOMPSON, HELEN B.: The Mental Traits of Sex.

TILT: Elements of Health and Principles of Female Hygiene.

TOPINARD: Anthropologie générale.

WARDLAW, R.: Lectures on Female Prostitution; its Nature, Extent, Effects, Guilt, Causes, and Remedy.

*WEININGER, OTTO: Sex and Character.

*WELLS, H. G.: First and Last Things.
A Modern Utopia.
Marriage.

WOLLSTONECRAFT, MARY: Vindication of the Rights of Women.

INDEX